I0828264

IMAGES
of America

AROUND MORGANTOWN

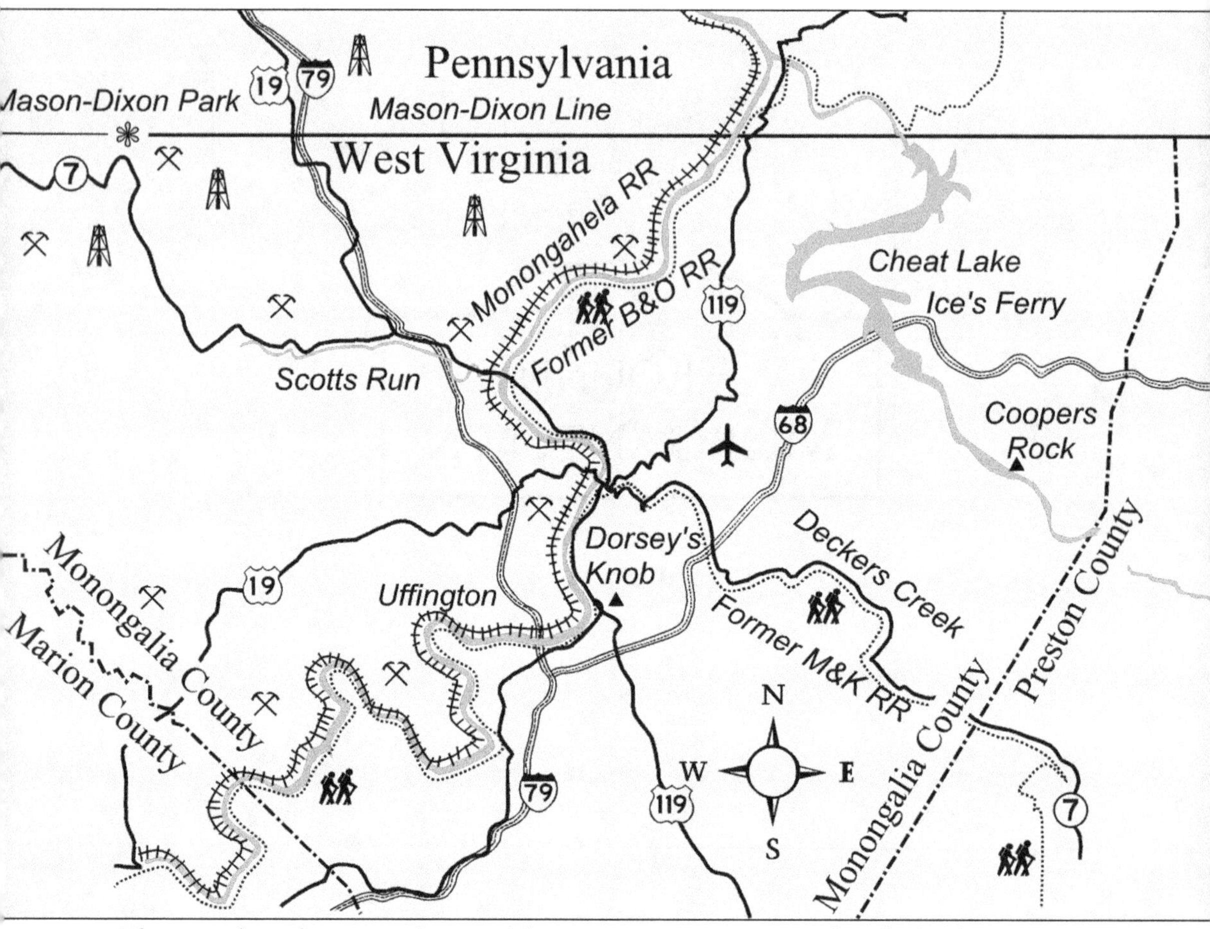

This map shows locations of some of the more remote sites pictured in the book.

On the Cover: The photographer caught the packet *Columbia* backing away from the Morgantown wharf. The maneuver was a little more complicated than usual because of a visit by *Price's New Water Queen* showboat and her towboat, the *Argand*. The prominent building with the twin towers is the new Central School. The photograph was taken about 1905. (West Virginia and Regional History Collection, West Virginia University Libraries.)

IMAGES
of America

AROUND MORGANTOWN

Wallace and Norma Venable

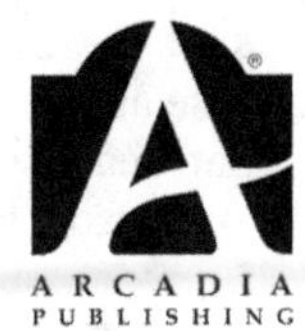
ARCADIA
PUBLISHING

ISBN 978-1-5316-2680-8

Published by Arcadia Publishing
Charleston, South Carolina

Library of Congress Catalog Card Number: 2006934734

For all general information contact Arcadia Publishing at:
Telephone 843-853-2070
Fax 843-853-0044
E-mail sales@arcadiapublishing.com
For customer service and orders:
Toll-Free 1-888-313-2665

Visit us on the Internet at www.arcadiapublishing.com

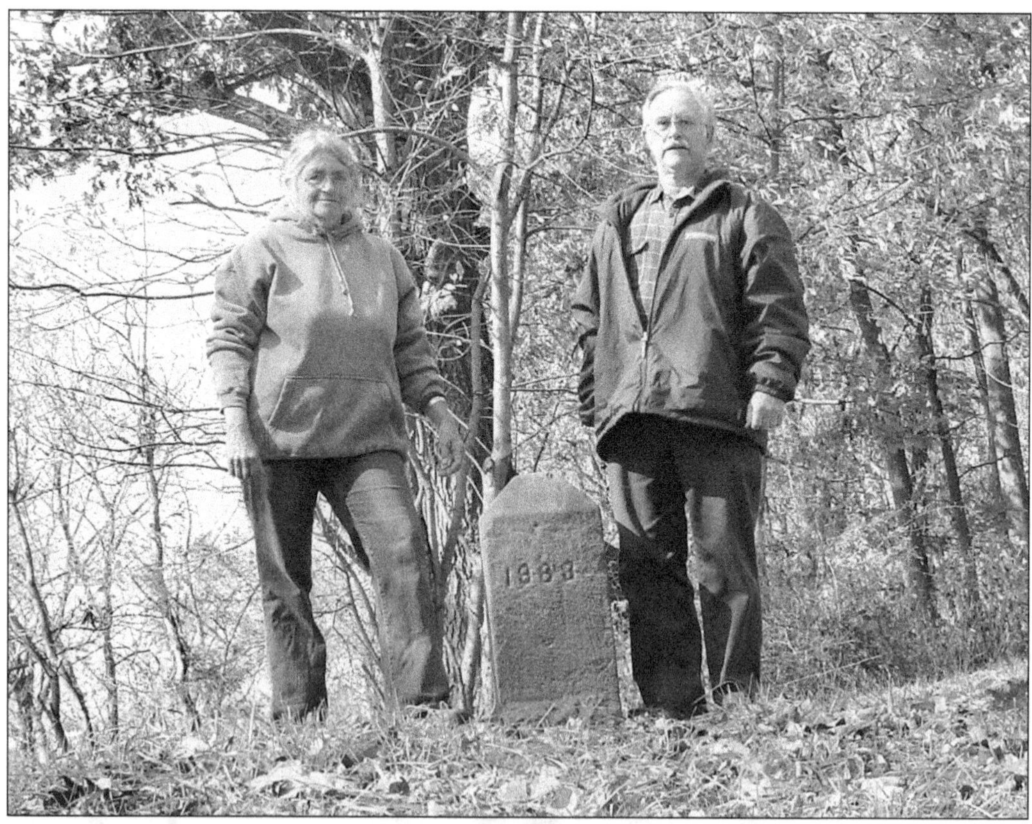

The authors, Wallace and Norma Venable, pose at the spot where Charles Mason and Jeremiah Dixon terminated their survey of the line that bears their names in 1767. The original marker was replaced in 1883. The site is in the Mason-Dixon Historical Park located near State Route 7 northwest of Morgantown.

Contents

ACKNOWLEDGMENTS

We owe a particular debt to the late Earl Core, whose bicentennial history *The Monongalia Story* has been a constant reference. The five-volume work, which he finished in 1984, was based not only on several previous county histories, but also on a search of most surviving newspapers.

The Morgantown Public Library has been particularly generous in granting us access to local publications and photographs. Unless otherwise noted, pictures are from the authors' collection.

We should also thank Kendra Allen of Arcadia Publishing, who solicited a book proposal from us, made sure we understood our commitments, and then gave us the freedom to carry out the work in our own fashion.

Finally we want to thank the many friends who have helped and encouraged us to become part of the Morgantown and Monongalia County communities since we came here as out-of-state "immigrants" some 40 years ago.

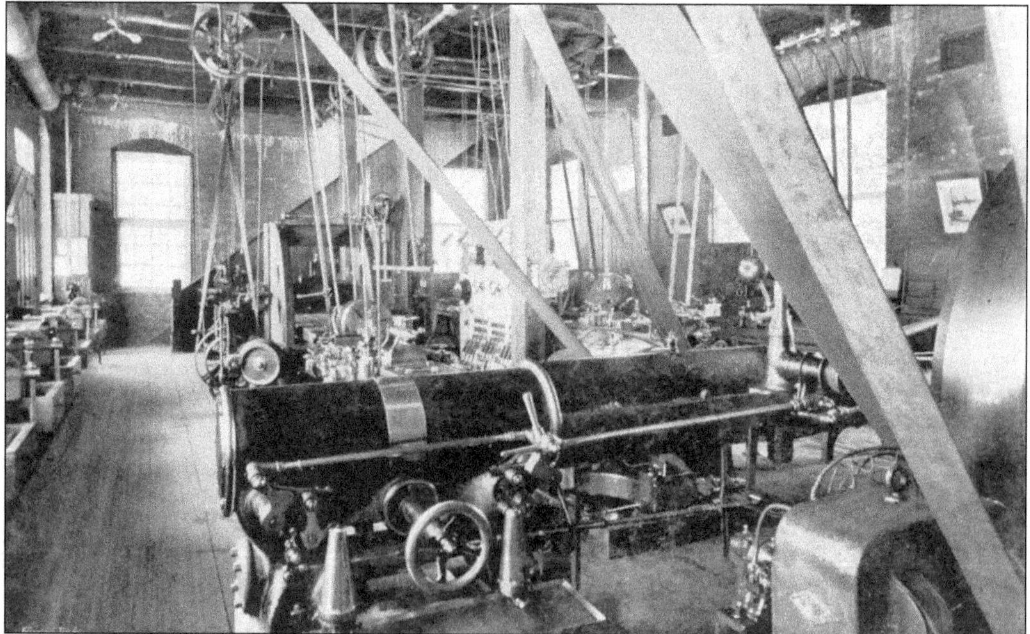

The 1896 *Monticola*, the West Virginia University yearbook, carried this picture of the machinery laboratory in the Mechanical Building. It contained both electrical and thermal machines. The unguarded belts were typical of 19th-century factory practice. Workplace safety was the responsibility of the student, not the college. (Morgantown Public Library.)

Introduction

Morgantown is on an ancient plateau cut by streams. The airport is near the top with an elevation of 1,220 feet, while the Monongahela River at the bottom has an elevation of 810 feet. Much of the area is on steep slopes with little naturally flat land.

The Monongahela flows north to Pittsburgh, where it joins the Allegheny River to form the Ohio. By air, the city is only 55 miles from Pittsburgh, Pennsylvania, but 125 miles from Charleston, the state capital. The difference in distance, plus the historical river connection, means that Morgantown has closer ties to Pittsburgh than Charleston on non-political matters. Pittsburgh is the big city to which Morgantown people go for serious shopping, major entertainment, and professional sports.

The Morgantown urban area includes four incorporated municipalities—the city of Morgantown, Star City, Westover, and Granville—plus many unincorporated suburban developments. Only about 60 percent of the 50,000 residents of the urban area, and about 40 percent of the Monongalia County population of 80,000, live within corporate boundaries. The line between city and country life is hard to draw.

Much of Morgantown's attention is focused on West Virginia University, known locally as WVU, which is situated within its borders. The university is by far the largest employer, and its athletic events draw people from all over the state to town. Most newcomers arrive as either students or faculty.

The area has a long history of struggling with the balance between freedom and morality. Known at times for large numbers of drinking establishments, at least twice in addition to national Prohibition the county has forbidden the sale of liquor, but today it hosts a large wine and jazz festival. While still a slave-holding territory before the Civil War, the county provided schooling for free black children. Once a tobacco growing area, it was one of the first communities in the state to regulate smoking in public places.

Morgantown has few major monuments. It has many good but few distinguished buildings. The community judges a structure on its ability to serve human needs, not on its attractiveness or age.

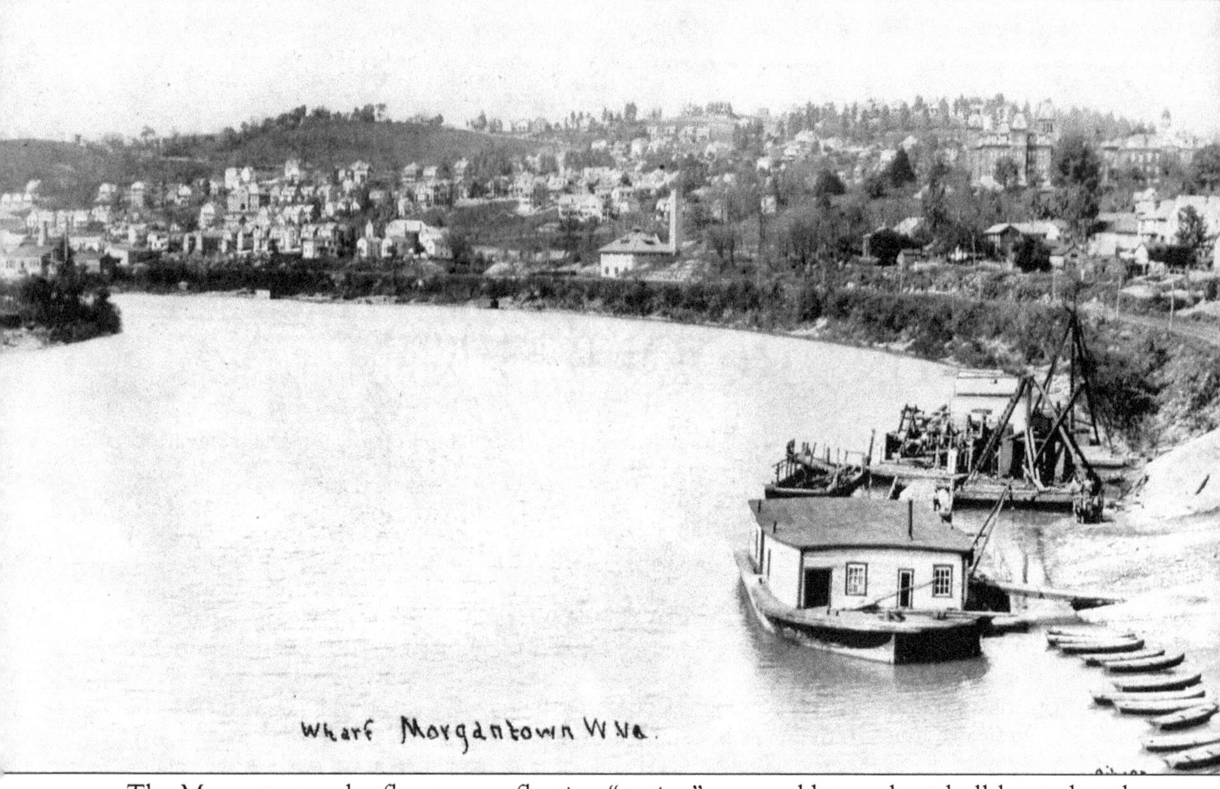

The Morgantown wharfboat was a floating "station" on an old steamboat hull located at the foot of Walnut Street. The Scott Gibson photograph is undated, but the construction barge suggests it was taken while the suspension bridge was being replaced with a steel bridge in 1908. Rental rowboats and floating boathouses tied to the bank indicate that the river was a place for recreation as well as commerce.

One

Early Days

The first attempt at settlement in the Morgantown area was established beside Deckers Creek in 1858 by Tobias Decker. His community was attacked by the Delawares in 1759, and those who survived left the immediate area.

Popular legend says Morgan's Town was established in 1772 by Zackquill Morgan. Although surviving documents leave some doubt about the details, he was certainly an early settler and leader. By 1773, Morgantown had a stockaded fort. In 1785, the Virginia Assembly granted a formal charter to the town.

When Monongalia County was established in 1776, it measured more than 130 miles from north to south and 60 miles from east to west. The location of the first county seat was north of what is now Point Marion, Pennsylvania. Zackquill Morgan became the first sheriff. By 1780, Marion, Randolph, Preston, and Tucker Counties had been split off from Monongalia, and the county's final configuration was established.

Morgantown continued to grow with exports of lumber, food, iron, and pottery, which could be transported by river.

In the Civil War, West Virginia sided with the North, and on December 31, 1862, Pres. Abraham Lincoln signed legislation forming the new state of West Virginia effective June 20, 1863.

West Virginia University was established at Morgantown as the state's land grant school in 1863, and much of Morgantown's name recognition is based on the success of West Virginia University.

Railroads and reliable river transportation only reached Morgantown about 1890. At the time, agriculture was the economic base. Agriculture declined after the 1940s. There are only about 400 farms in the county today, and much agricultural land is sold for housing.

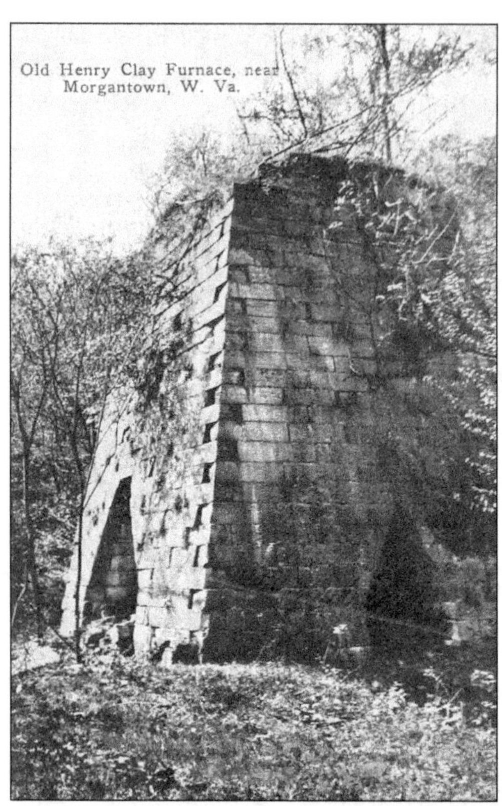

Remains of the Henry Clay Iron Furnace can be seen in Coopers Rock State Forest. The furnace, built about 1836, used local iron ore, limestone, and charcoal to produce pig iron. Iron was important to the economy for nails and iron implements. Today visitors can hike the half-mile forest path to see the historic stone-cut furnace, which was placed on the National Register of Historic Places in 1970.

Potential army recruits lined High Street during the Civil War. After Virginia seceded from the Union in 1861, leaders from northwestern Virginia began the political process that resulted in the formation of West Virginia on June 20, 1863. West Virginia is the only state formed as a result of the Civil War. (West Virginian and Regional Collection, West Virginia University Libraries.)

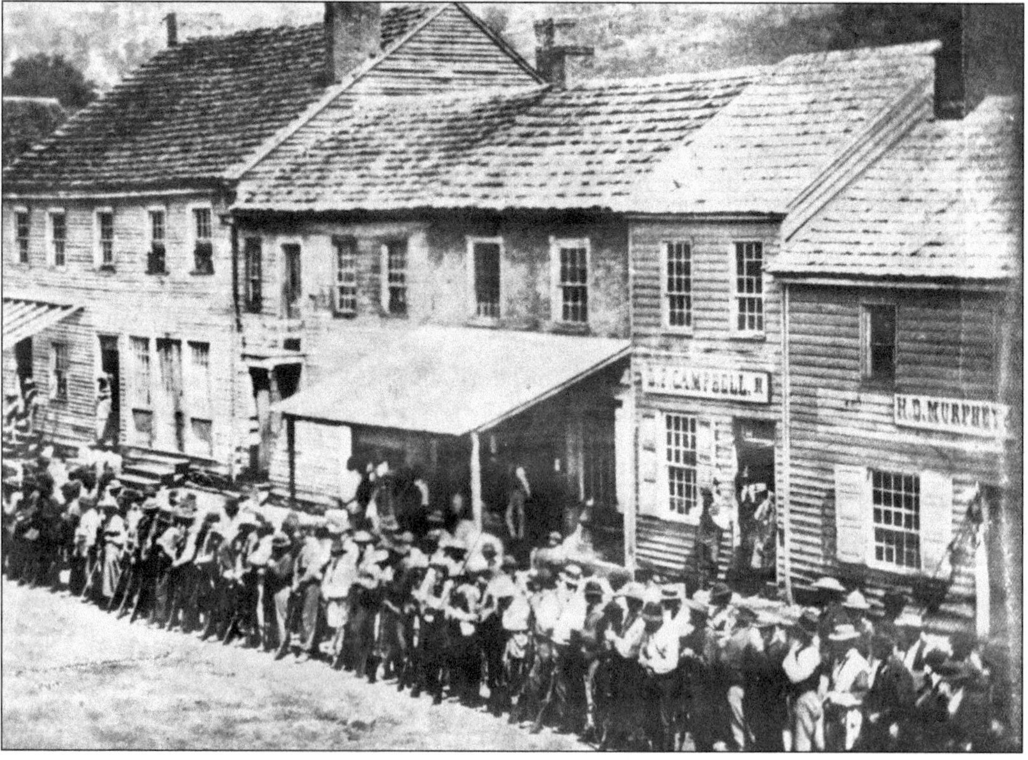

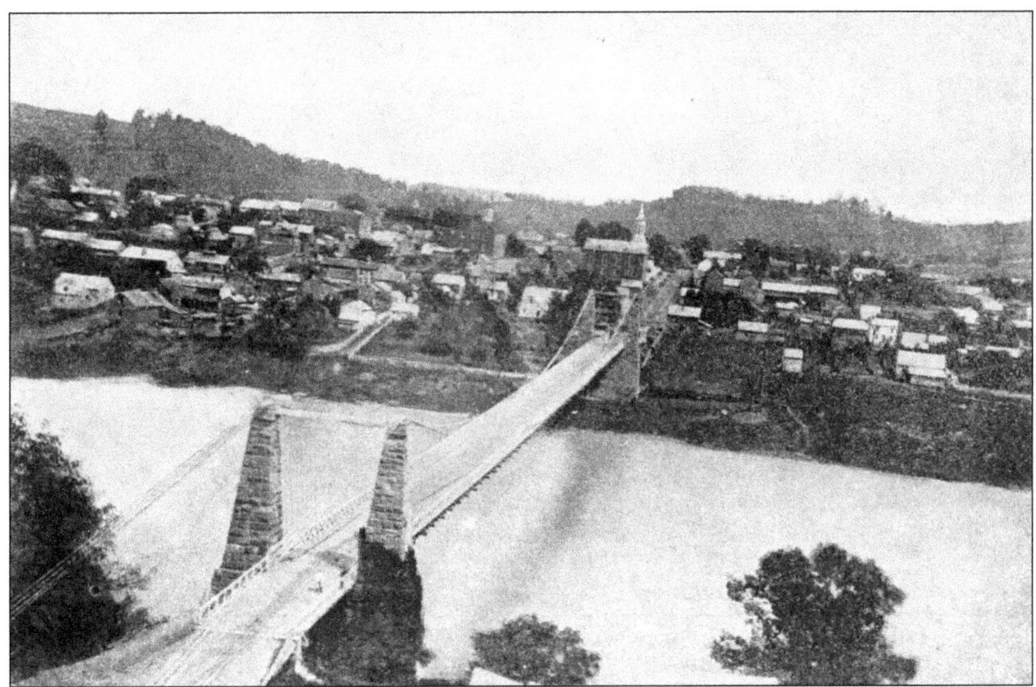

This photograph of Morgantown was taken in 1865 when the town had a population of 684. There is no clear evidence of a wharf or other waterfront activity. At that time, boatbuilding was done on Deckers Creek, which is out of the picture to the right. (Morgantown Public Library.)

This is the Methodist Episcopal Church, which was built in 1849 on Pleasant Street and used until 1904. Following the War of 1812, Methodists, Presbyterians, and Episcopalians started planning to build houses of worship, but it was not until 1819 that the Methodists constructed Morgantown's first church building at the northeast corner of Pleasant Street. The Presbyterians and Episcopalians joined together to build a church, which was completed two years later.

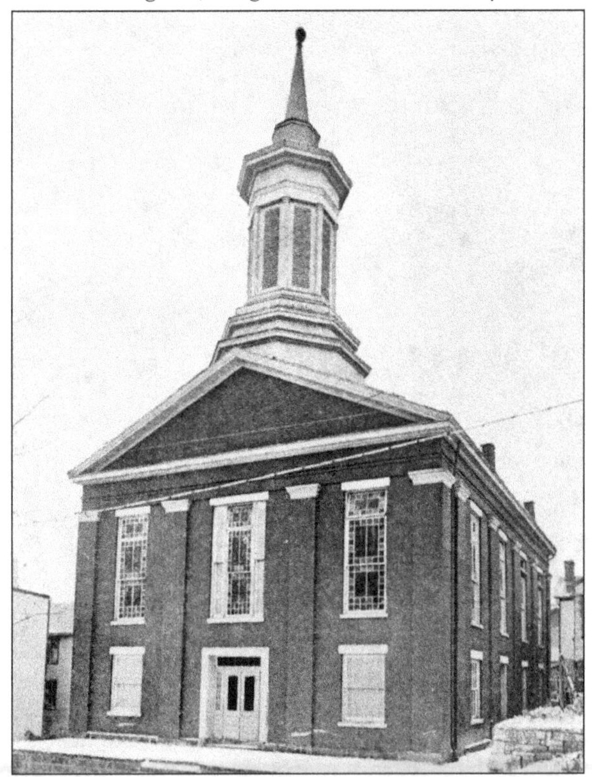

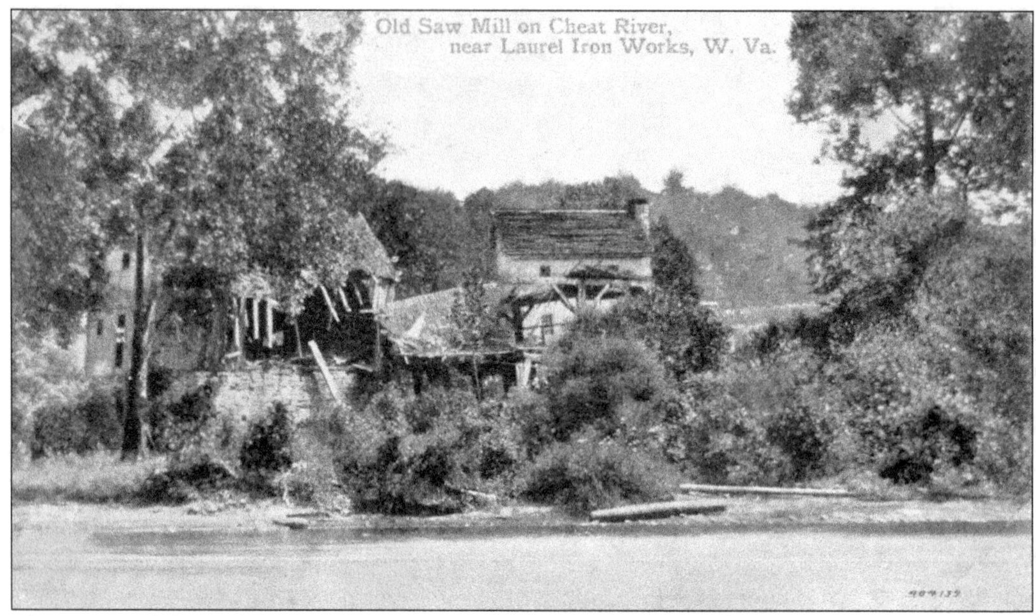

This postcard shows the remains of a sawmill next to the remains of the Laurel Iron Works along the Cheat River about 1915. According to tradition, the furnace supplied iron to Commodore Oliver Hazzard Perry and Gen. Andrew Jackson during the War of 1812. A sawmill on this site may have provided lumber for the construction of the flatboats that delivered the iron. The site is now under Cheat Lake.

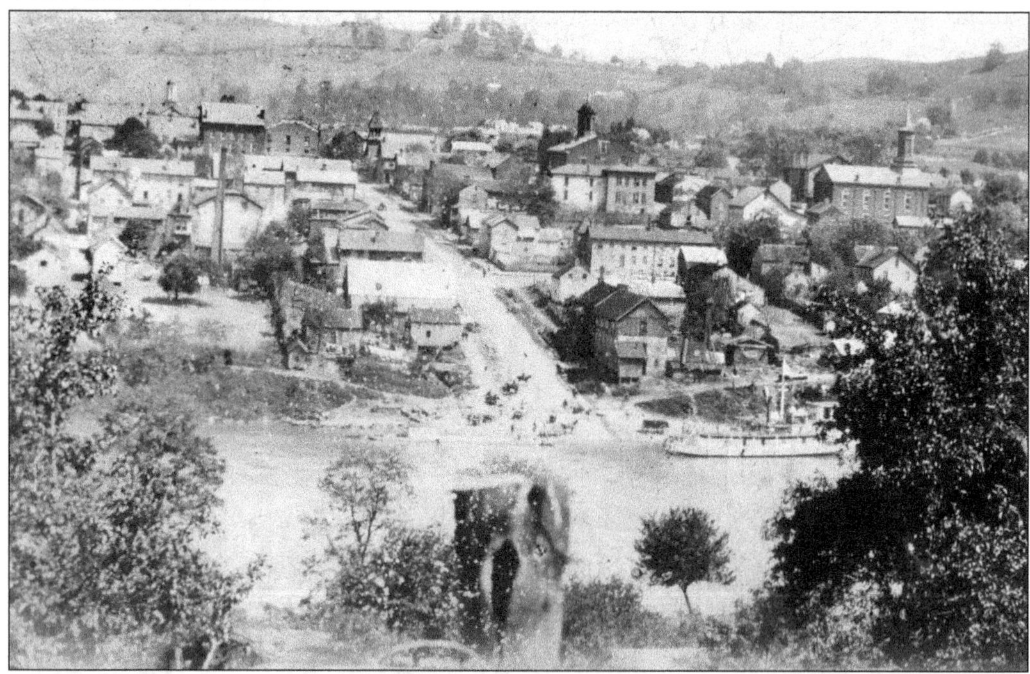

In 1884, the first railroad tracks from Fairmont were completed and work began extending the line to the north. The steamboat at the Walnut Street wharf was delivering supplies to the track construction crew. The building with a spire near the center of the picture is the courthouse, which had a wooden statue of Patrick Henry on top. (Morgantown Public Library.)

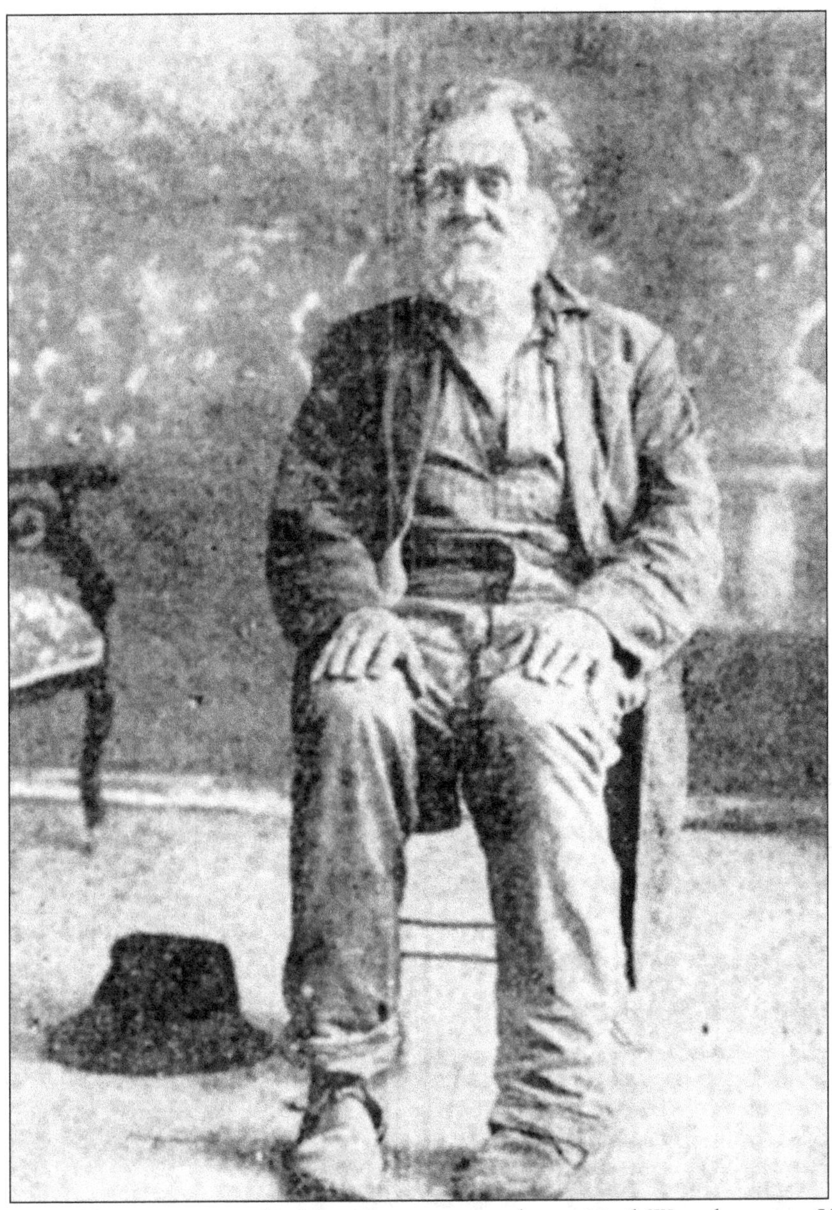

The Uffington Hermit was a colorful and controversial pre–Civil War character. His name, Napoleon Bonaparte Alsoupe, reflected his French extraction and supposed relation to Napoleon. Dr. Alsoupe, as he was called, was a medical student, and people remembered him as refined and intelligent. He also drove a fancy rig pulled by two black horses. For several years, Dr. Alsoupe lived near present-day Uffington on an island on the Monongahela River. Locks and dams were not then built, so the river level was lower. Dr. Alsoupe left the area, and when he returned in 1850, his character had completely changed from debonair to derelict and he appeared slovenly and unkempt. He built a rude hut on the river and claimed the nearby island. His neighbor Phillip Shuttleworth grazed his cow on what the Uffington Hermit regarded as his property, and in the ensuing trouble, the hermit murdered Shuttleworth. The hermit was tried and sent to prison, from which he was pardoned, but later confinement and death in an asylum was the fate of the enigmatic Uffington Hermit.

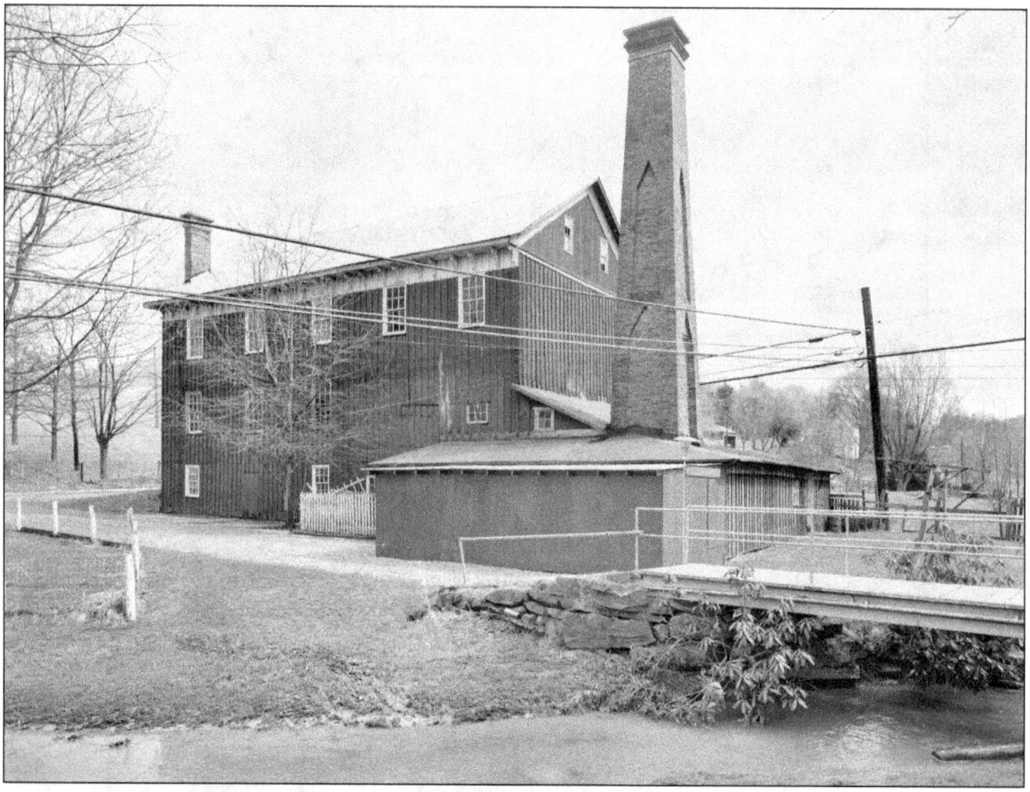

The Easton Roller Mill was built about 1864. Wheat was ground into flour to make bread, rye was processed to make the famous Monongahela rye whiskey, and oats and corn were processed for feeding livestock. The mill's grinding stones were powered by a steam engine. The mill worked until the 1930s. The mill was placed on the National Register of Historic Places in 1978. (HABS/HAER Library of Congress.)

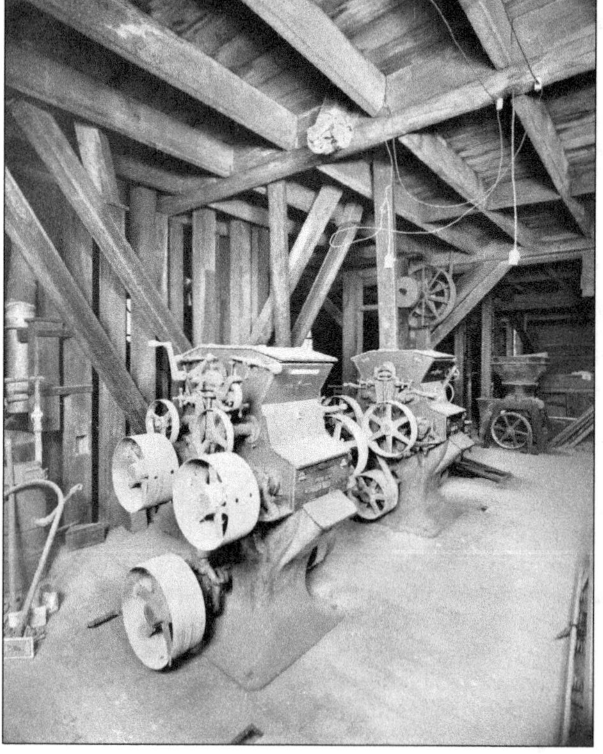

Many mills of the time were water-powered, but the Easton Mill used a steam engine. For about 30 years, traditional millstones were used to process grain. In 1894, the mill's owner added these roller mills. Roller mills were considered superior to grist stones since they produced much finer flour as well as producing much more flour than the old millstone technology. (HABS/HAER Library of Congress.)

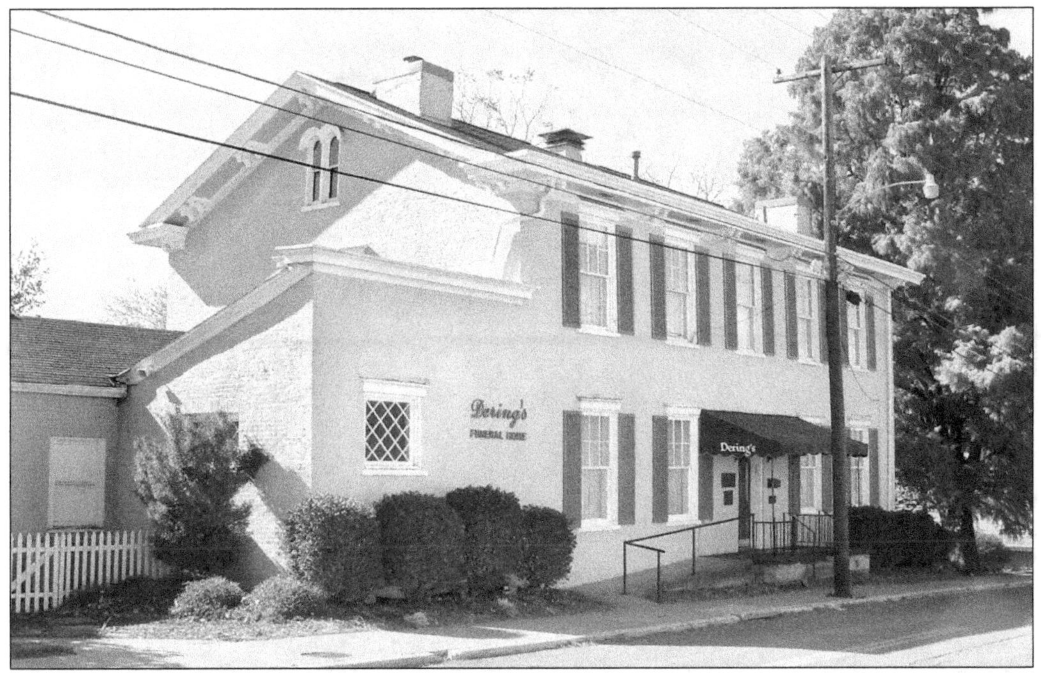

The John Rogers home is one of the oldest major structures in Morgantown. When the house was built in 1840, it was on a working farm. It has not moved, but today it is downtown at 156 Foundry Street and houses the Dering Funeral Home.

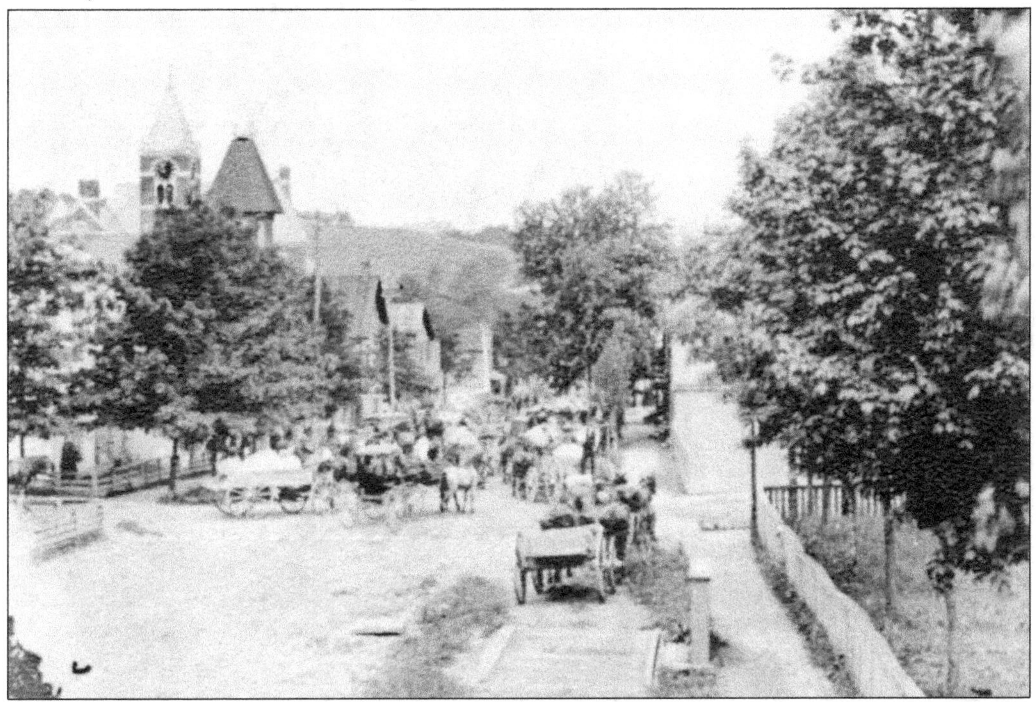

This photograph of North Walnut Street was taken on a wool market day in 1892. In those days, Morgantown had a thriving agricultural economy and no market building. Conducting business in the street created traffic congestion. (Morgantown Public Library.)

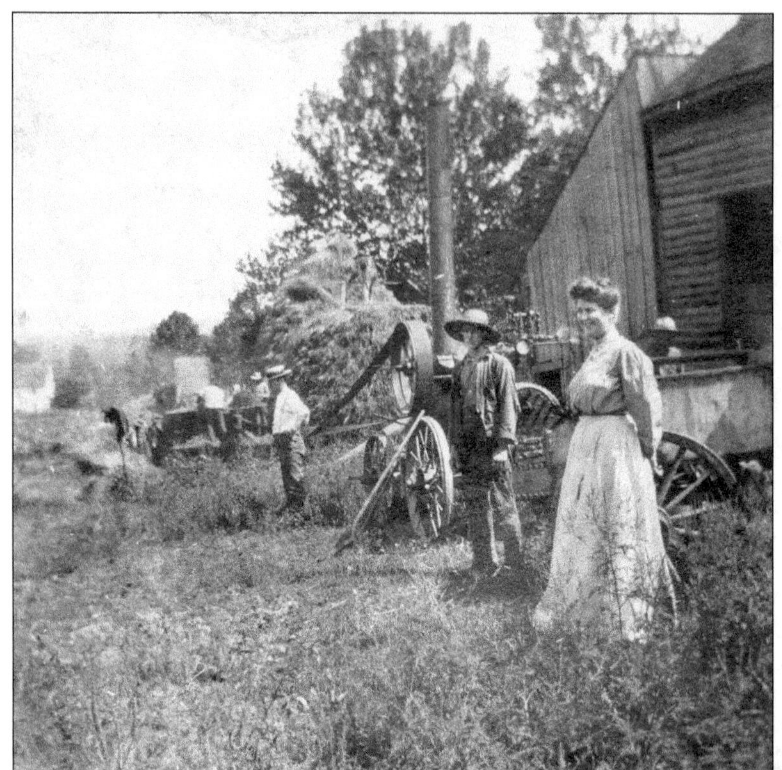

The photographer caught a threshing crew on the farm of James L. Krepps at the Flatts near Morgantown. The site is now part of the Evansdale Campus of the university. Little evidence of this area's farming past is visible today. (West Virginia and Regional History Collection, West Virginia University Libraries.)

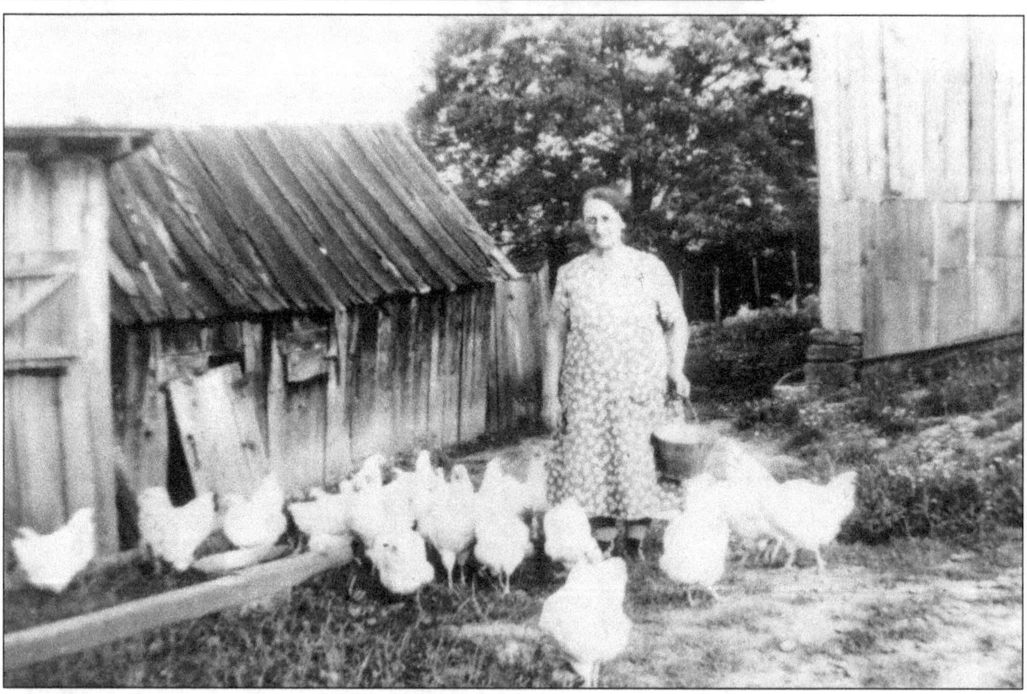

Until the 1950s, most farm wives kept hens on a free-range management system. Eggs not used for the family were sent to Morgantown for sale. Occasionally as many as 100 dozen eggs were sold. Eggs once sold for 5–10¢ a dozen.

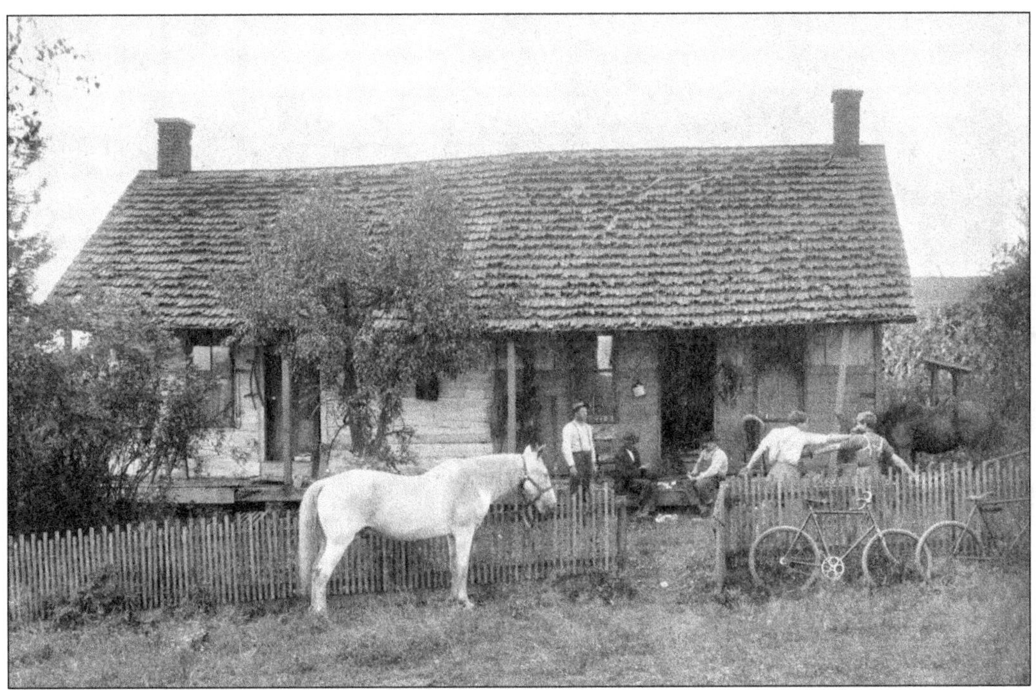

Perhaps this picture records a visit home for a Sunday dinner by a college boy and his roommate. Two gents on the porch are playing cards, and the boxers are wearing boxing gloves. The bikes are safety models. The picture was taken about 1900. (Morgantown Public Library.)

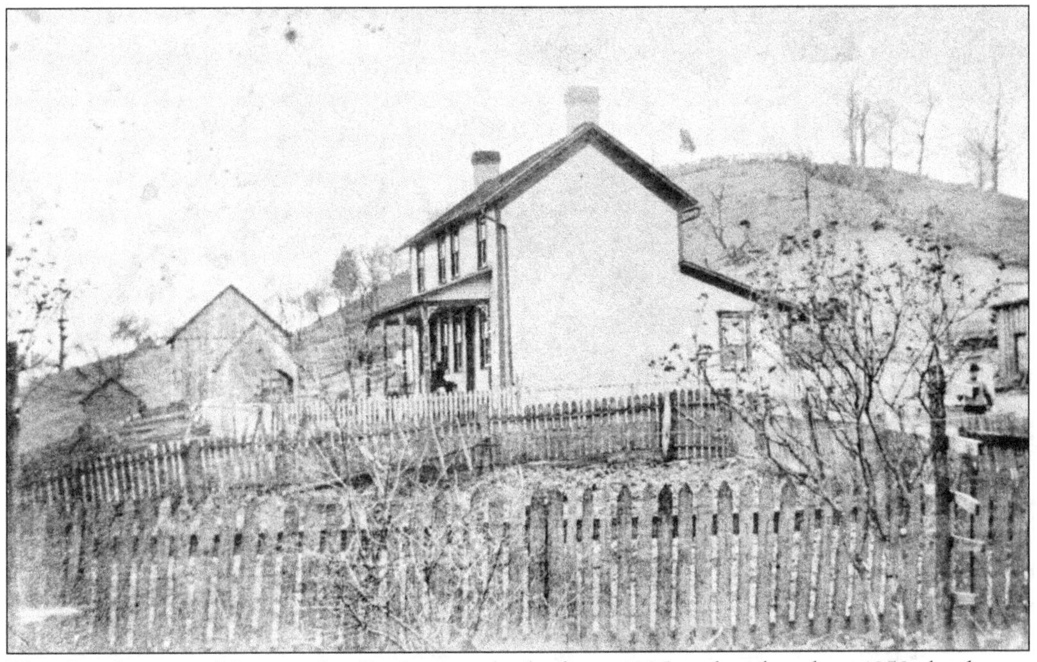

This farmhouse in Monongalia County was built about 1905 and replaced an 1850s log house that had been the original pioneer family home. In this modern home, a fence of wooden stakes surrounds the garden to keep out farm animals. The hill or "knob" in the background behind the house has been cleared for use as pasture.

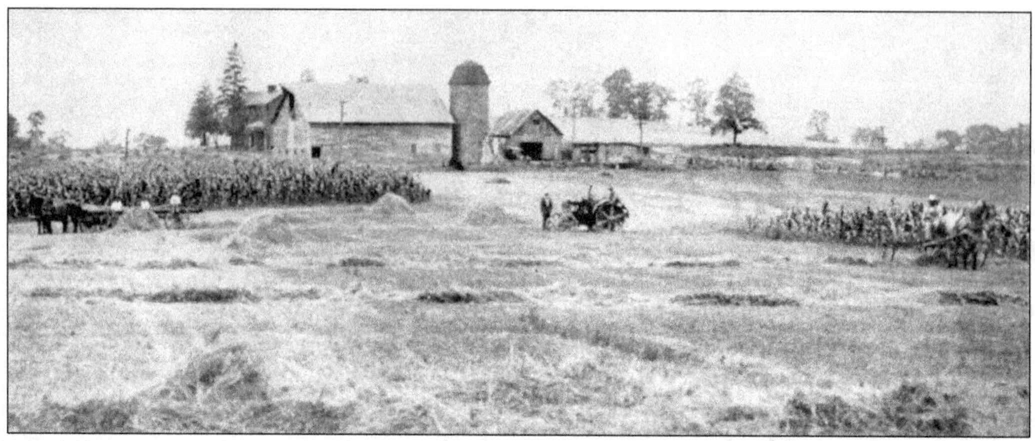

The West Virginia University Experiment Farm, as seen in the early 1900s, served the state's agricultural economy based on crops including corn, wheat, oats, and tobacco. The farm was located north of Morgantown.

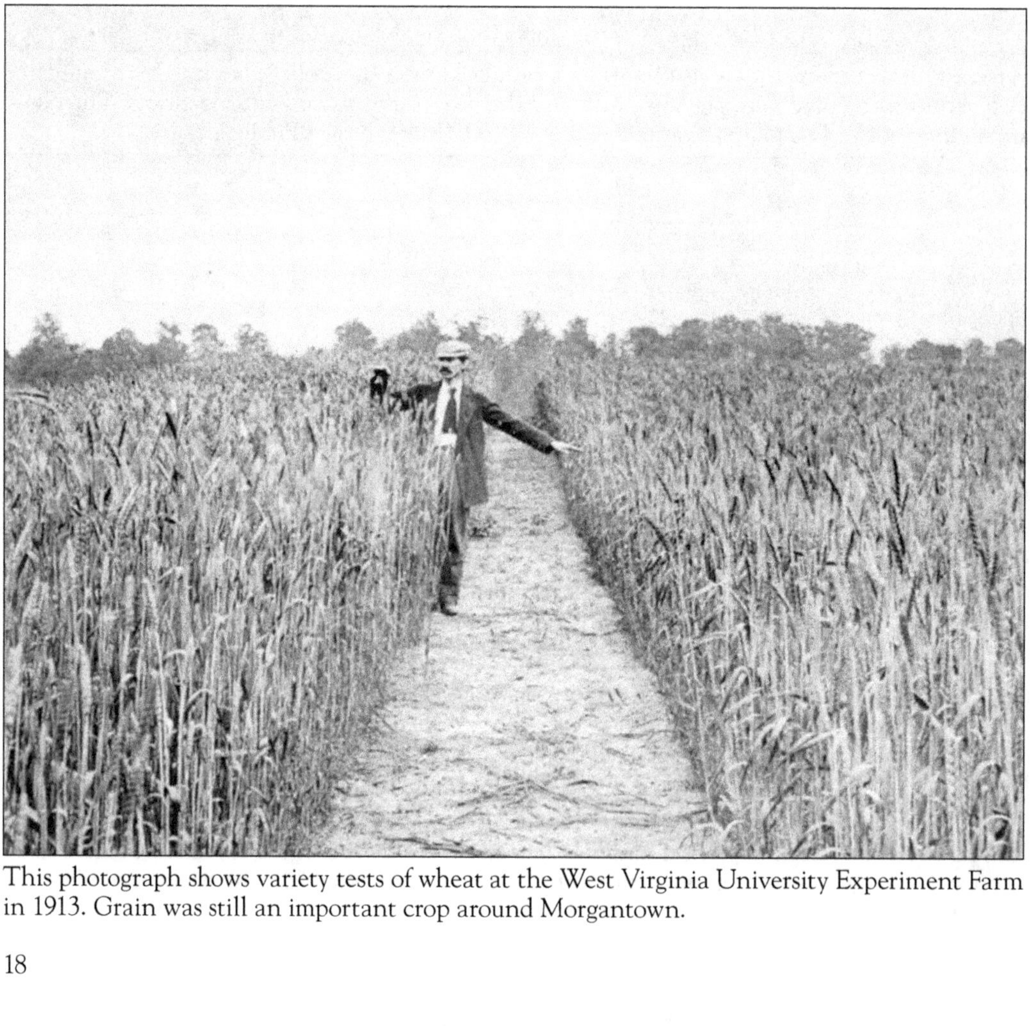

This photograph shows variety tests of wheat at the West Virginia University Experiment Farm in 1913. Grain was still an important crop around Morgantown.

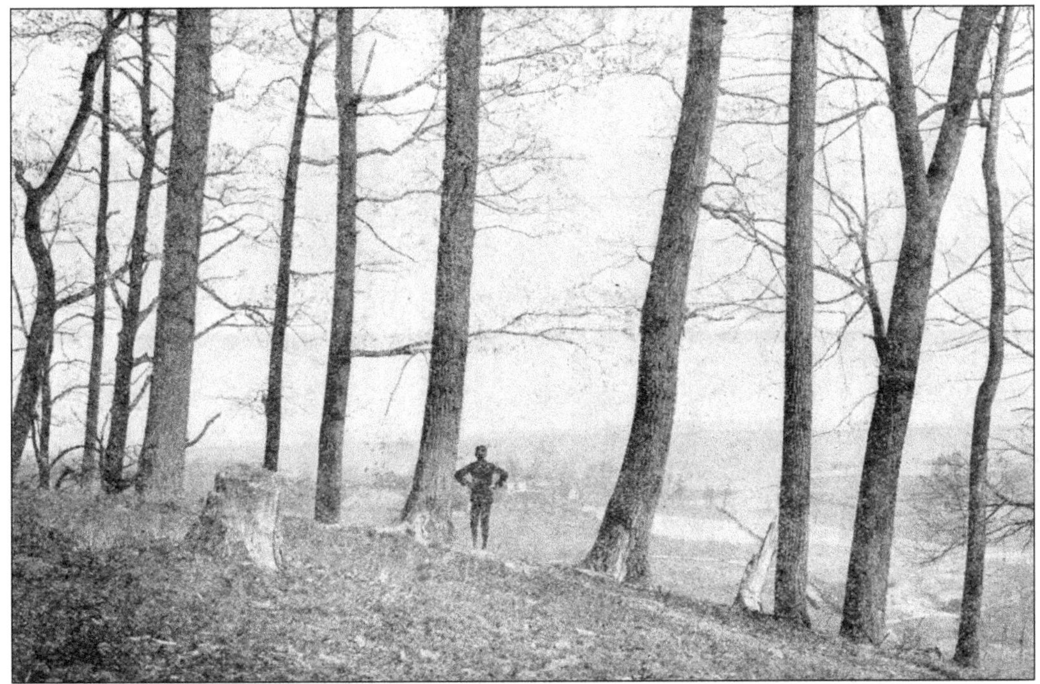

When this photograph was taken in the early 1900s, most land around Morgantown had been cleared for farming. Farming activities included raising cattle and growing crops such as wheat.

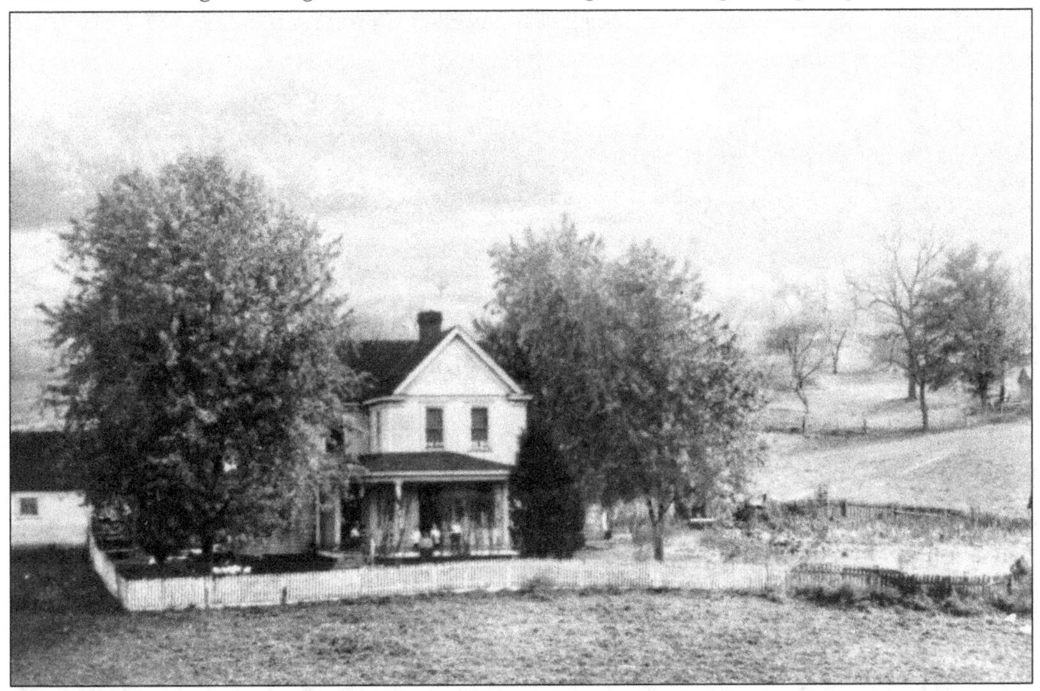

This is another typical farmstead in the early 1900s. A picket fence surrounds the frame home to exclude free-ranging chickens. Land around the farm is cleared for use as hay meadows and pasture. Large trees provided shade in summer since homes of the time had no air-conditioning, and the trees also served as a windbreak in the cold of winter.

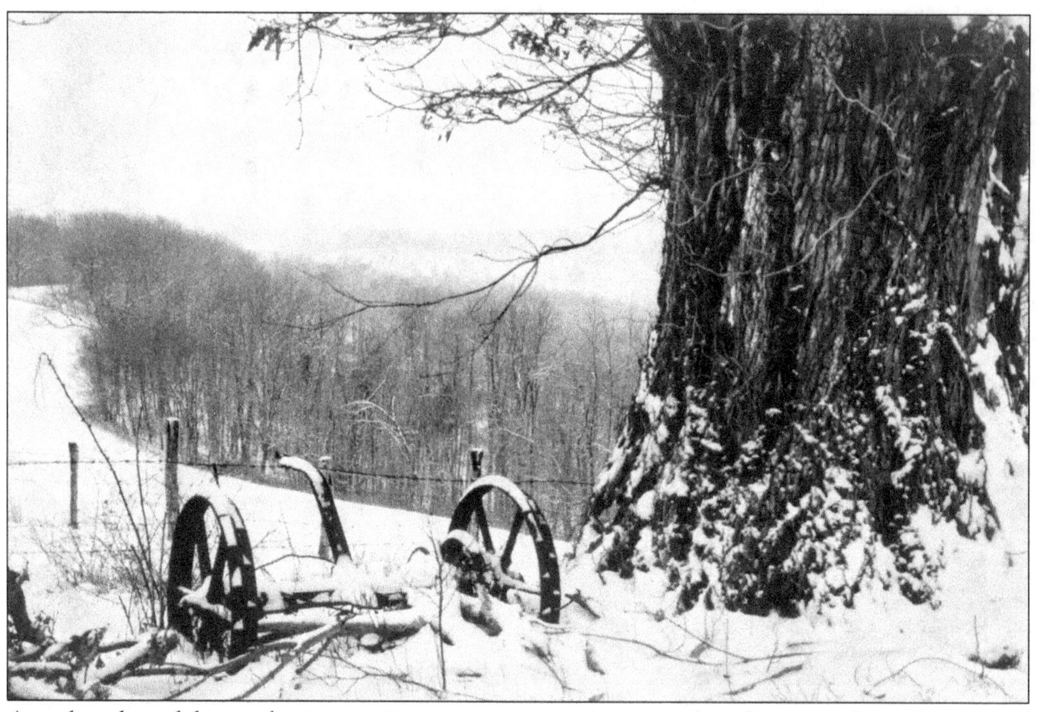

An abandoned hay rake in a wintry scene remains as a lonely reminder of a way of life long gone.

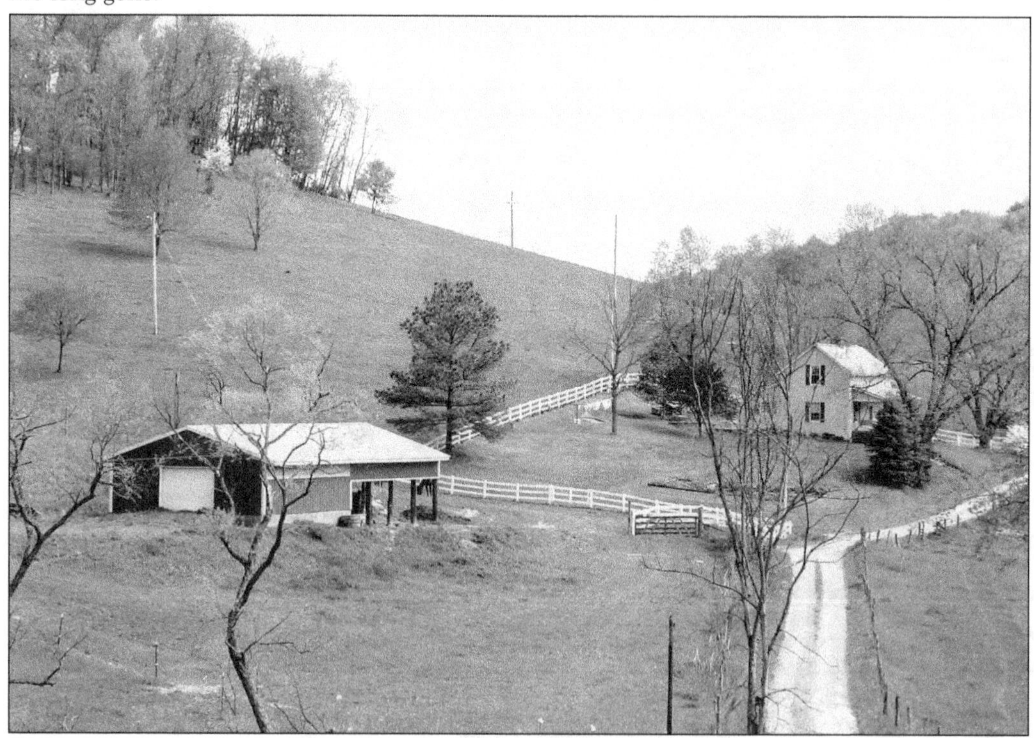

There are still about 400 farms in Monongalia County, mostly located on back roads. Although farms produce a variety of crops and animals, most focus on beef cattle.

Two

Rivers, Rails, and Roads

Before 1776, travelers reached Morgantown by walking buffalo paths and Indian war trails. Cargo was carried on pack horses. Fording was the only way to cross streams. The first wagon roads reached the area about 1790, and dirt or corduroy roads provided the only land transportation to Morgantown for about a century thereafter.

Westbound cargo leaving Morgantown went by water. Locally made pottery, iron from the Cheat Valley, hides, and farm products typically were shipped on locally built flatboats, simple disposable craft that were intended for a one-way trip. Boats that escaped the dangers of swift water, rocks, and attacks by Native Americans and pirates might even go as far as New Orleans.

The first steamboat, the *Reindeer*, reached Morgantown in 1826. The Monongahela River drops some 90 feet between Morgantown and Pittsburgh. Without dams, much of the river consisted of scenic stretches with exposed rocks, and boats traveled only during periods of high water; thus, for over 50 years, steamboat visits were special events and often many months apart.

A "slackwater navigation" on calm pools created by dams and connected by locks finally connected Morgantown to Pittsburgh in 1889. Railroad tracks from Fairmont reached Morgantown in 1886. Soon after, both riverboats and railroad trains provided through service between Fairmont and Pittsburgh for both passengers and freight.

Before 1910, roads into Morgantown were so poor that the first car in town arrived by steamboat. The first paved roads connecting Morgantown to the north and south were completed in 1923. Four-lane roads out were not available until Interstate 79 South reached the county in 1970, and the full route north to Pittsburgh took even longer. Improved connections to the east began in 1970 with the construction of Appalachian Corridor E, now I-68.

A local experimenter began flying an airplane here shortly after the Wright brothers proved flight was possible. In 1935, construction of a good regional airport was started.

In 1975, the university opened the first phase of the Personal Rapid Transit system, which now connects three campuses and downtown with automated cars on elevated tracks.

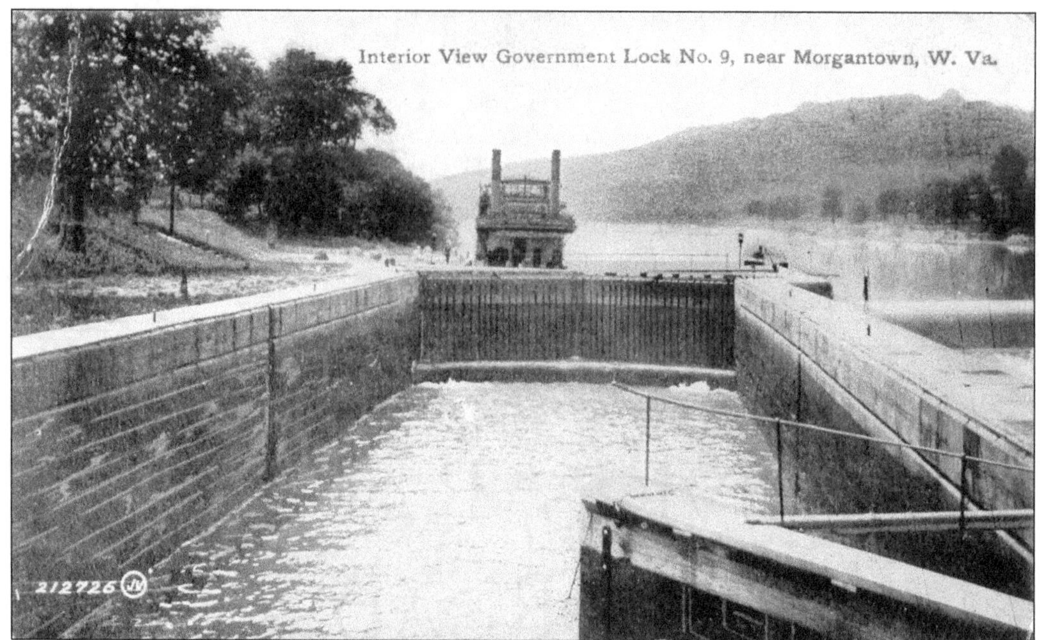

This postcard shows Lock Number Nine about 1910. It was 10 miles north of Morgantown and the first of six locks on the Monongahela River in West Virginia. The towboat is waiting for the lock to be filled so it can enter. It was probably pushing coal barges, which were pulled out of the lock by hand because the combined size of the tow was too large for the lock.

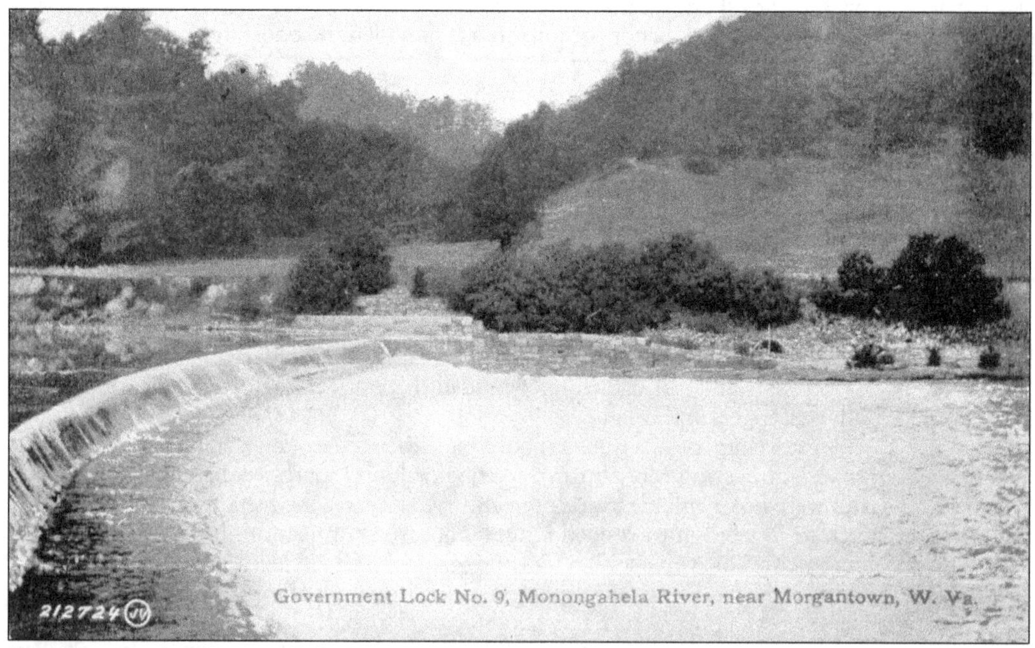

Dam Nine on the Monongahela River was a unique structure. It was built of stone, whereas previous river dams had been constructed with "cribs," structures similar to log cabins filled with rocks. The dam also had an arc shape, which created a large eddy and caused serious problems for boats coming upriver. The site was called Hoard Lock and Dam since it was built at Hoard Rocks.

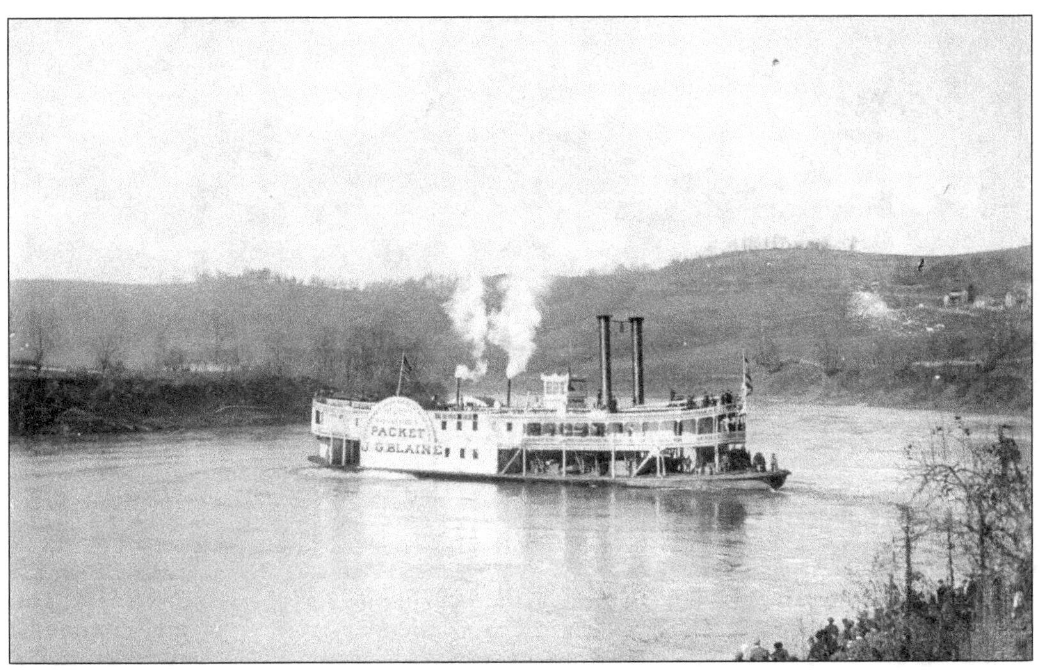

The packet steamboat *J. G. Blaine* was the first boat to reach Morgantown on "slackwater" in 1889 when Lock Nine was completed. Packets carried both passengers and freight on a regular schedule. On signal, packets stopped at farm landings as well as towns. A Morgantown group traveling to Pittsburgh for business or pleasure could have sleeping cabins and enjoy good meals and entertainment on board. (Morgantown Public Library.)

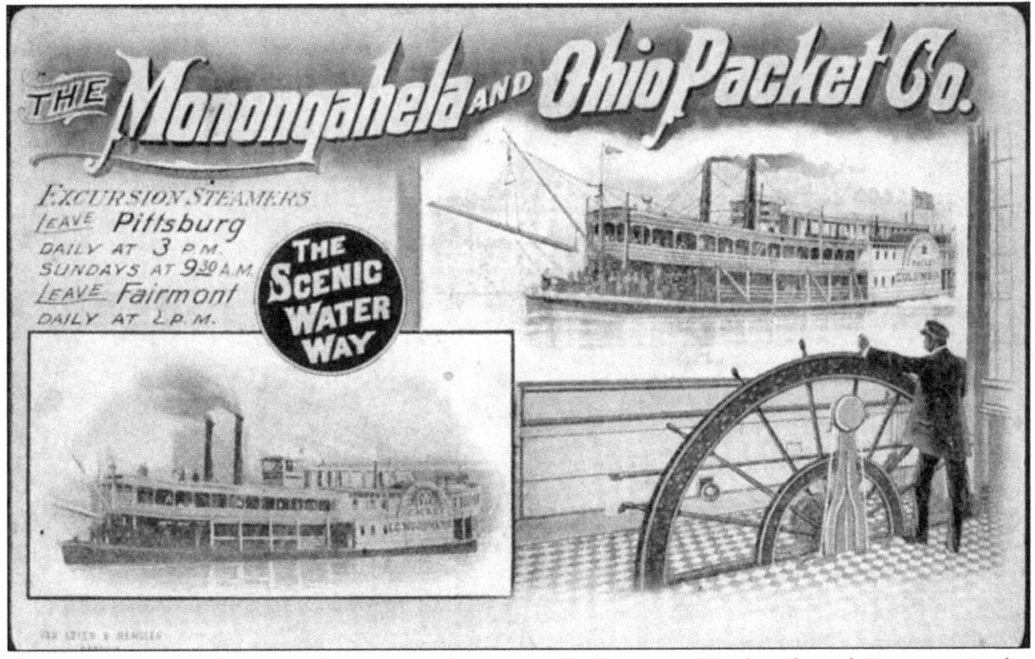

There were two packet boat lines competing for traffic between Pittsburgh and Fairmont in the early 20th century, so advertising was important. This postcard promoted the notion that the trip might be a nice two-day vacation.

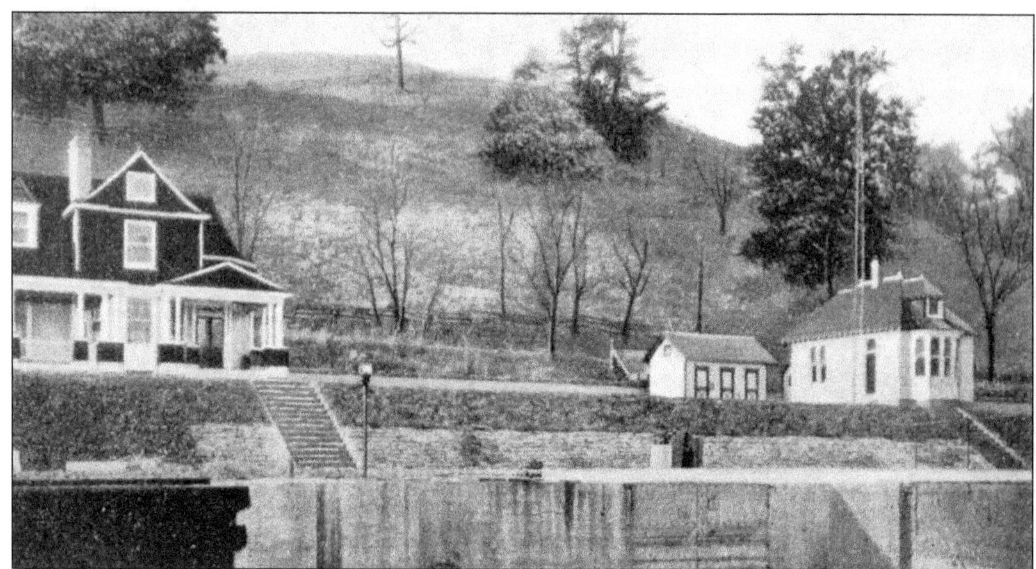

Early lockkeepers were responsible for operating the locks 24 hours a day, seven days a week. The U.S. Army Corps of Engineers, which built and operates the locks, provided them with government-owned houses. This 1908 picture of the Morgantown Lock depicts a typical lockkeeper's home on the left and the lock operation building on the right. Four sets of lock buildings survive on the Monongahela River in West Virginia.

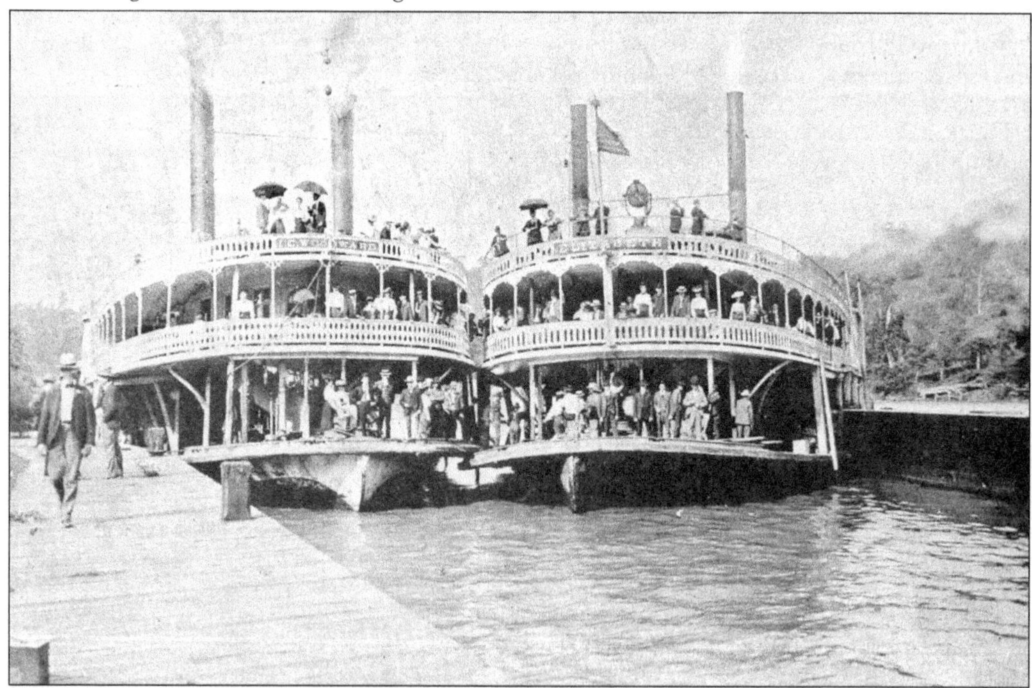

In July 1902, Monongalia County was host to a funny steamboat race. The packets *Elizabeth* and *I. C. Woodward* left Morgantown simultaneously. The captains knew that Lock Nine could only take one boat at a time, and the first boat through would get most of the business between Point Marion and Pittsburgh. An informal race ensued, and they reached the lock together. No one was injured, and the damage was minor.

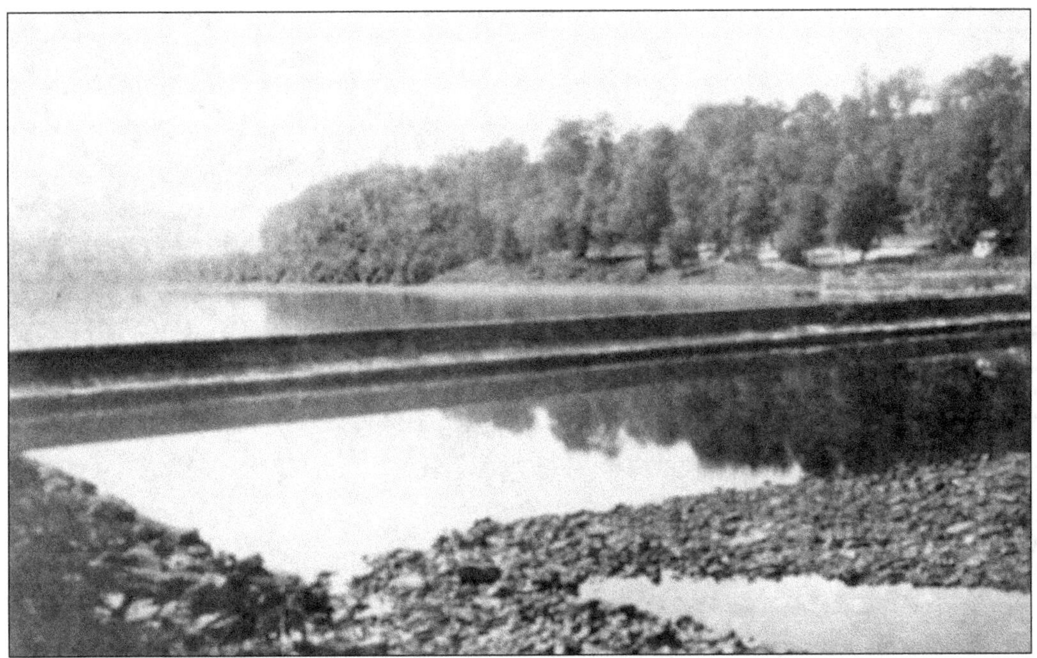

In 1930, a dry summer resulted in an empty river. This is a photograph of the situation at Lock and Dam 11, the next above Morgantown. The need to maintain river traffic provided the justification for the construction of the Tygart River dam, near Grafton, which also provides flood control and recreation. The construction of the Tygart Reservoir was a major New Deal project.

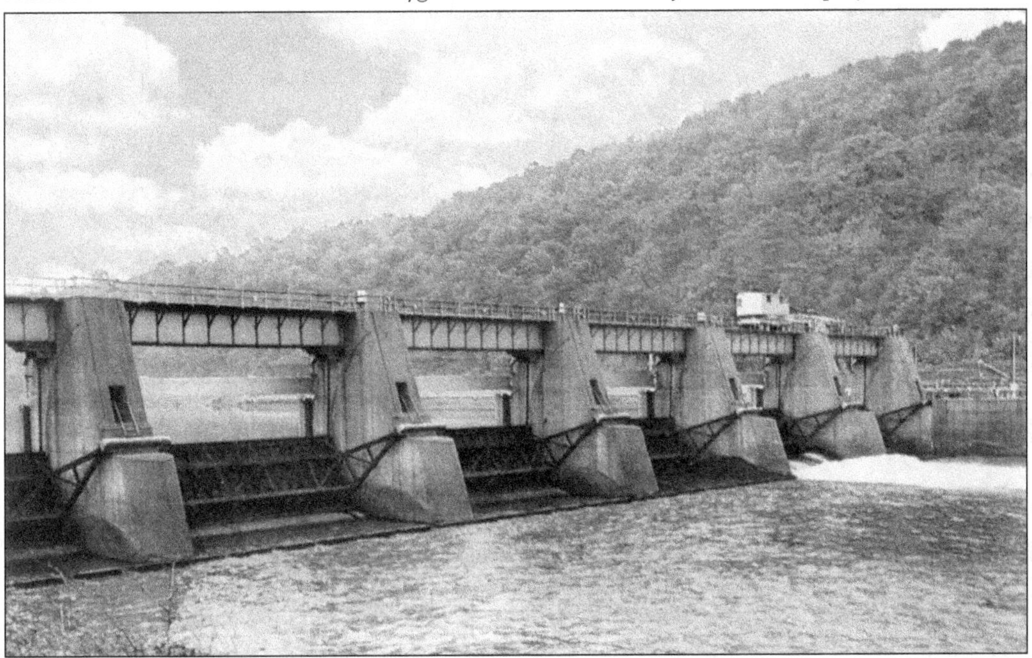

This photograph shows the present Morgantown Lock and Dam shortly after its completion in 1950. The dam has rotating gates, and the water flows out beneath them. The original series of locks and dams was built for passenger boats, and the locks were too small to handle six-barge tows of coal efficiently. The new facility was part of a modernization program started in the 1940s.

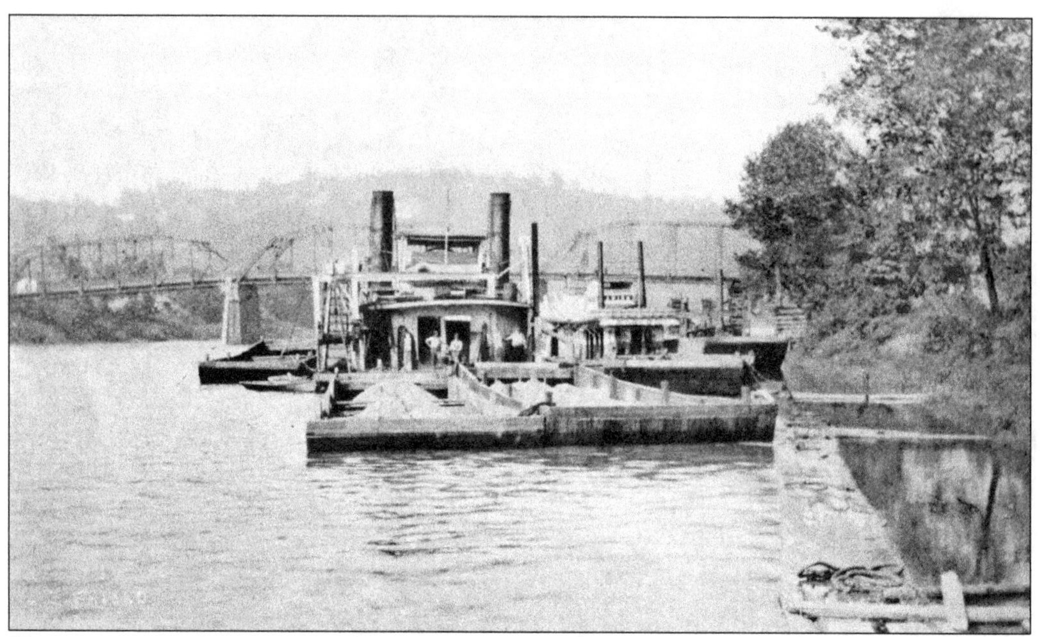

The McLean Sand Company dredged sand and gravel from the Cheat River for area construction. Although their major operations were in Point Marion, Pennsylvania, much of the production was unloaded beside the Westover Bridge for use in the Morgantown area. The McLean Sand boats and barges were the closest thing Morgantown had to a hometown river fleet.

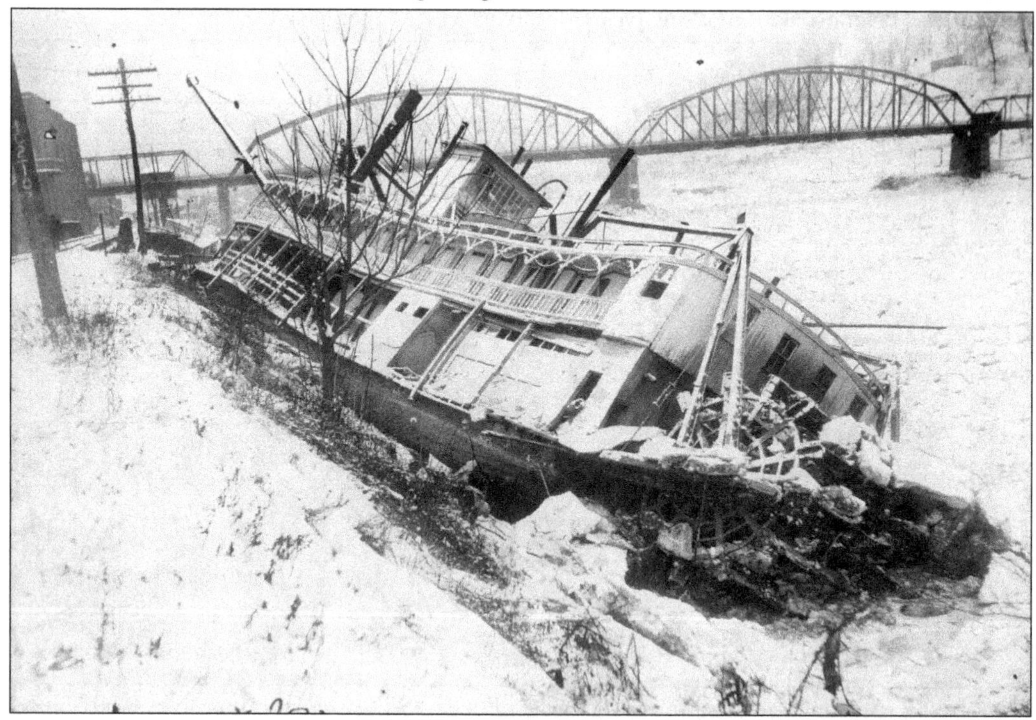

There was a heavy freeze in 1918. River ice formed a "jam" and damaged many boats and facilities in the Monongahela and Ohio Valleys. The *Valley Gem* packet boat was caught at Morgantown and destroyed. (Bunny Javins.)

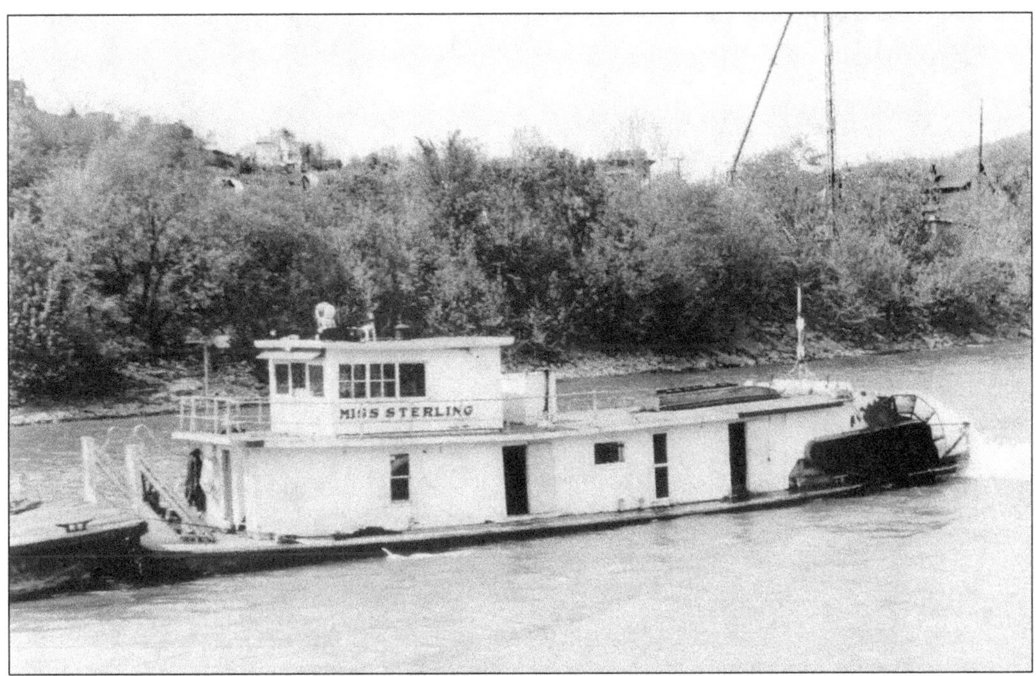

River people call a boat that moves barges a "towboat," even though it actually pushes them. The diesel-powered towboat *Miss Sterling* was the last sternwheel towboat to work pushing barges on the Monongahela River. *Miss Sterling* was built at Point Pleasant in 1926. She retired from commercial work in 1983 and since then has been a pleasure boat in Charleston.

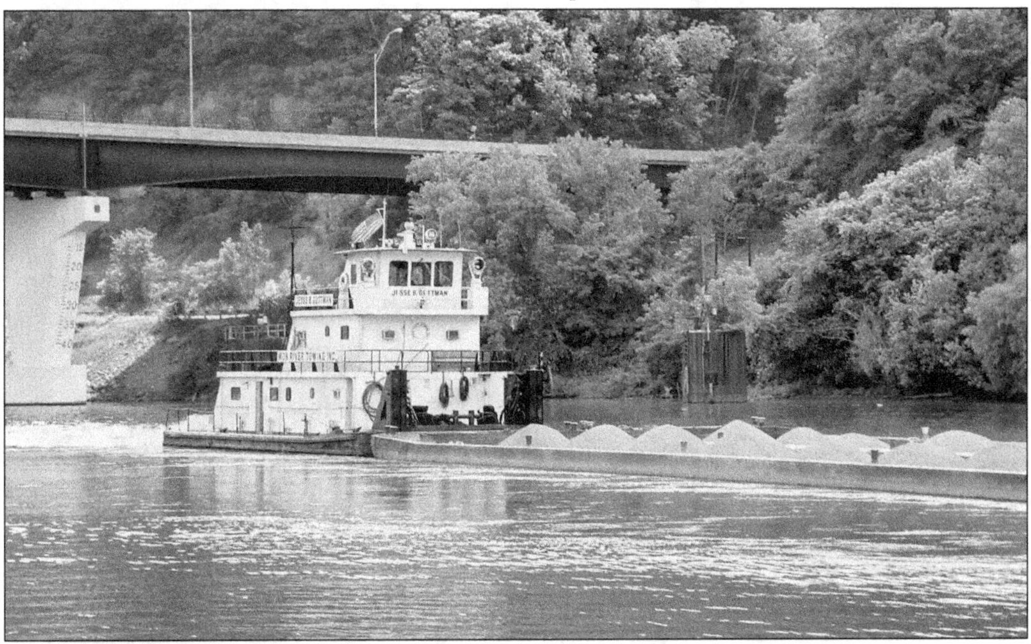

The *Jesse B. Guttman*, built in 1966 at Brownsville, Pennsylvania, is shown pushing barges under the new Star City Bridge. The barges, filled with limestone mined by Greer Limestone Company in the Deckers Creek valley, are probably bound for the Kanawha River. Coal and gasoline are also regularly moved through the Morgantown area by river.

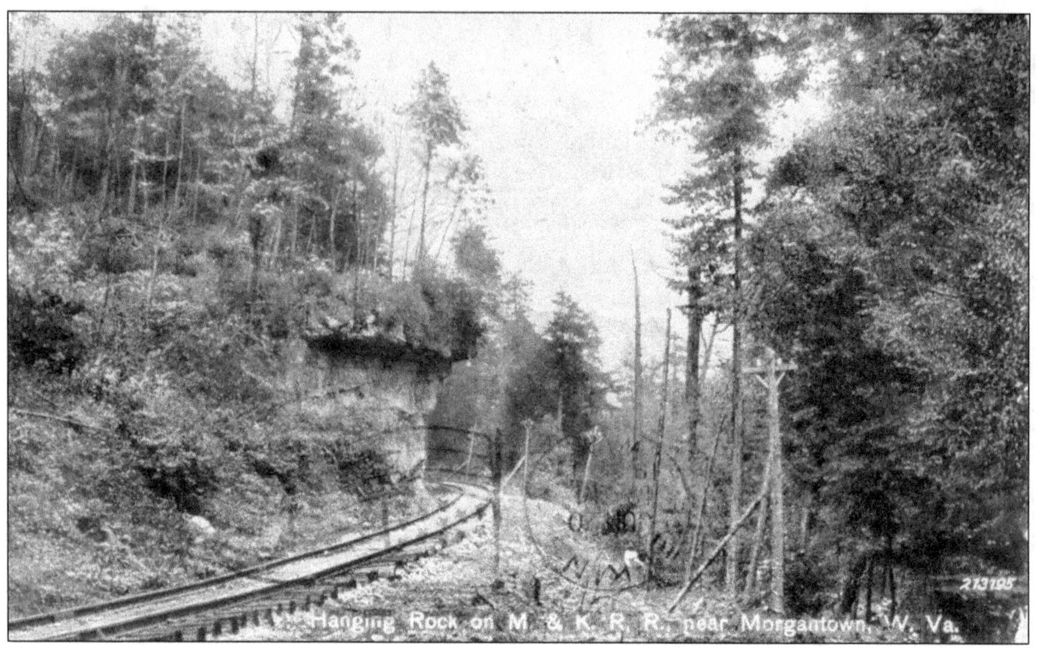

This rock cut on the Morgantown and Kingwood Railroad was one of many scenic spots. Passengers were thrilled to think it might fall. It did collapse, and the railroad ran excursion trains so the public could see reconstruction efforts. The route, without the tracks, survives as the Deckers Creek portion of the Monongahela River Trail.

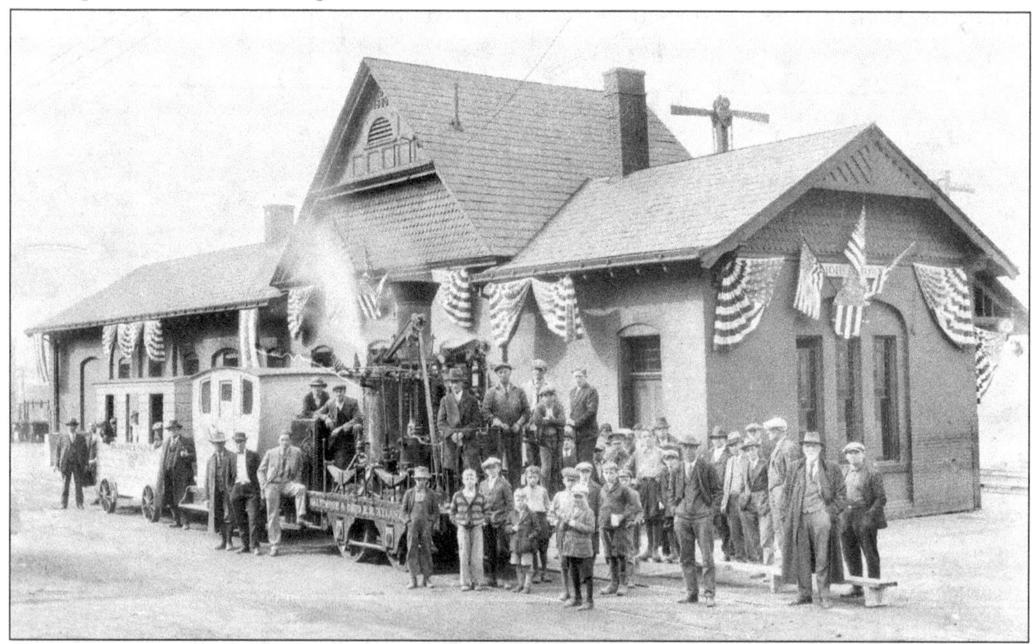

The Baltimore and Ohio Railroad exhibited this replica of its first train at the Morgantown Station during the 1926 celebration of the sesquicentennial. Parades, speeches, floats, bell ringing, and other activities took place to honor Monongahela County's 141st anniversary as well as national independence. (West Virginia and Regional History Collection, West Virginia University Libraries.)

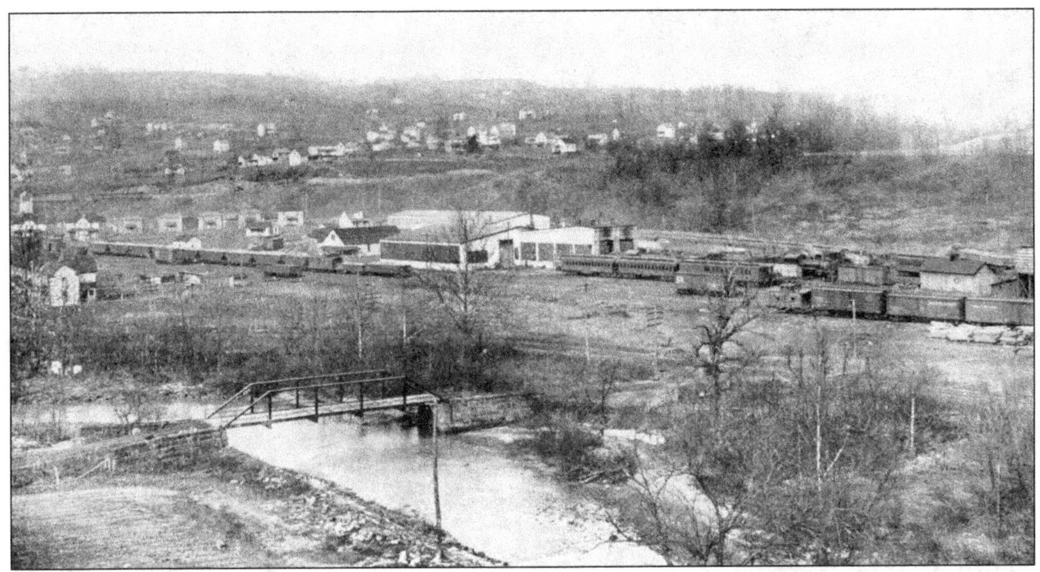

The Morgantown and Kingwood Railroad was chartered in 1899. It started at the Baltimore and Ohio (B&O) main line station in Morgantown and ran along Deckers Creek. By 1906, it provided passenger service to Kingwood twice a day. The rail line also served a variety of mines and industries. These maintenance shops, photographed about 1920, were in Sabraton.

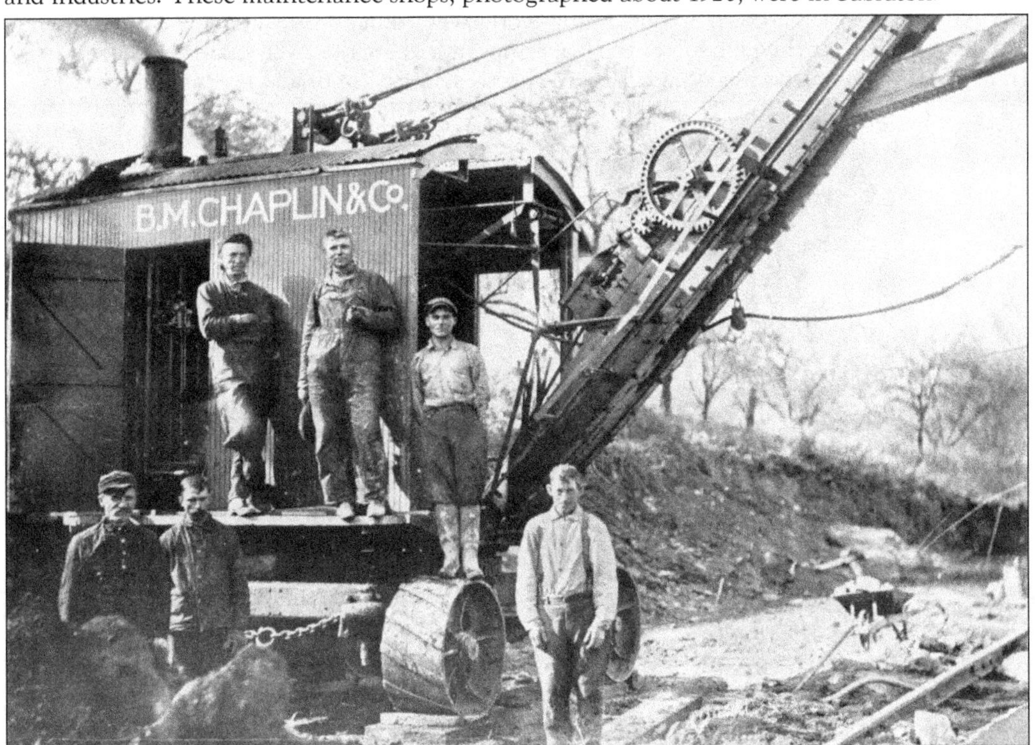

B. M. Chaplin and Company, construction contractors with offices in Morgantown, was also involved in mining coal. They advertised that they built roads, railroads, mines, and bridges. This is a steam-powered shovel. When this picture was taken in 1921, the Chaplin shovel was constructing a railroad near Pittsburgh.

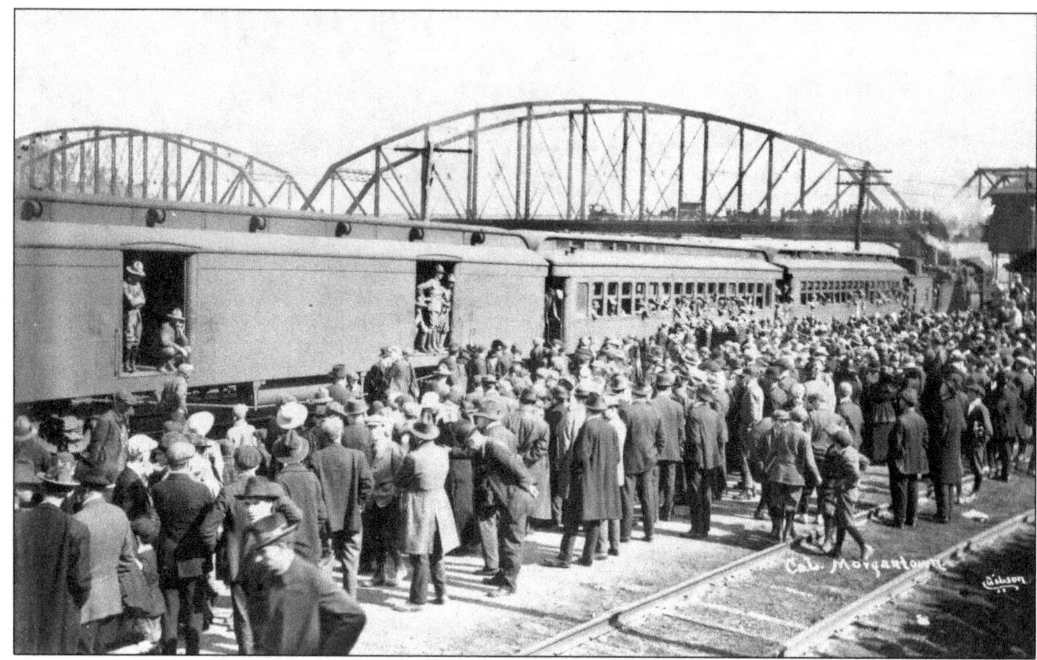

Local photographer Scott Gibson took this photograph of the community send-off for Company L, U.S. Army, at the Morgantown Station during World War I, around 1918. Today the station stands in Riverfront Park at the junction of the Caperton Trail along the river and the Deckers Creek Trail. (West Virginia and Regional History Collection, West Virginia University Libraries.)

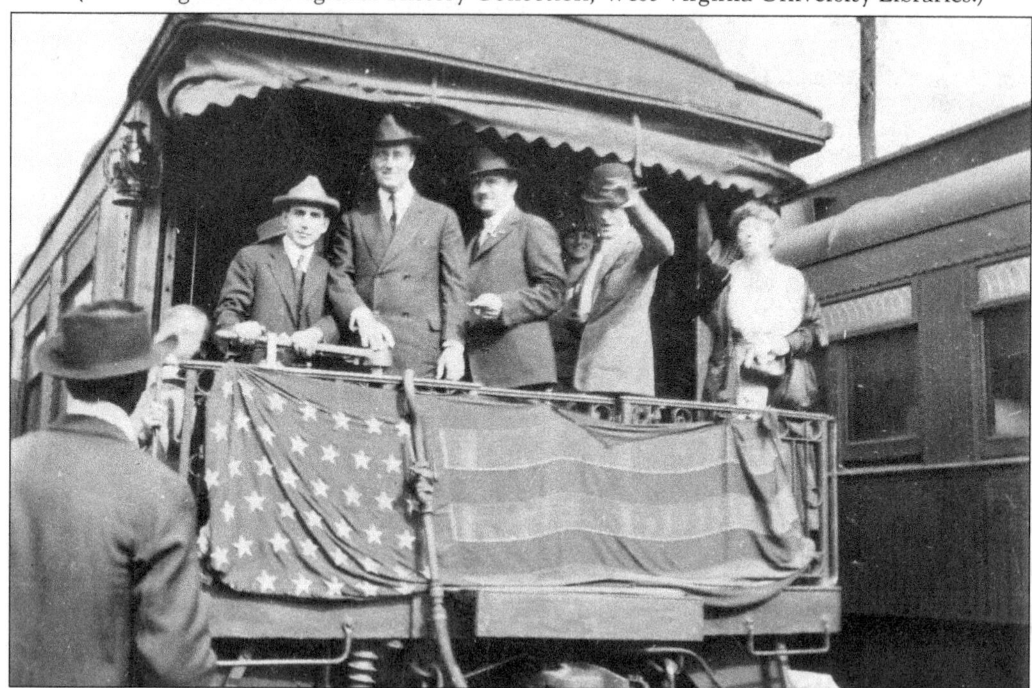

Franklin D. Roosevelt (second from left) rode the train to Morgantown on September 29, 1920. Roosevelt was a candidate for vice president, and he spoke at the Strand Theater. (National Archives, Roosevelt Library.)

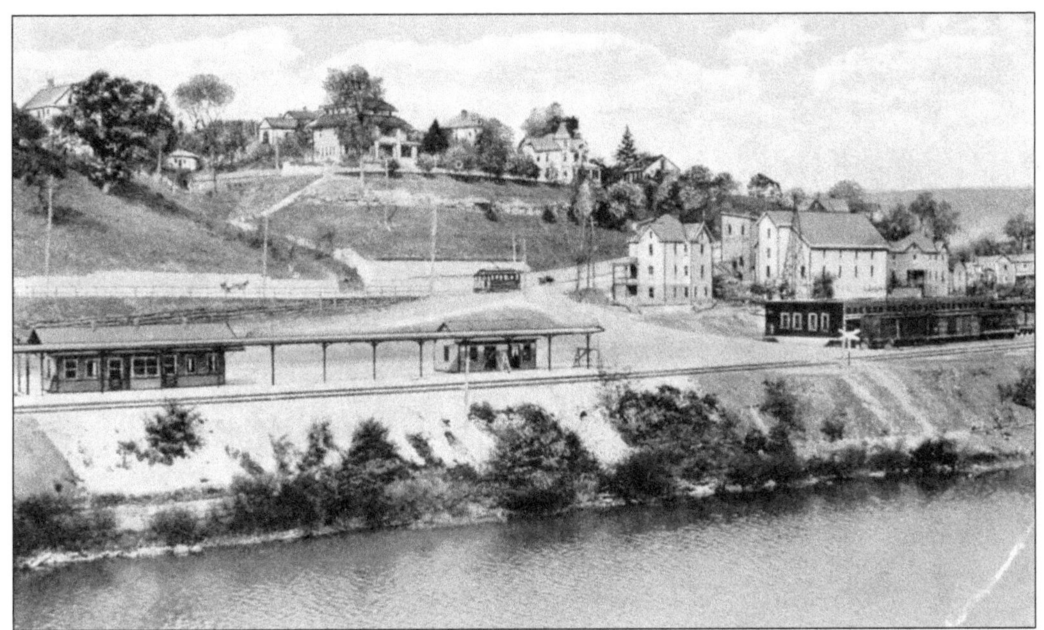

This postcard shows the Monongahela Railroad passenger and freight station in Westover. By 1921, the Monongahela Railroad provided a second passenger service from Fairmont to Pittsburgh and served many coal mines along the west side of the river. Passenger service ended in the 1950s. The tracks are now part of the Norfolk Southern system and still carry mile-long coal trains.

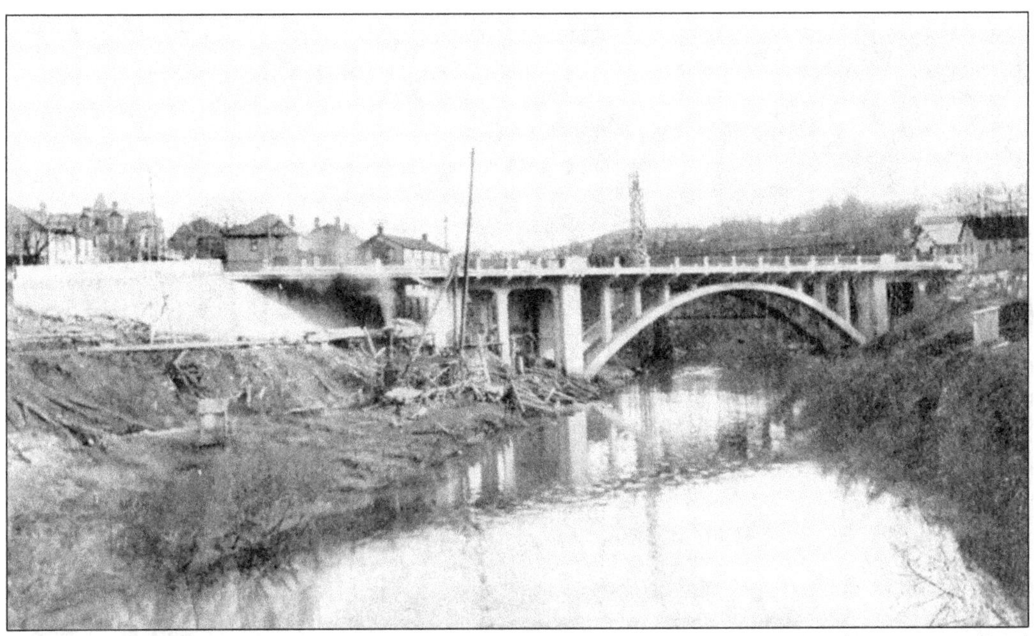

When construction of the 150-foot concrete arch in the South Morgantown Bridge was completed in 1915, it was the longest in the state. Today the street it carries is known as University Avenue. Sand and gravel for the bridge came by river from Point Marion, while limestone aggregate and concrete from local plants came down Deckers Creek.

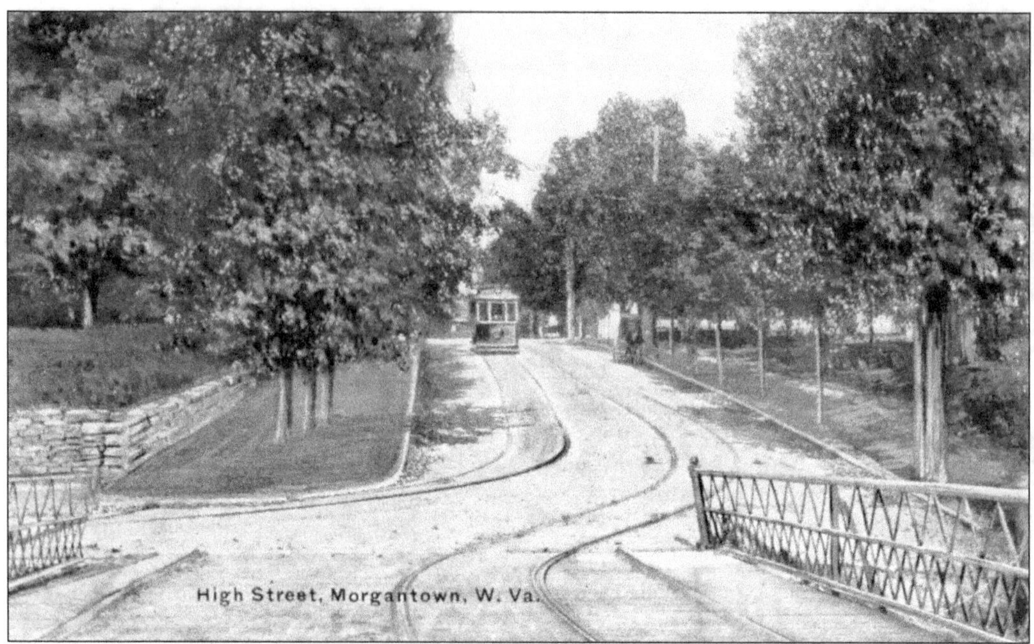

In 1910, the downtown business district ended at Pleasant Street. The trolley on High Street will be heading down Kirk. The tracks in the foreground lead onto the High Street Bridge to South Morgantown.

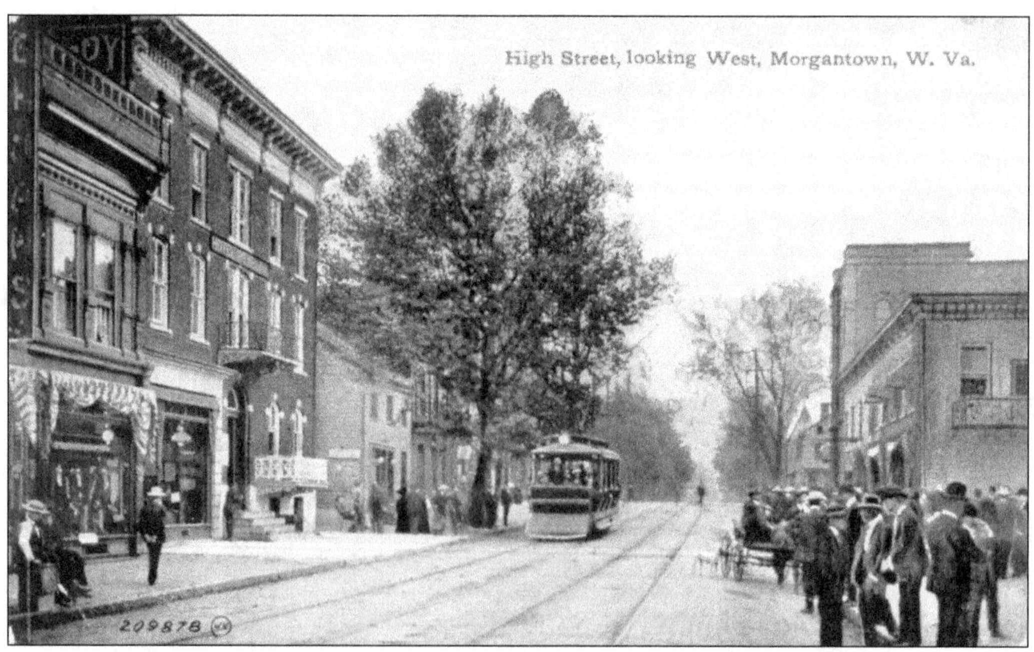

This postcard view was captured around 1910. Although nothing in the picture survives today, it appears that an upbound trolley was stopped at Wall Street on High Street. Streetcars and other traffic ran in both directions.

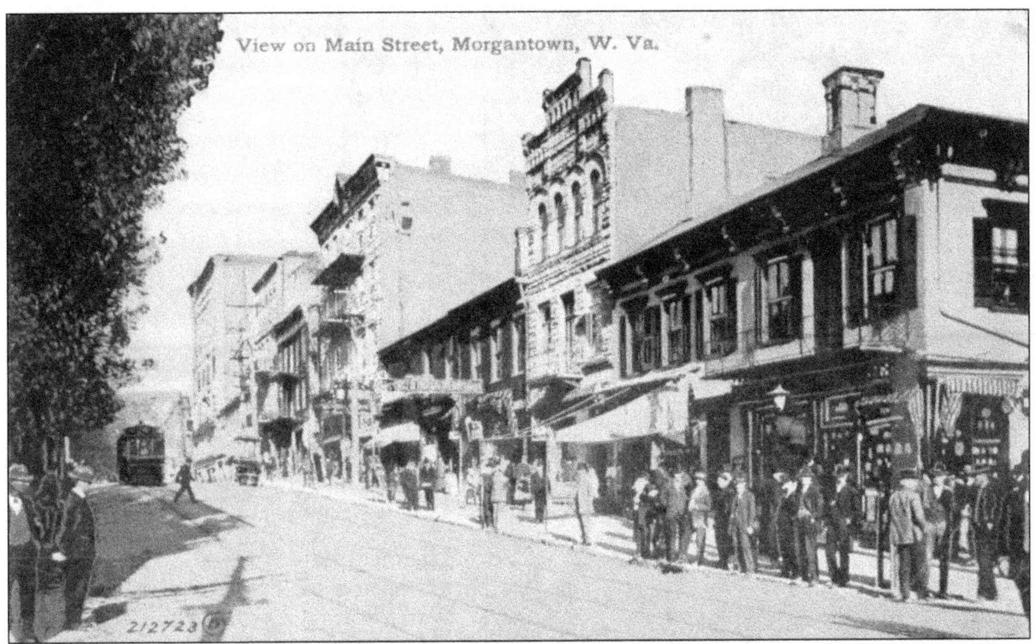

This 1915 postcard shows a trolley coming down High Street from Fayette Street toward Walnut Street.

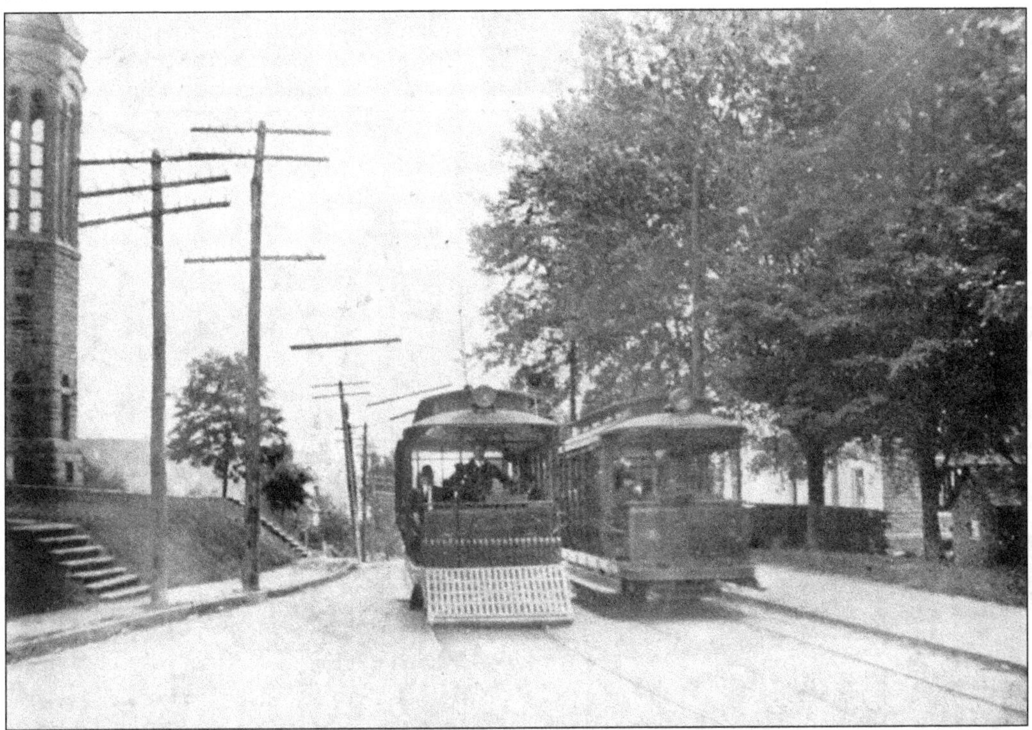

These trolley cars are in front of the West Virginia University Library. The first trolley system was opened by the Morgantown Traction and Electric Company in 1903. At its peak, the network of trolley lines provided service from downtown to the Seneca industrial district, Sabraton, Westover and Scotts Run, and South Morgantown. By 1923, trolley service had been discontinued.

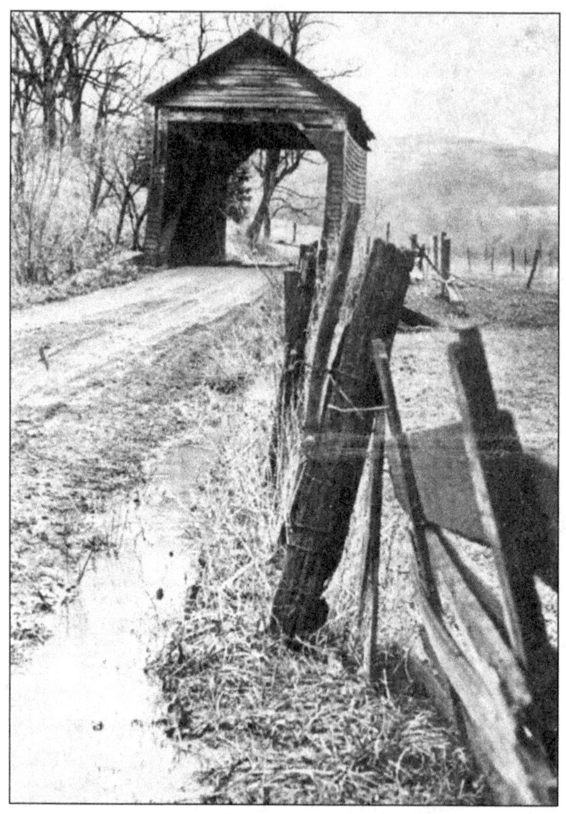

Morgantown's location near a river and large creeks necessitated building many bridges. As early as 1802, there is a report of a bridge across Deckers Creek. Covered bridges, such as this one near Laurel Point, were roofed to protect the wooden truss structure from the weather.

The first bridge across the Monongahela was opened in 1854. During the Civil War, it was used by both Union and Confederate armies. This picture was taken about 1908, shortly before it was torn down. Detailed examination of the photograph discloses a banner on the bridge that says, "This bridge is dangerous."

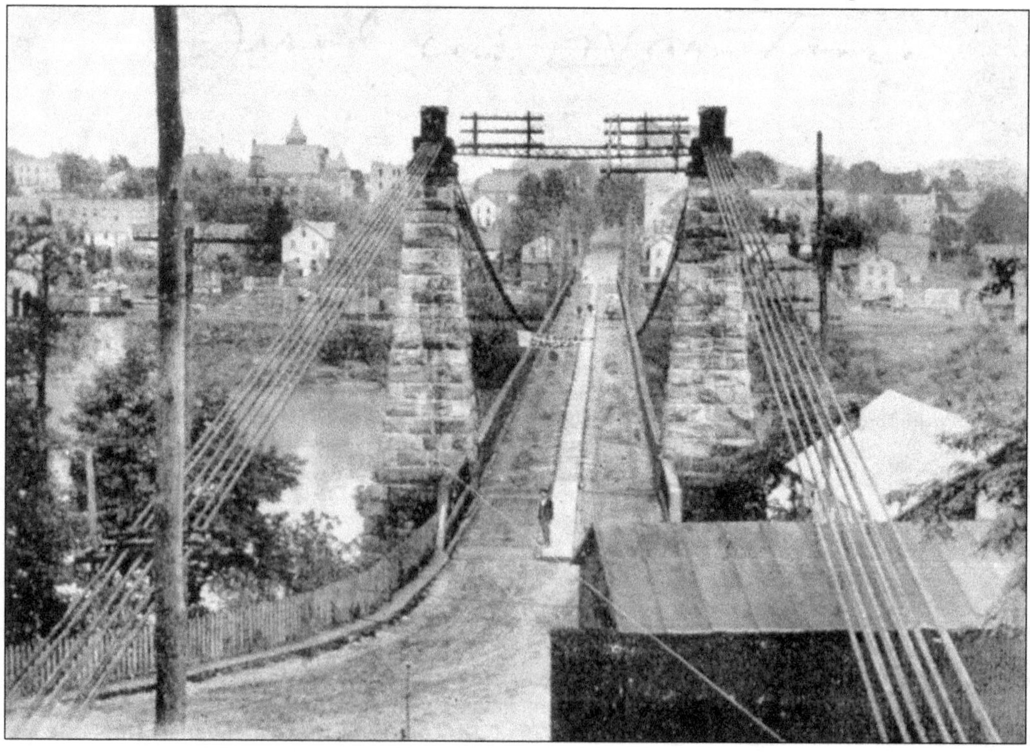

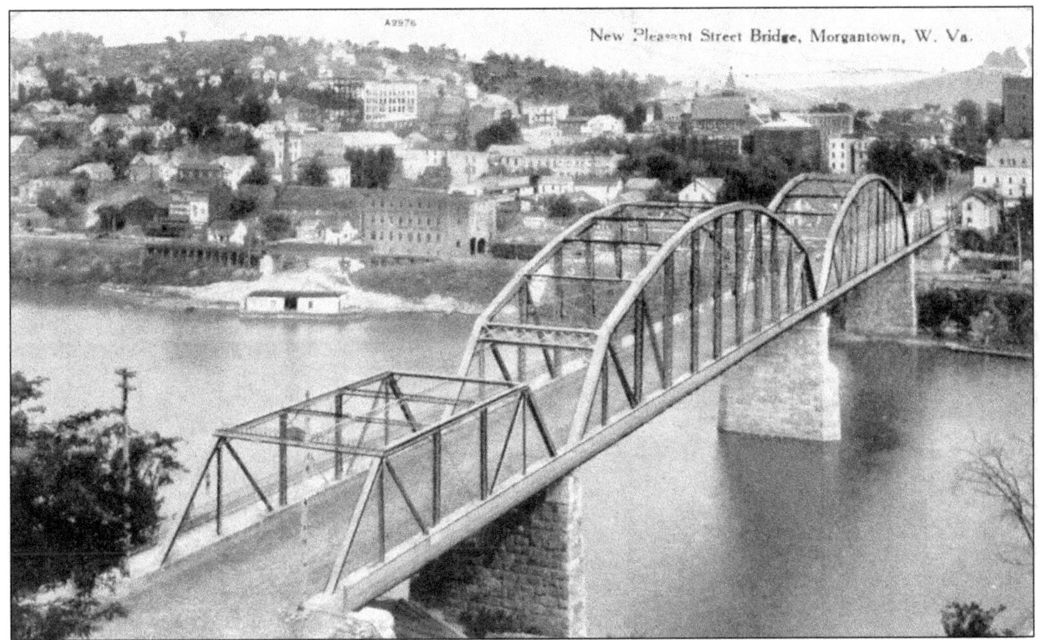

The steel-truss Westover Bridge at Pleasant Street was opened in 1909. The Morgantown wharfboat, a sort of floating station constructed as a building in an old steamboat hull, can be seen at the foot of Walnut Street.

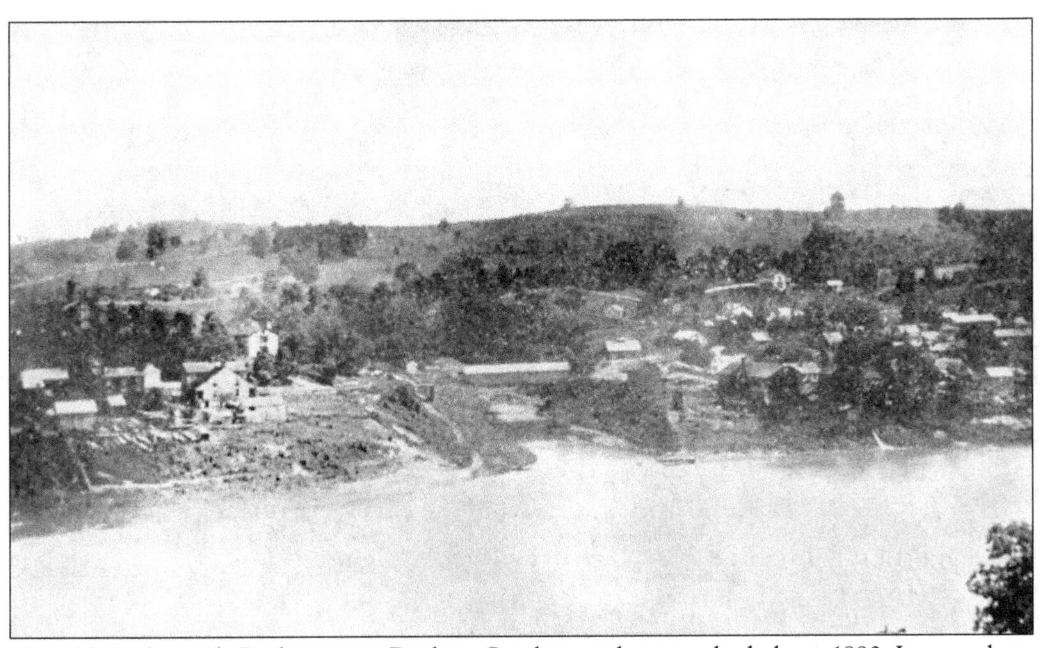

The old Durbannah Bridge across Deckers Creek was photographed about 1880. It was a long covered bridge. The area south of Deckers Creek included an iron foundry and tanneries. The hillsides behind the town show how rural the area was. (Morgantown Public Library.)

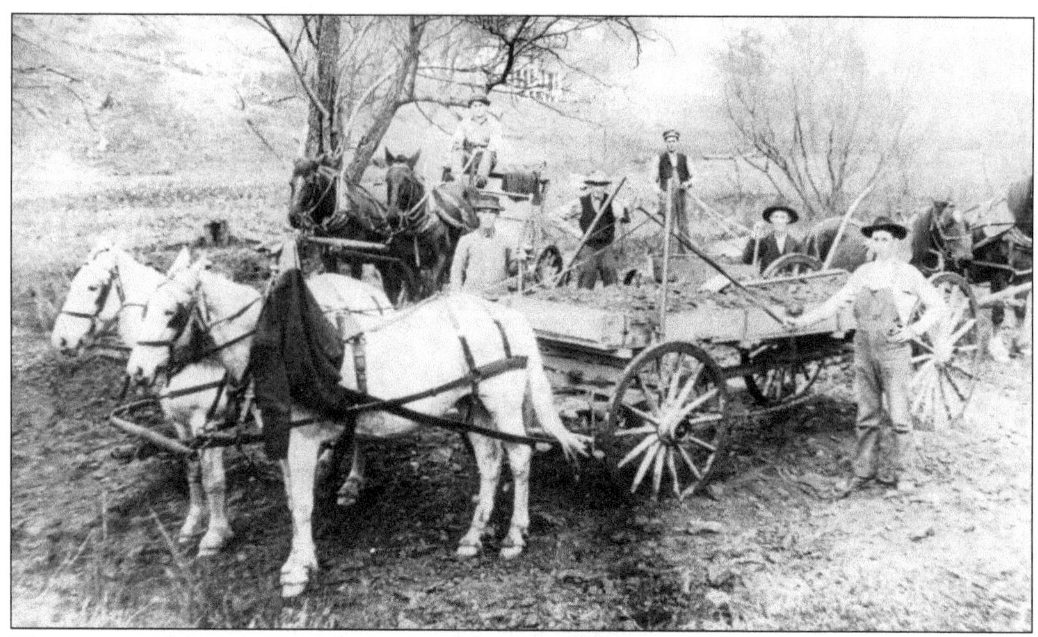

These men and their teams and wagons are hauling gravel from a creek bed. The gravel could be used to improve local roads, many of which were unpaved earth and gravel "all-weather" roads.

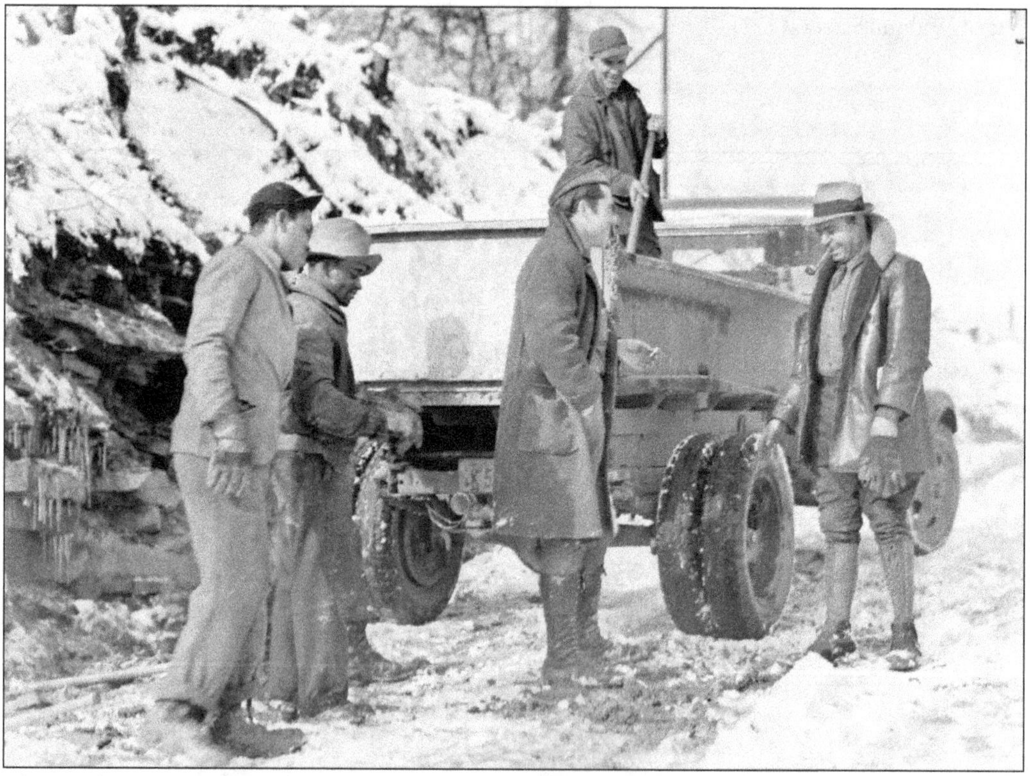

This road crew at work in 1937 in Scotts Run was spreading cinders by hand during a late snowfall. While some winters produce little snow, sometimes there is plenty. The legendary storm was at Thanksgiving in 1950, when about 30 inches fell. (National Archives.)

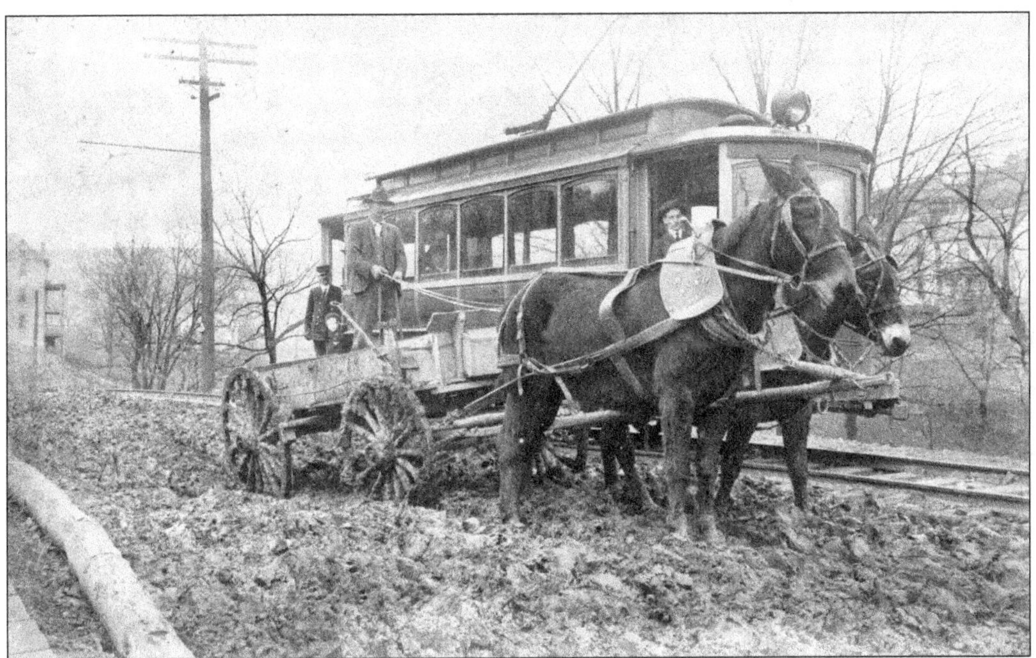

Before the construction of paved streets and roads, a team of horses, or in this case mules, sometimes provided more reliable transportation than an engine-powered vehicle. This 1906 scene was on North Willey Street.

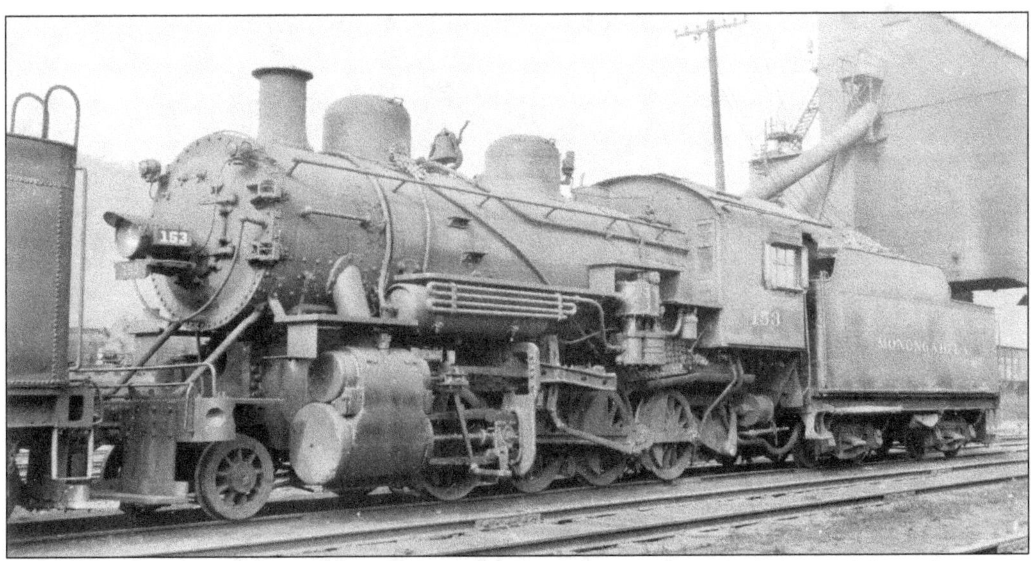

Steam locomotives such as Monongahela Railroad Engine 153 moved the coal from the mines west of the river to the steel mills around Pittsburgh. This engine was built by Alco in 1918 and was still in service when photographed in 1949. Not only did these engines move coal, they were also powered by it and threw huge clouds of black smoke along their routes.

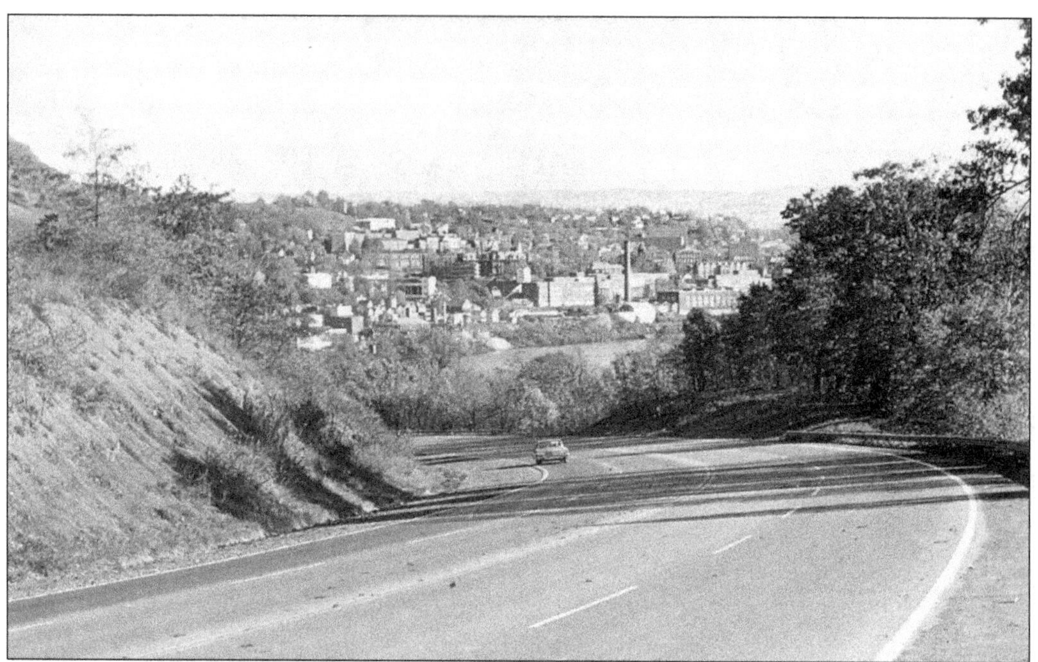

In 1950, a new highway to the north was constructed. From downtown, the route followed Beechurst Avenue past the glass factories, and then this four-lane boulevard was cut into the hill to Evansdale. The road descended to Star City, where a new bridge crossed the river to Scotts Run. Route 19 got an almost straight new path to Mount Morris, Pennsylvania.

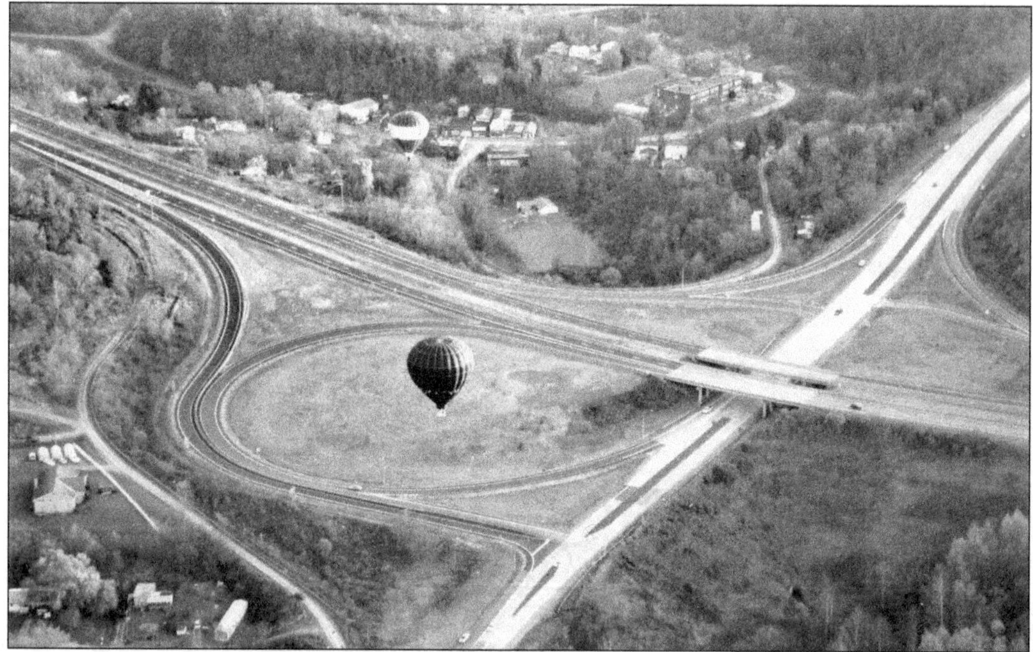

The construction of Interstate 79 in the 1970s brought major changes to Morgantown by cutting hours off residents' trips to Charleston and Pittsburgh. It also brought in many more people from outside West Virginia for activities like the Mountaineer Balloon Festival. (University Motors Mountaineer Balloon Festival.)

Pres. Lyndon Johnson attended the dedication of the Morgantown airport on September 20, 1964. Here he posed with Walter L. "Bill" Hart, for whom the airport was named, and Mrs. Hart. Construction of the field actually began as a Depression relief project in 1935, and scheduled service began in 1937. (Morgantown Public Library.)

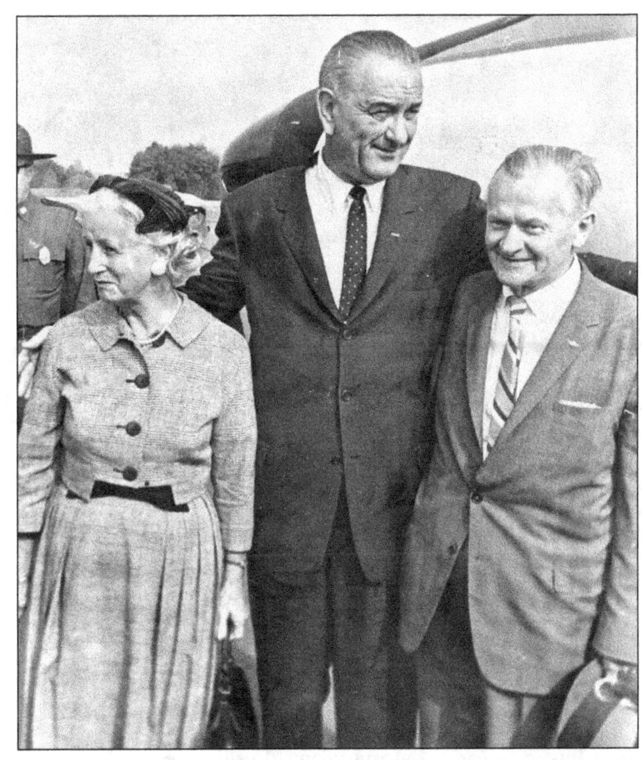

Air Force One parked on the ramp at Morgantown's Hart Field in 1964 when Pres. Lyndon Johnson spoke at the dedication ceremony. The ceremony marked the construction of an extended runway, new terminal building, and Flight Service Station at the airport. (Morgantown Public Library.)

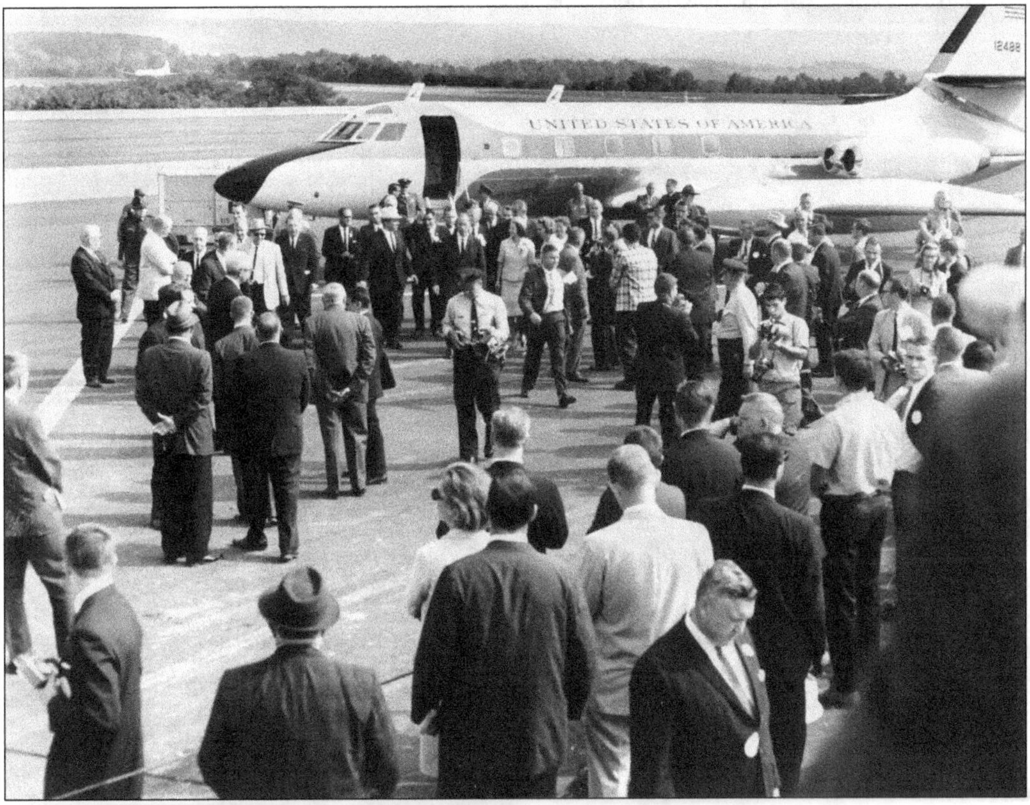

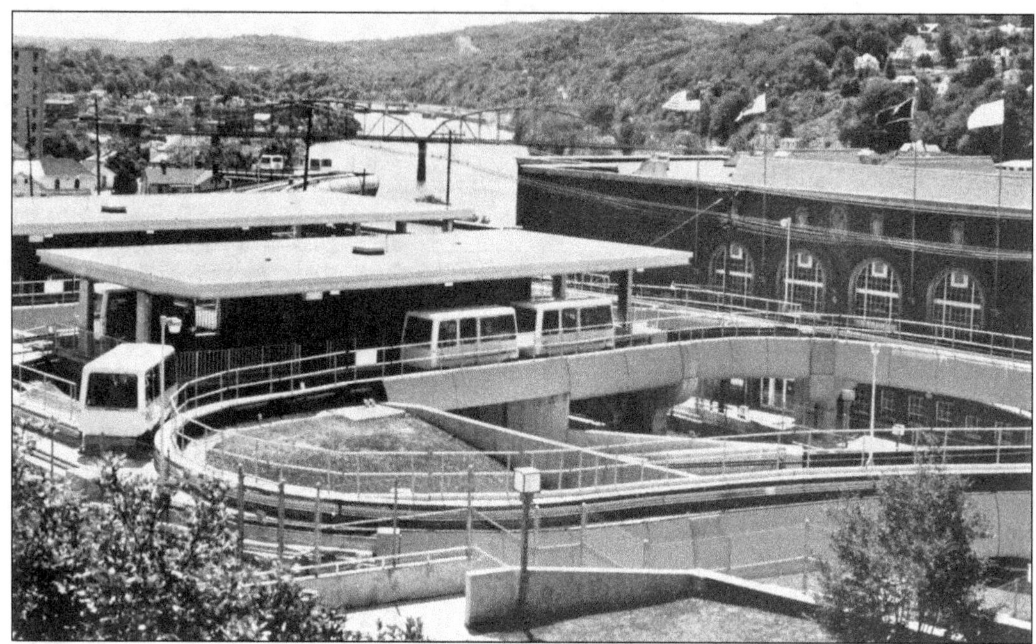

Opened in 1975, West Virginia University's Personal Rapid Transit System, locally called the PRT, has carried over 30,000 students in a single day. Visitors also enjoy riding the rubber-wheeled cars, which offer scenic views of the Morgantown area. Visitors often compare the PRT with something from Disney World. (Morgantown Public Library.)

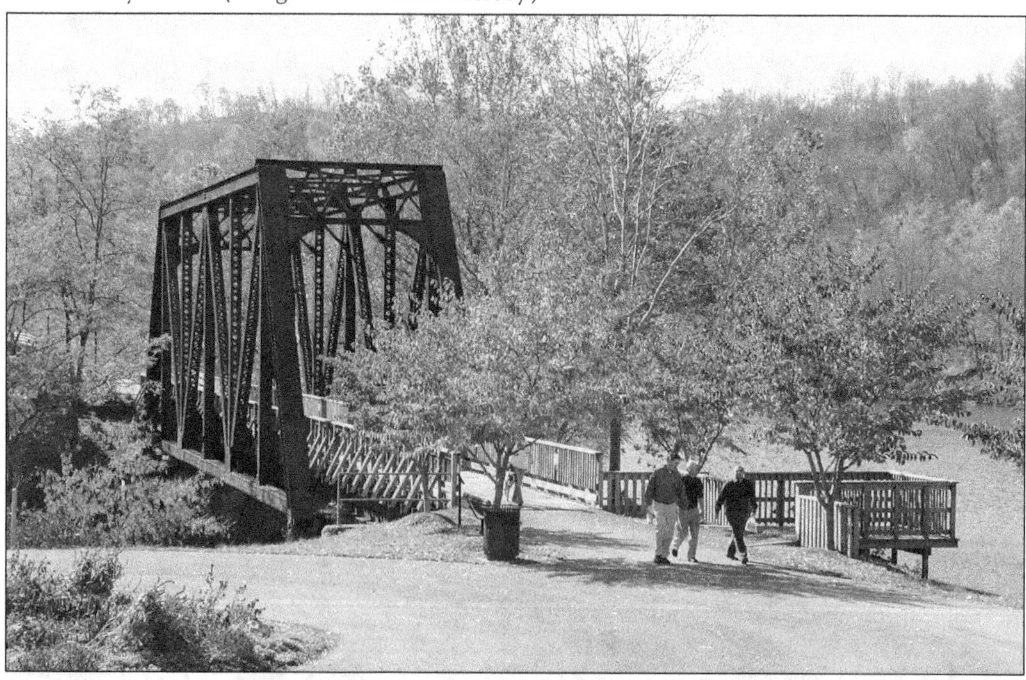

The right-of-way of the former B&O Railroad tracks was converted to a rail-trail in the 1990s. The trail along the Monongahela River bank runs from the Pennsylvania line to Fairmont, and a connecting trail runs up the Deckers Creek valley. This photograph shows the bridge across Deckers Creek at Hazel Ruby McQuain Riverfront Park in downtown Morgantown.

Three

GLASS

In 1895, local developers found themselves with a large supply of natural gas for which they had a very small market. They offered the Seneca Glass Company, then in Fostoria in Seneca County, Ohio, a free factory site and a forgivable loan for construction. Within six months, the entire company had moved to Morgantown. Two hundred employees were at work producing three railroad car loads of tableware per week. Seneca Glass was unusual in that the stockholders were actually glass workers.

In 1899, local businessmen organized the Morgantown Glassworks, later known as Economy Tumbler and then Morgantown Glassware Guild, to produce tableware. The Beaumont company moved to Morgantown in 1918, giving the community three producers of mouth-blown glass for table use.

Tableware was not only mouth-blown but also hand-cut with grinding wheels or acid-etched with intricate designs. This glass was sold through department stores across America and used in homes and hotels, on trains and ships, and in government facilities. Production at Seneca continued until 1984 and at Beaumont until 1992. While industry leaders complained about high fuel costs and overseas competition, the primary reason for the end of the American hand-crafted tableware industry has been a decline in interest in owning and using sets of fine glassware.

In 1901, the W. R. Jones Company began producing mouth-blown window glass. They were followed in that trade by Marilla Window Glass, then specialty window glass producers making pressed and rolled products joined the industrial community. Machine-made window glass put the blown producers out of business by 1925.

Later plants produced a variety of lighting products. These included chimneys for oil lamps, lamp shades, and lamp base parts. The Davis Lynch Glass Company, established in 1946, continues to produce mouth-blown lamp shades today.

Most of the glass produced in Morgantown was sold through wholesale jobbers or retailers who put their own brands on the products, so only a small portion of the millions of pieces of locally made glass was ever popularly associated with Morgantown.

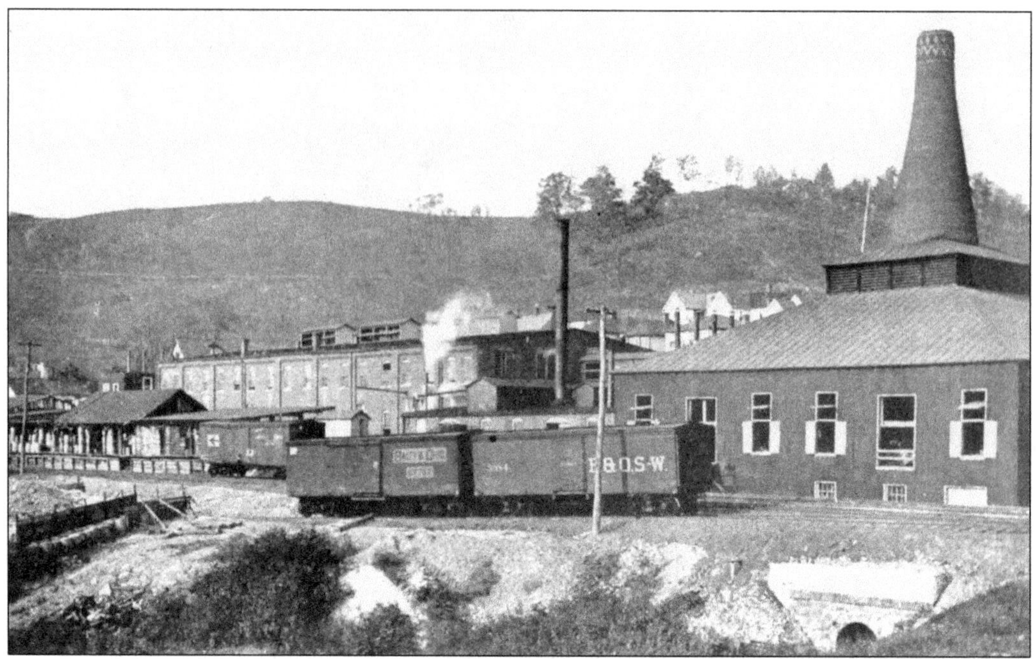

The Seneca Glass Company factory was built in 1896. The building on the left in this 1902 photograph burned in 1906 and was replaced by the one designed by prominent Morgantown architect Elmer Jacobs, which now houses the Seneca Center retail complex. The original furnace building is still standing.

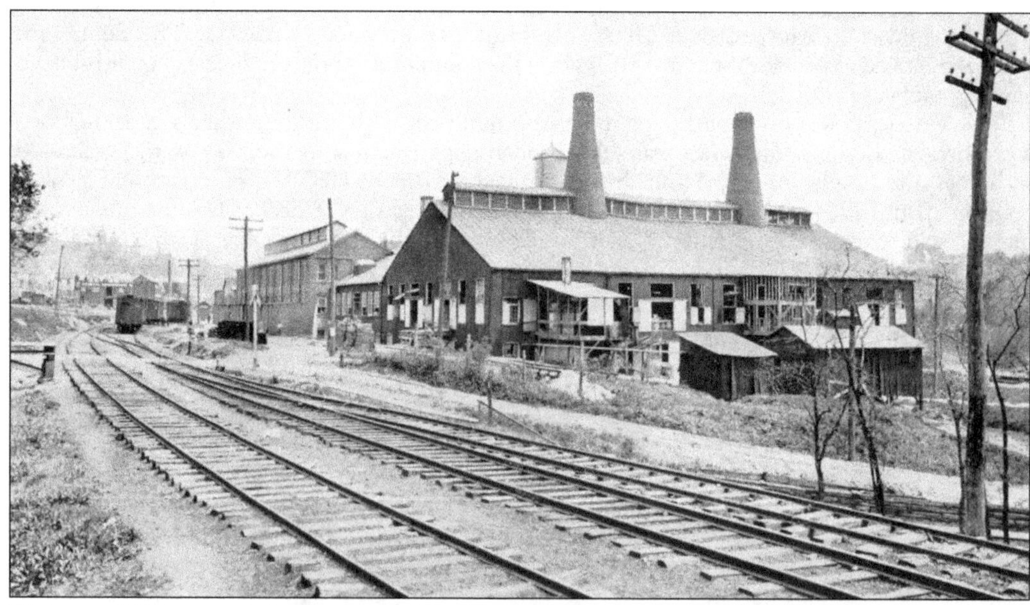

This is a 1902 view of the Economy Tumbler Company, founded by local businessmen. The company, better known today by its later name, Morgantown Glassware Guild, closed in 1975. The company is best known for blown stemware with pressed stem shapes.

Before World War I, child labor was common in American industry. This 1908 photograph shows a boy at Seneca Glass Company operating a mold for a glass blower. The molten glass, at about 1,700 degrees Farenheit, moves within inches of his hands and face. His workday would have been 10 hours long. These conditions would have been common across the country in glass factories. (National Archives.)

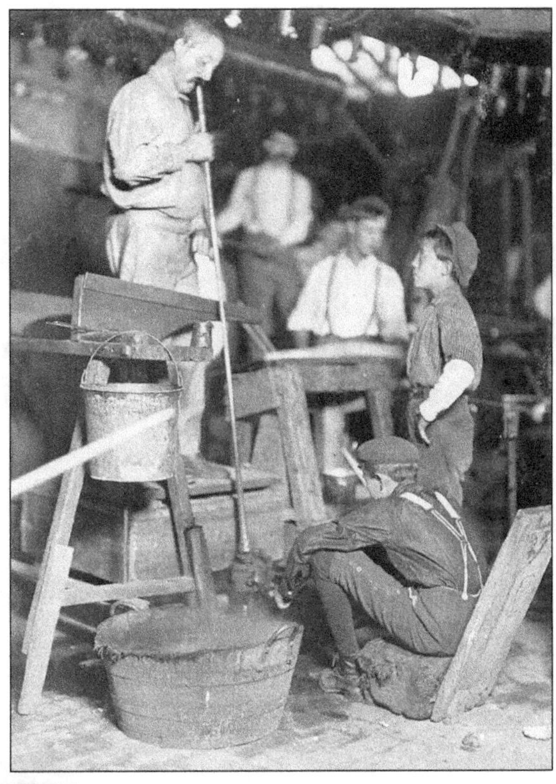

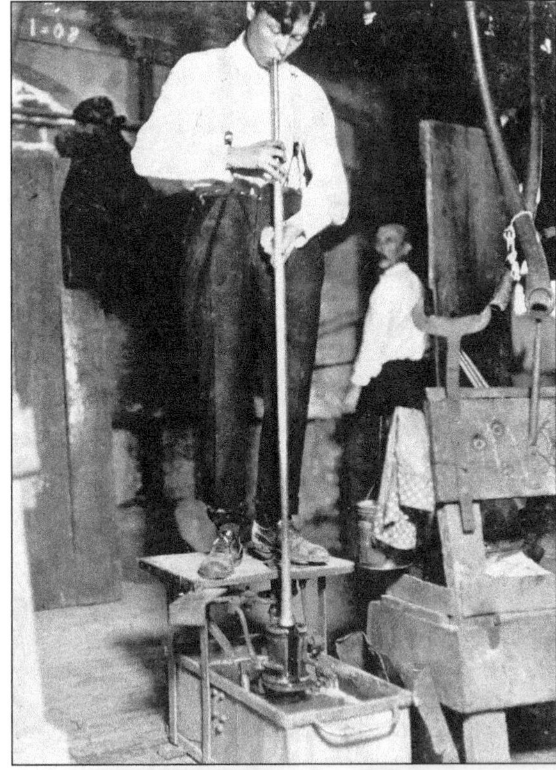

A blower in another part of the same furnace room is operating his mold with a foot pedal. Even today, this mechanism is known in glass plants as a "boy." Each blower would be expected to produce between 700 and 1,200 pieces of blown glass each day. The two photographs on this page were taken by Lewis Wickes Hine as part of a federal investigation of child labor practices. (National Archives.)

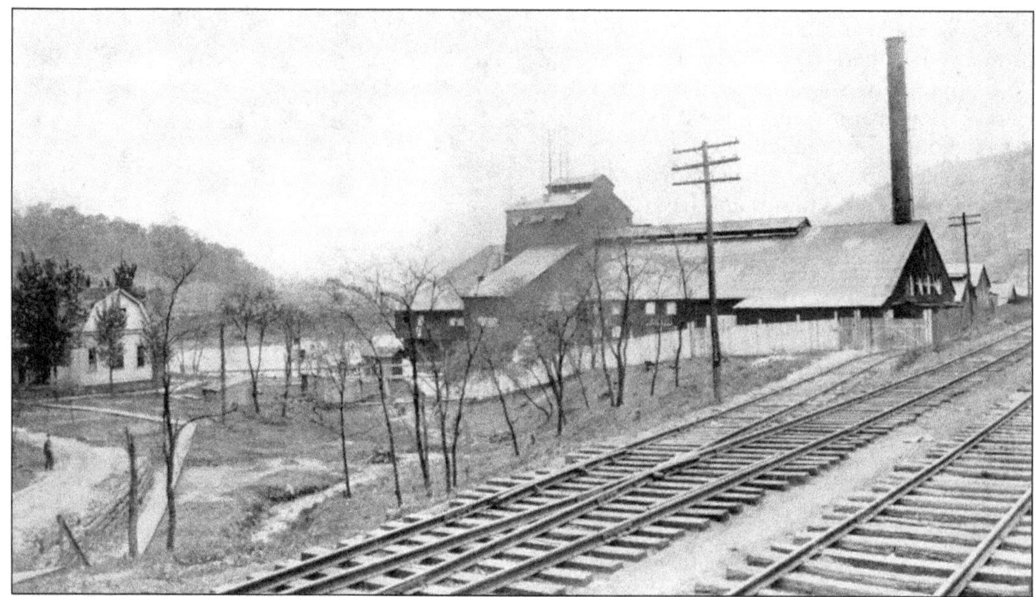

The W. R. Jones Company began producing mouth-blown window glass on this location in 1901. The first factory burned, was rebuilt, and became part of United States Window Glass. This shows the factory at the north end of the Seneca district in 1920. The development of machines forced the plants producing mouth-blown window glass out of business by 1925.

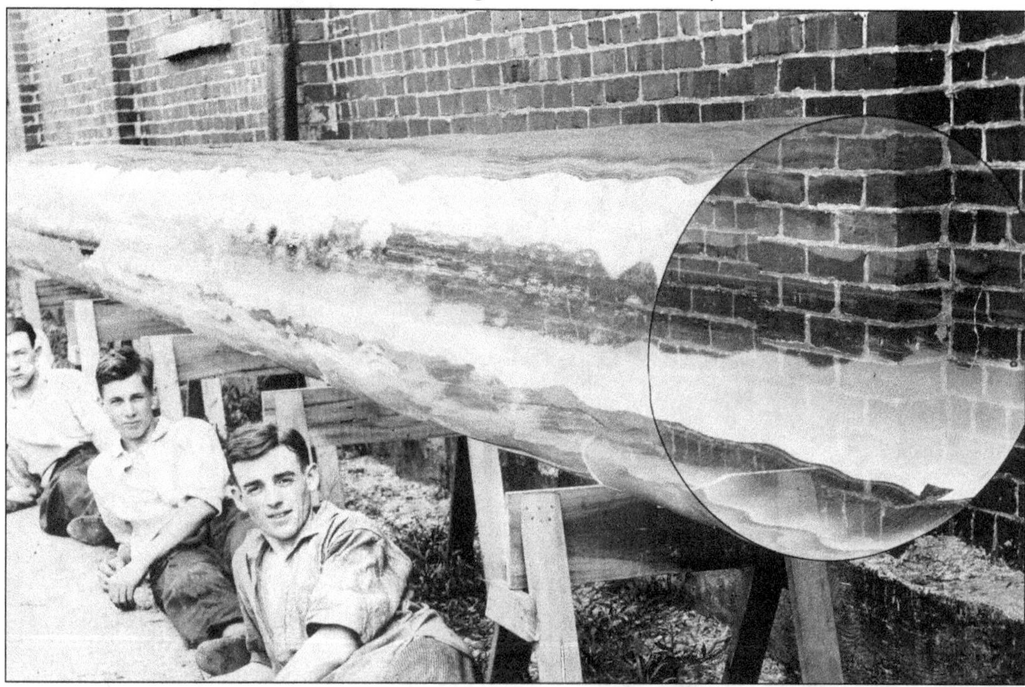

Morgantown window glass factories made their products using the cylinder method. These boys are merely posing with a cylinder. Large bottles were mouth blown, then cut and flattened to make the sheets. It took years to acquire the great strength and specialized skill required to handle the large size and heavy weight of the cylinders. (West Virginia and Regional History Collection, West Virginia University Libraries.)

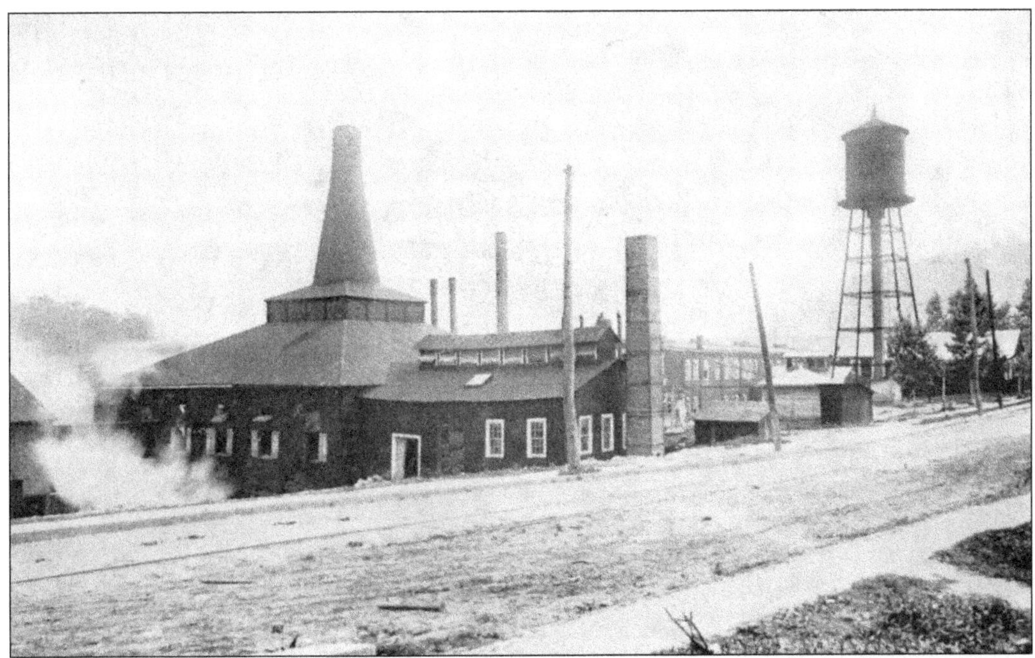

This shows the Seneca factory in 1921. At that time, the trolley line and Beechurst Avenue ended here. It was not until 1950, when the first Star City Bridge was constructed, that the road was extended up the hill and became U.S. Route 19. The chimney on the furnace and the water tank are still prominent local landmarks.

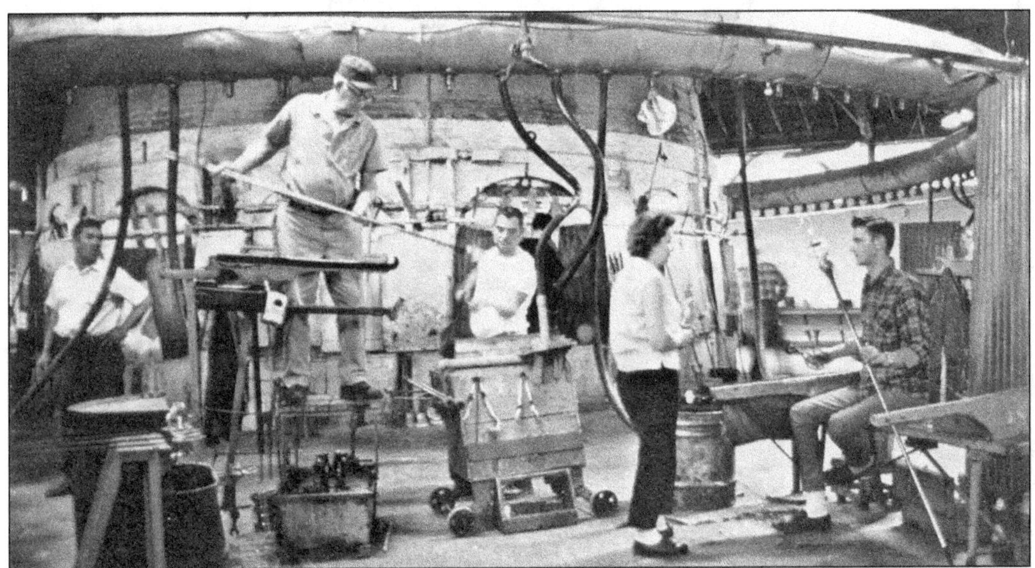

This photograph shows glass blowing at the Seneca Glass Company in 1969. A worker from 1896 would have been surprised to find a woman, no boys, and electric lights but otherwise could have stepped into position and gone straight to work.

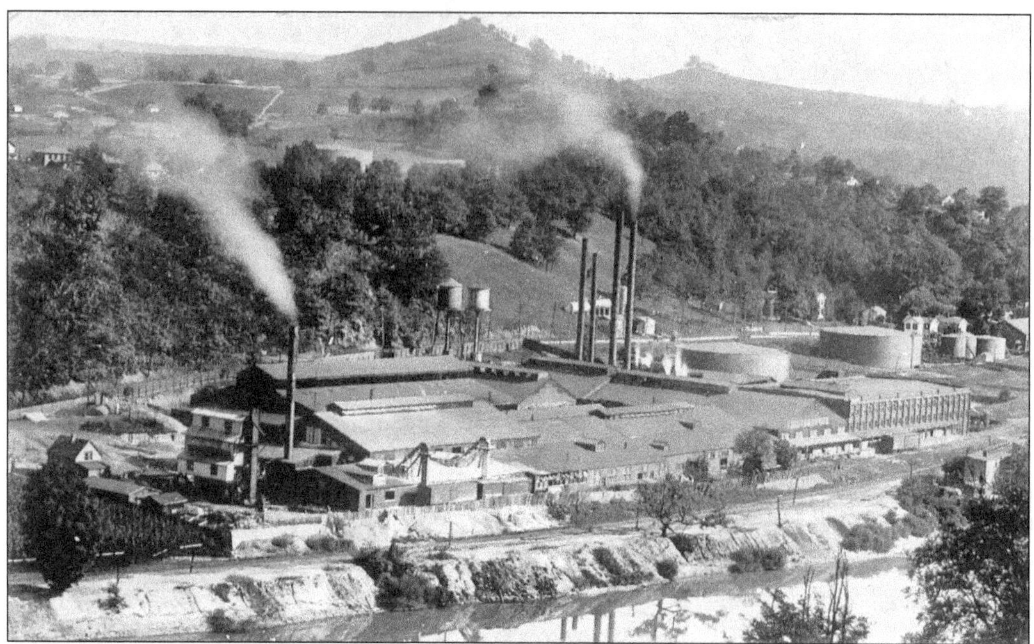

The large factory in the center of the picture is the Mississippi Glass Company. Their primary product was "chicken wire" safety glass. The factory was located on what is now Don Knotts Boulevard. The factory opened in 1902 and closed in 1937. The hilltop in the center is Dorsey's Knob. The tanks on the right were part of the Standard Oil tank field.

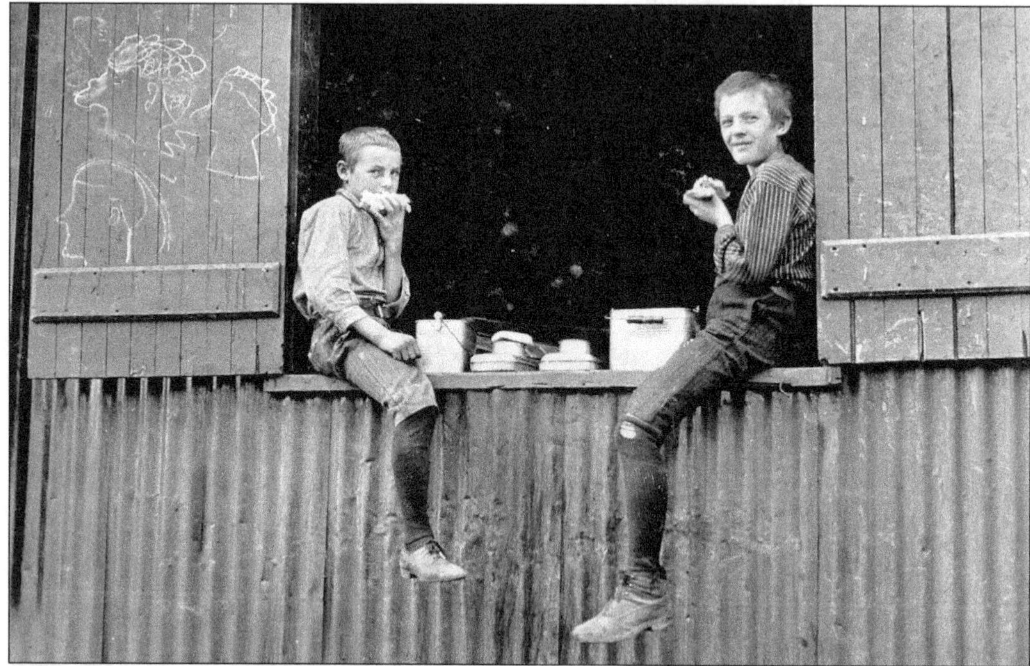

During the 1908 investigations of child labor, Lewis Hine took this picture at the Economy Tumbler Company (later Morgantown Glassware Guild) factory. Two workers, possibly a father and son or two brothers, open their dinner buckets between the five-hour morning and afternoon turns in the blowing shop. (National Archives.)

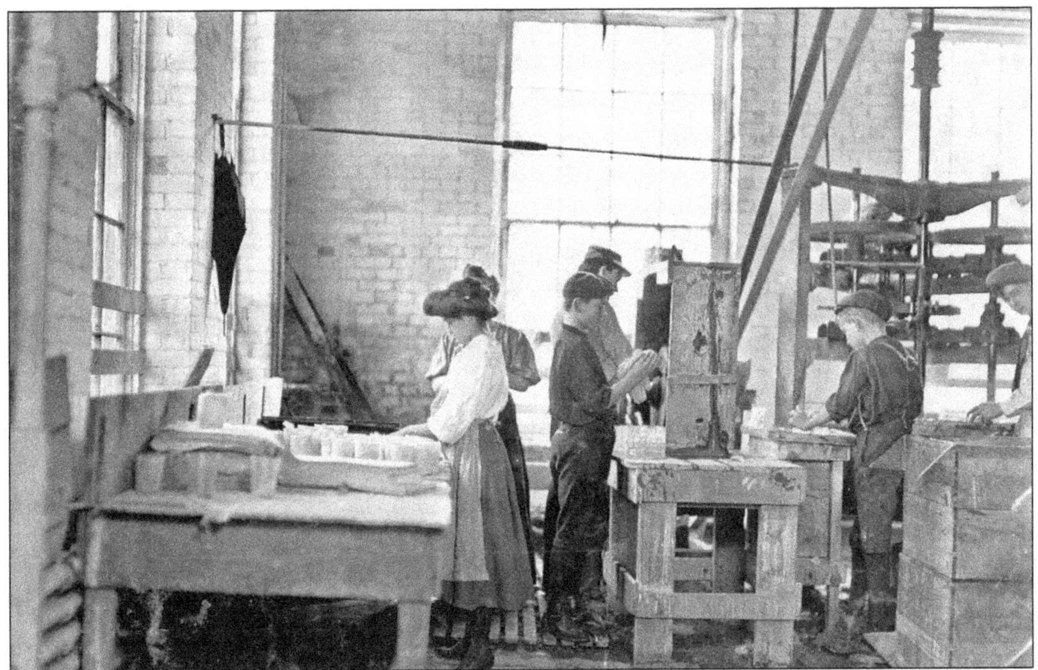

Women and girls also worked in the glass factories. In connection with this photograph taken in the Union Stopper Company, the 1908 investigators said, "Girls, boys and men, polishing and wrapping, working together: morals in glass factory are proverbially bad." Reformers considered simply having both sexes working in the same space to be unacceptable. (National Archives.)

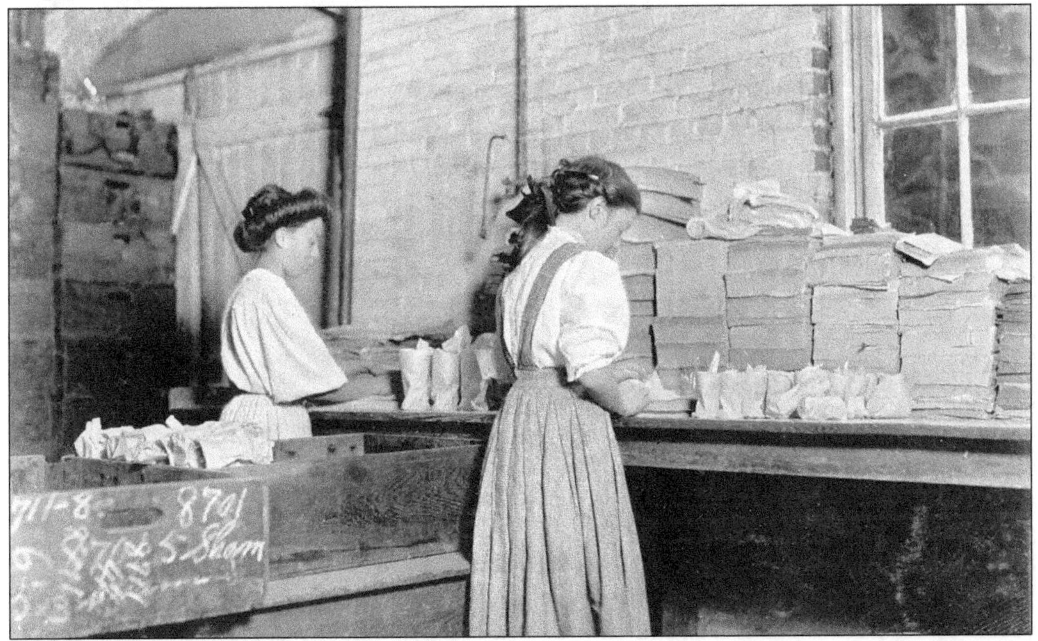

Child labor investigators photographed these girls wrapping and packing in the Seneca Glass Works. The girl in the center said she was 13. The Seneca factory was owned by glassworkers, and whole families were often involved in various phases of the work. After wrapping, the glassware would be packed in wooden barrels with straw for shipment to retailers. (National Archives.)

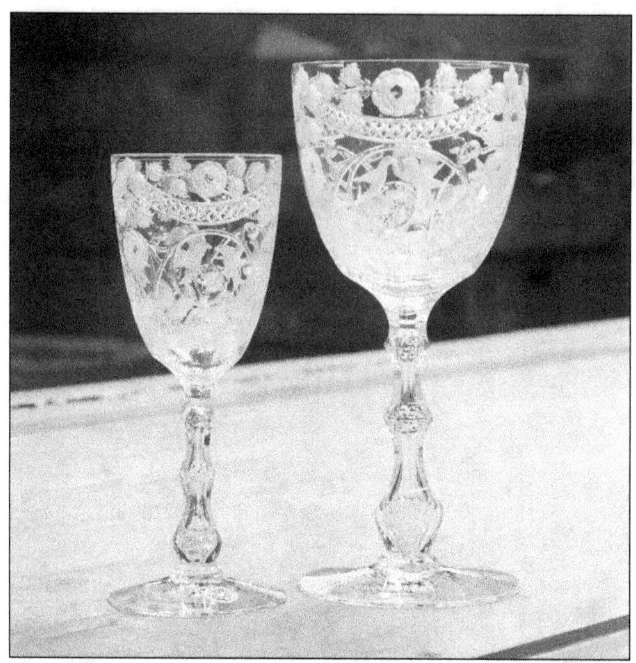

The Love Bird pattern was created at Seneca Glass as a special exhibition set for the 1939 New York World's Fair. The blowers created a blank with a hollow stem. Arner Linquist spent as many as 13 hours cutting the design in a single goblet using stone grinding wheels. Cut stemware from at least six local "cutshops" was shipped to department stores across the country. (HABS/ HAER Library of Congress.)

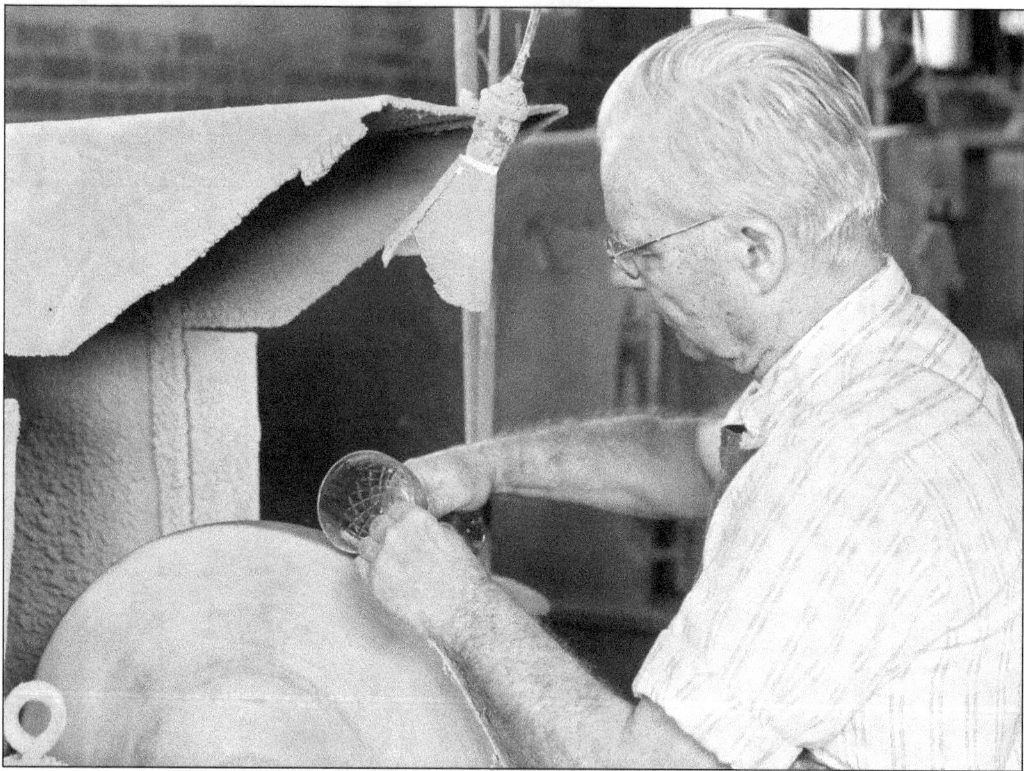

This photograph by William E. Barrett shows a glass cutter in the Seneca Glass factory polishing a design on a piece of stemware. It is one of many photographs taken in the study that a Historic American Engineering Record (HAER) team did on behalf of the Library of Congress in 1977. (HABS/HAER Library of Congress.)

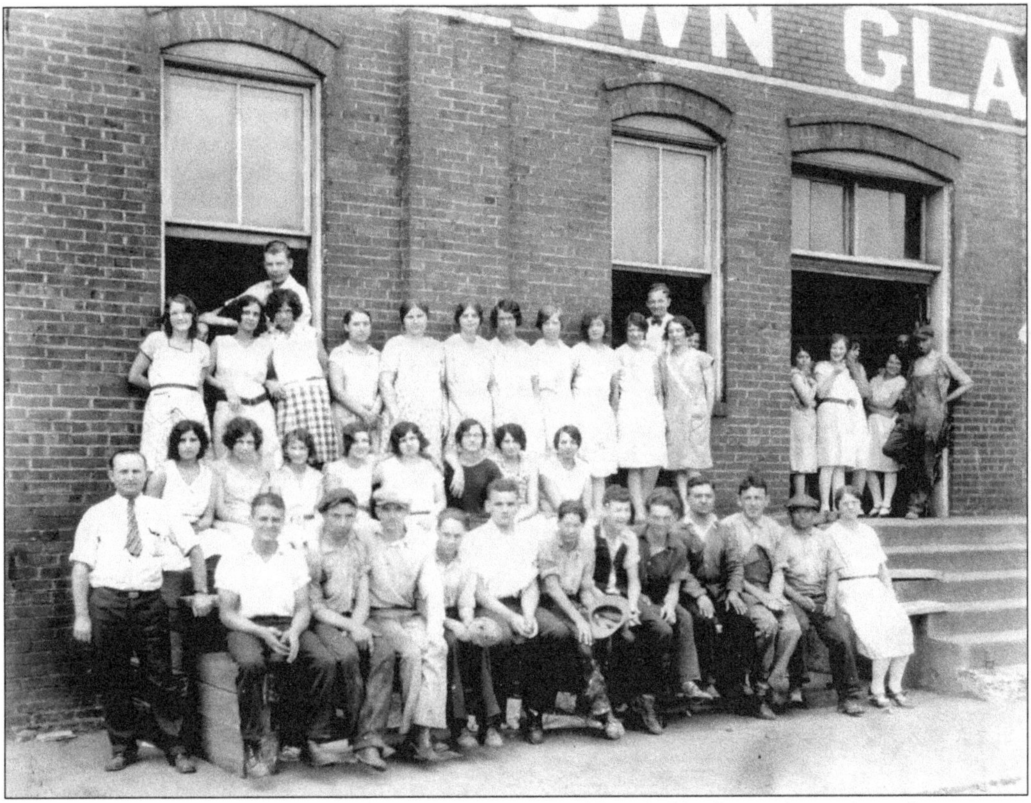

This group photograph at Morgantown Glassware Guild probably shows the packing department employees. There are a large number of girls because every piece of decorated ware, whether cut, etched, or transfer decorated, had to be washed by hand before packing. The picture was taken in the late 1930s. (John Gentile.)

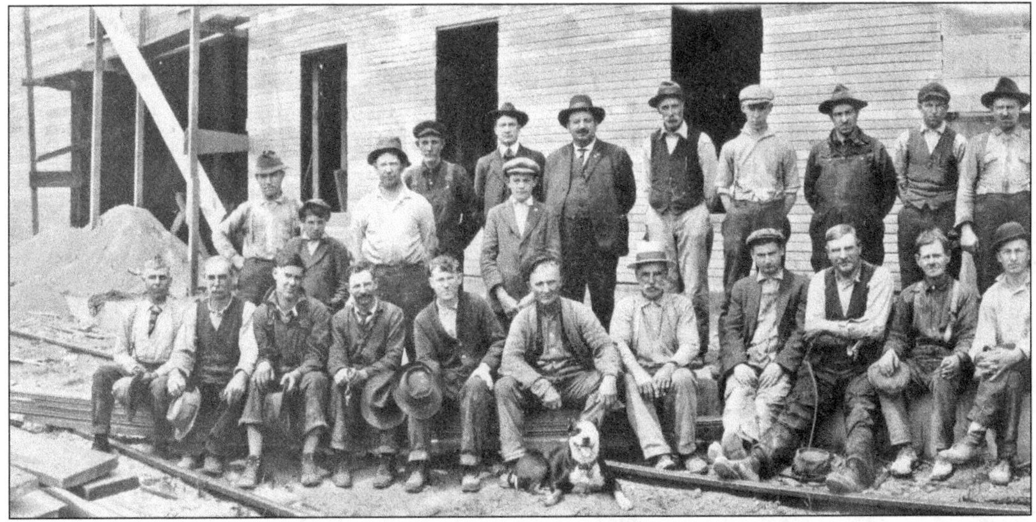

Workers at the Star Glass Company, from which Star City took its name, take a break for a photograph while doing construction work. The factory burned on December 11, 1917, and was rebuilt by the employees themselves in only 97 days. (Morgantown Public Library.)

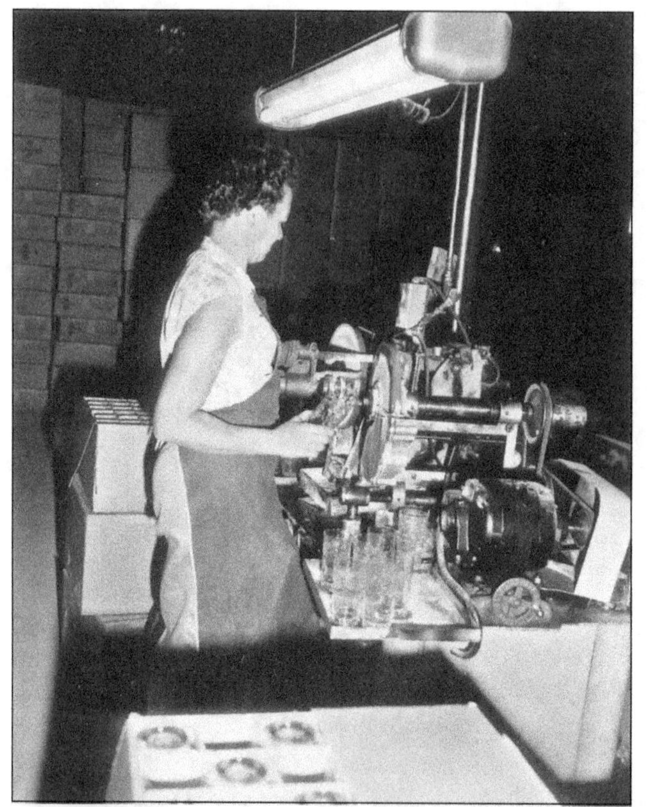

In 1953, local resident Victor Walker patented a machine that allowed production of cut glass with semi-skilled labor. The duties of this woman working at the Valcraft plant in Morgantown were to load and unload the machine and to inspect the glasses. (Terry Jones.)

Workers at the Davis Lynch Glass Company in Star City still mouth-blow and decorate large glass lamp shades. These products are sold under the trade names of the lamp makers, and few buyers know of their origin in West Virginia.

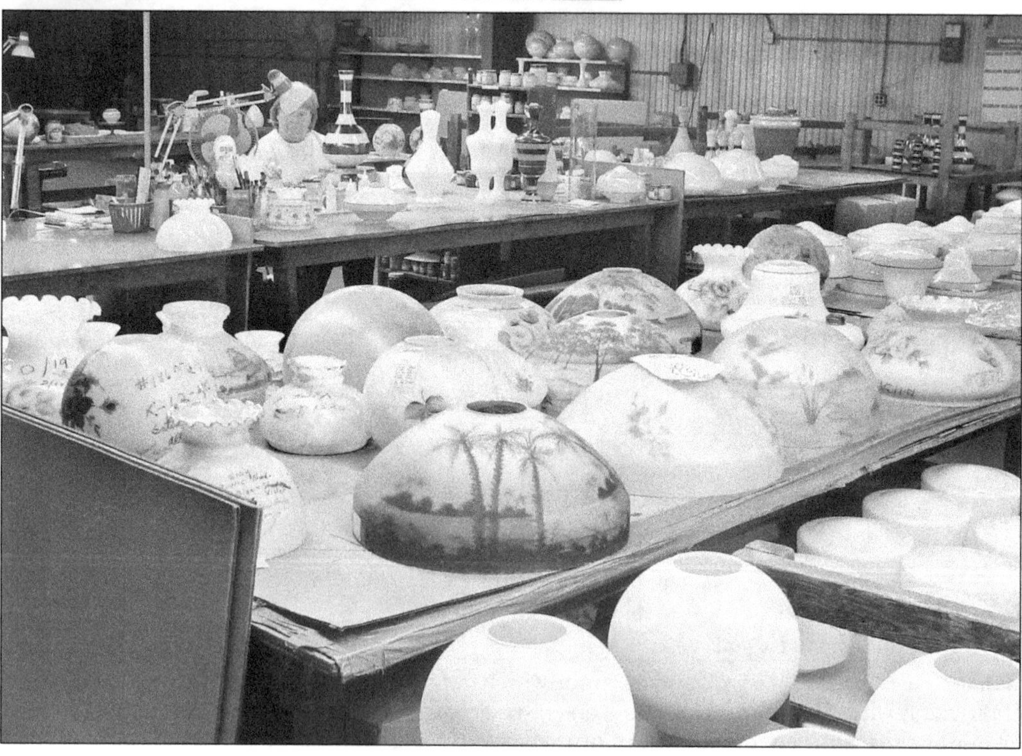

Four

COAL

In 1767, Charles Mason and Jeremiah Dixon noted in the journal on their survey of the famous Mason-Dixon Line, "Coal is found very plenty here" in the Monongahela and Cheat River valleys. At least as early as 1832, local landowners were operating "coal pits." These small surface mines operated with picks and shovels provided fuel for home heating and small industrial operations. The lack of good transportation meant that sales were limited. The 1870 census reported that the value of coal produced in Monongalia County was $2,400, while the value of locally produced wool was $11,000 and the value of flour amounted to $80,000.

With the construction of the railroads and Monongahela River locks and dams, larger markets for coal emerged. Supplying metallurgical coal to the Pittsburgh steel mills was particularly important, but the rapid growth in the production of electrical power also had a dramatic effect.

Coal production in 1900 was about 80,000 tons. By the start of World War I, this had jumped to over 2 million tons, and the increase continued through 1926, when production involved about 83 mines and 4,000 miners producing over 9 million tons of coal. Then, as now, some coal miners earned more in a year than most university professors.

While the financial segment of the economy collapsed quickly following the 1929 stock market crash, demands for coal fell more slowly. By 1932, production had fallen to less than 5 million tons with only 38 mines remaining in production. This left thousands of miners unemployed, and investigators from federal relief agencies such as the Works Progress Administration (WPA) found Morgantown a good base for documenting the resulting deprivation in photographs.

The demands of World War II restored the industry to prosperity. Prosperity did not completely restore employment to former levels, because between 1936 and 1940, machine mining replaced pick-and-shovel operations in the local coal mines.

Production increased to 12,550,000 tons in 1972, and the county led the state in 1974–1976. Coal production has declined since then, but mining remains an important segment of the local economy.

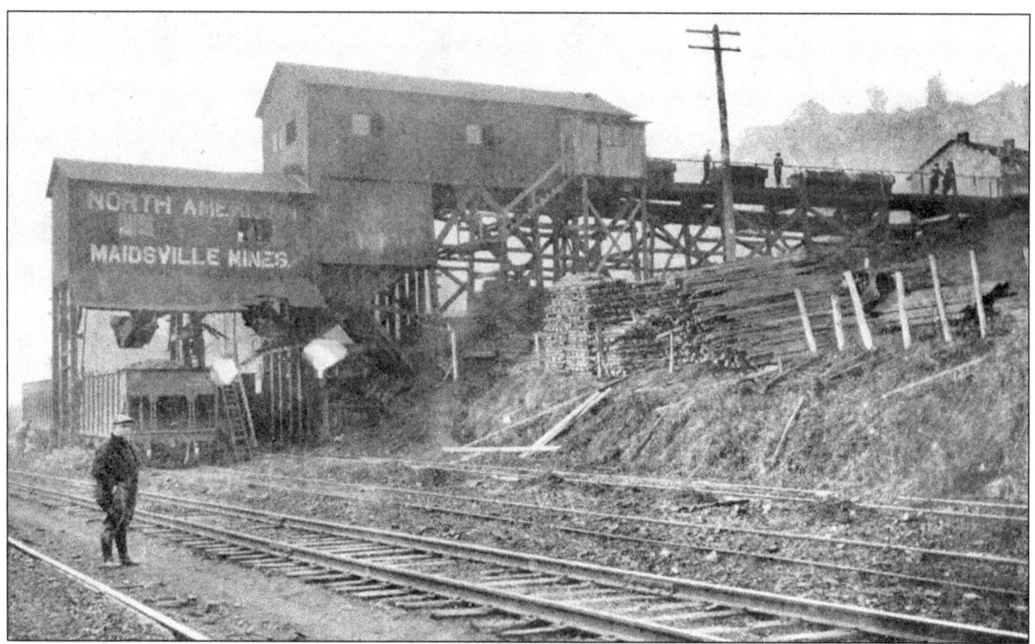

Early mining was done in seams near the hilltops on the eastern side of the Monongahela River. Large-scale industrial coal production in Monongalia County takes place in deeper seams west of the river. The Maidsville Mine, located at the mouth of Robinson Run, was the first of the mines to be located on the new Monongahela Railroad tracks. This picture appeared in a 1921 chamber of commerce booklet.

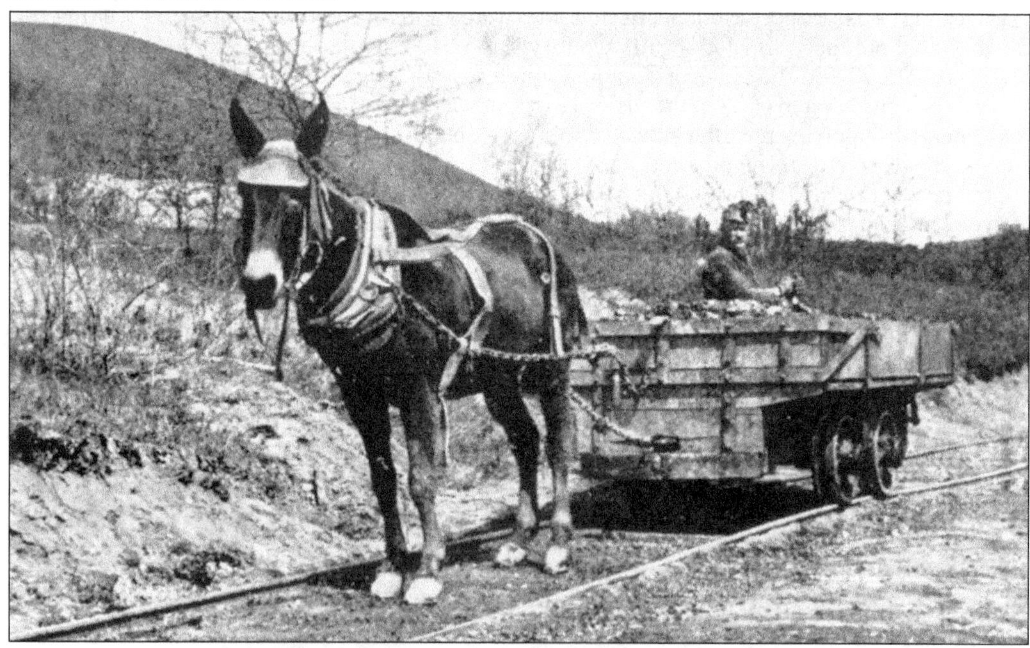

Before electrification, animals supplied the "pulling power" underground. This mule, pulling a mine car, was luckier than other mine mules and ponies, which spent their entire working lives underground and never saw the light of day. However, mine temperature is a constant 50 degrees, a comfortable temperature for long-haired ponies and mules.

Farm Security Administration photographer Marion Post Wolcott took this picture of coal miners buying supplies in a company store in 1938. Even when coal companies paid wages in cash, the availability of credit at the store led some families into financial problems similar to those created with credit cards today. (National Archives.)

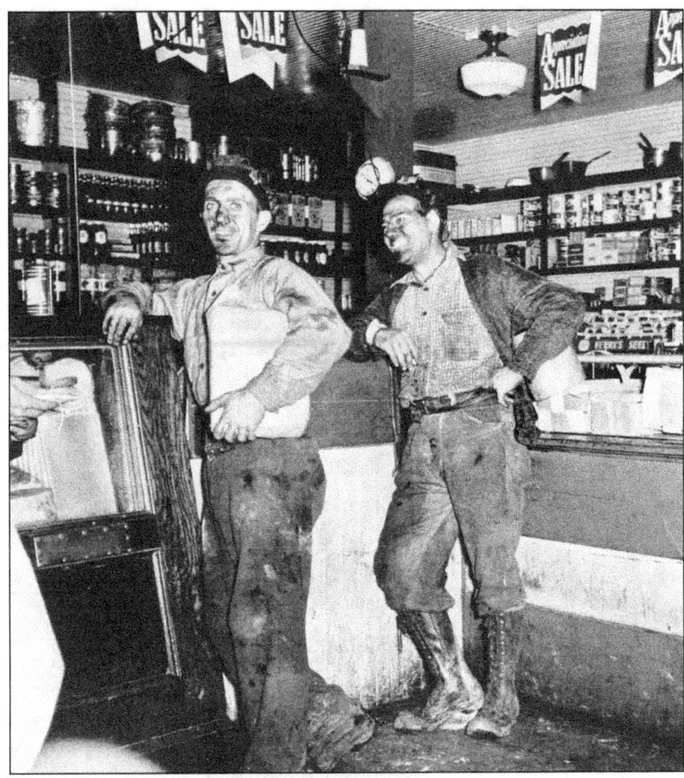

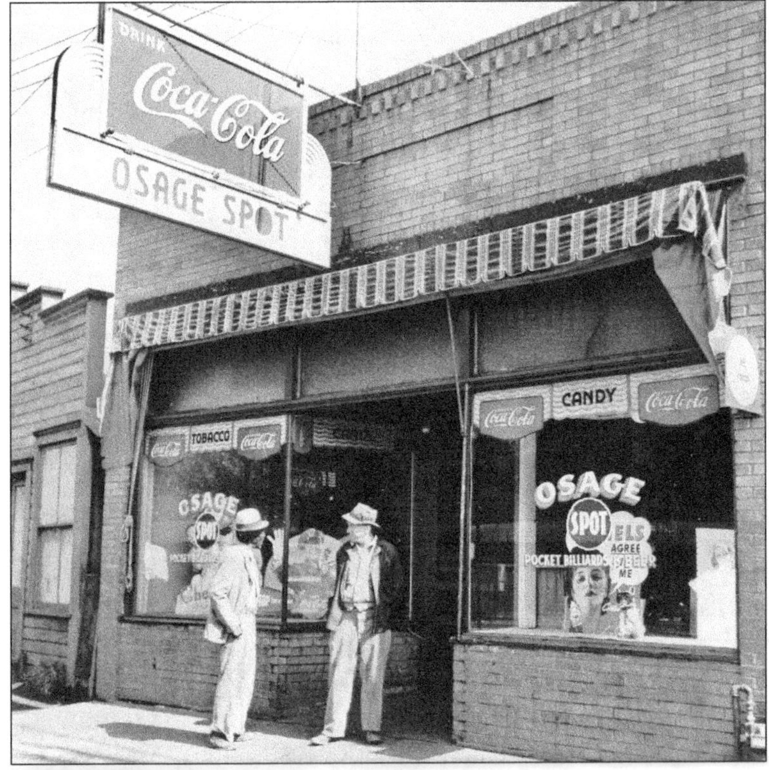

The coal mining town of Osage, near the mouth of Scotts Run, had substantial stores. A large new shopping complex called University Town Center has recently been built within half a mile of this site. (National Archives.)

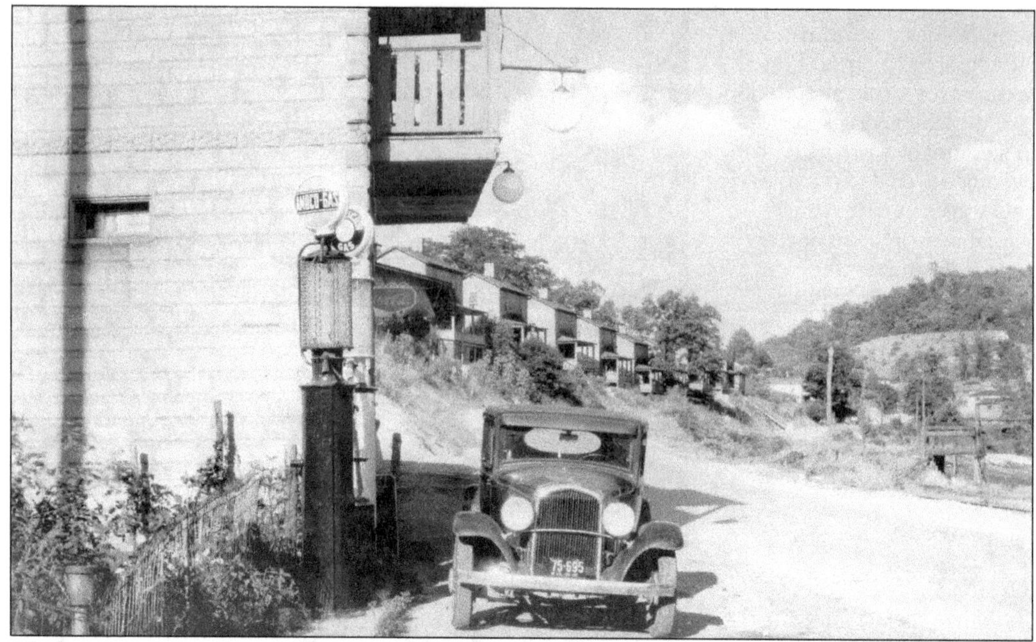

Those who regularly travel between Morgantown and Core or Blacksville will immediately recognize this photograph as having been taken just about at the intersection of Routes 7 and 19. A few of these houses are still standing. When the picture was taken in 1936, the road and railroad tracks shared the narrow valley. The main road went west, and Route 19 would not be located here until 1950. (National Archives.)

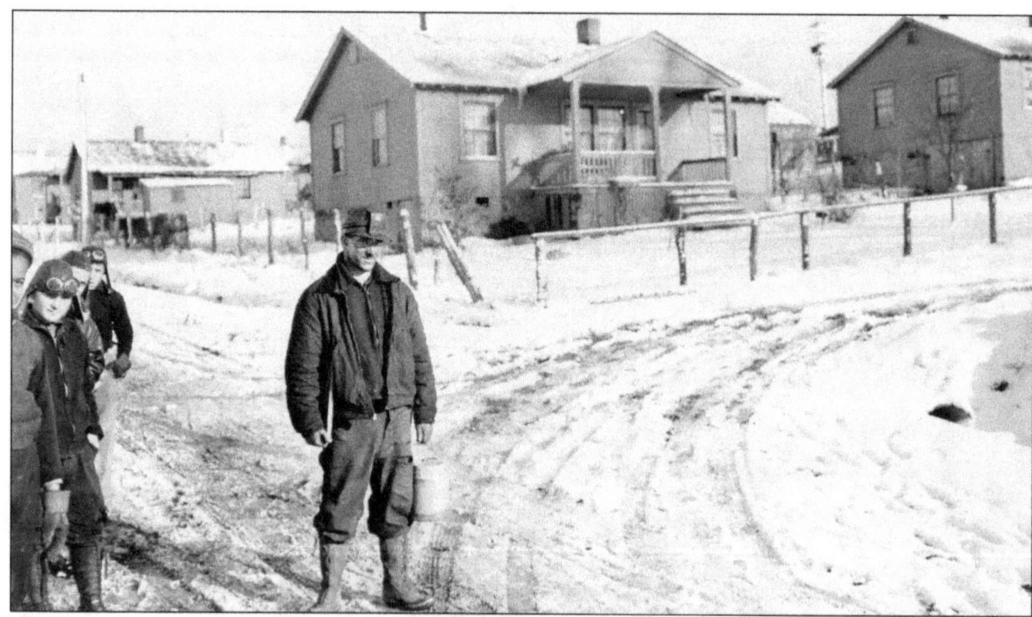

A Scotts Run miner returns from work in 1937. Mines of the time did not provide wash houses. Miners changed clothes and washed in tin tubs at home, bringing mine dirt home with them. He is carrying a dinner bucket, a vital part of a miner's equipment, in which he carried his food and water. The company houses appear to be well constructed and have decent yards. (National Archives.)

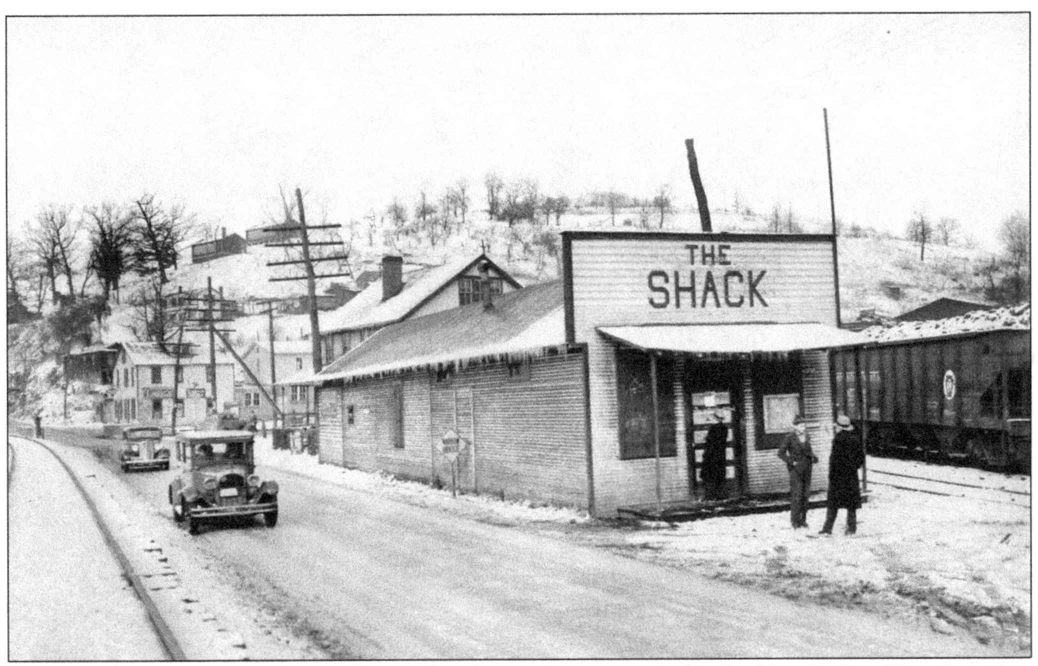

The Shack Community Center, located in Scotts Run, was established by the local Presbyterian churches. This scene, captured by a WPA photographer in 1937, is typical of crowded space in the center of the valley. Today the Shack occupies a substantial building. It has a gym and a large outdoor swimming pool. (National Archives.)

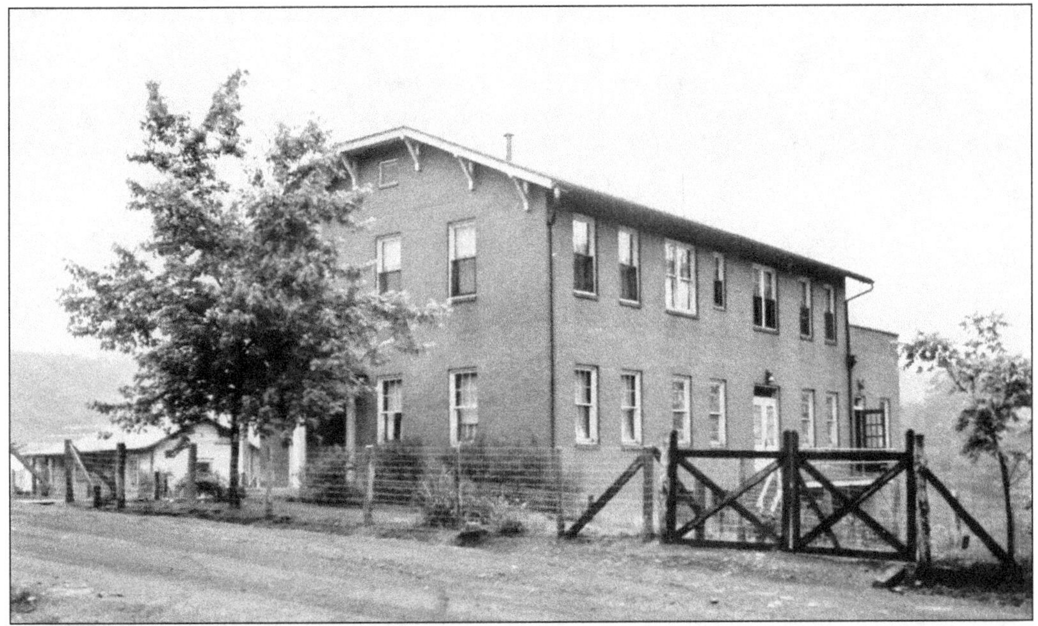

Churches in Morgantown established missions to assist in the "Americanization" of immigrant workers and their families. This 1946 photograph shows the Scotts Run Settlement House begun in 1922, when the Woman's Home Missionary Society of Wesley Methodist Church established a Bible school for children. The permanent building for the Settlement House in Osage was completed in 1927 and continues to this day as a community center. (National Archives.)

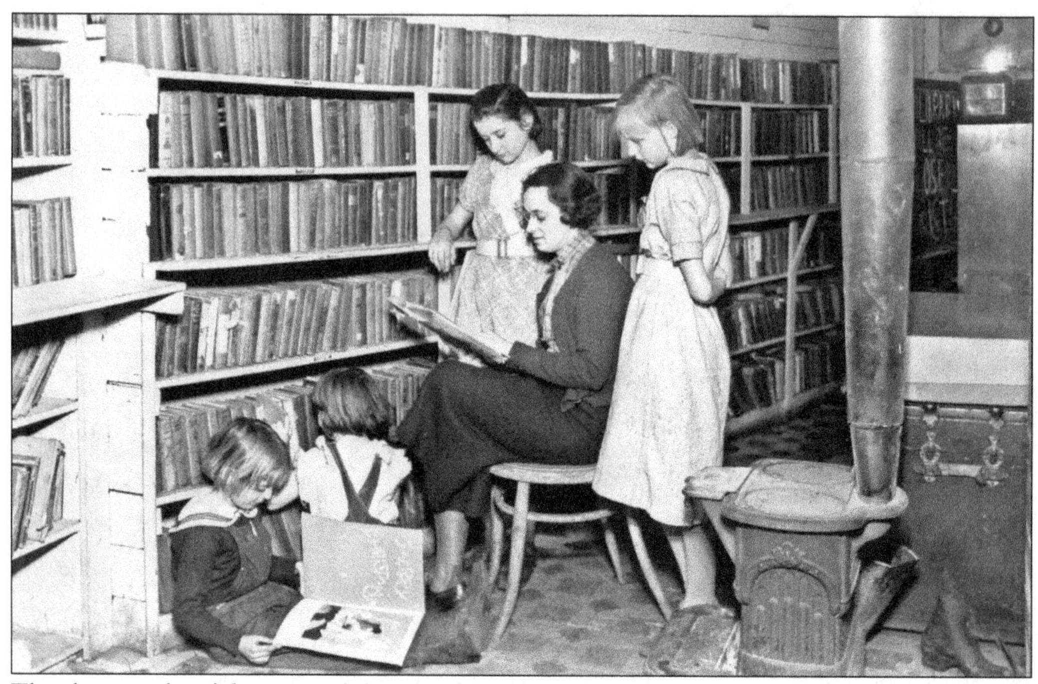

The photographer did not record the exact location of this coal camp library. It was probably either in the Shack or the Scotts Run Community Center. The collection of books is more impressive than the small coal stove used to provide heat. (National Archives.)

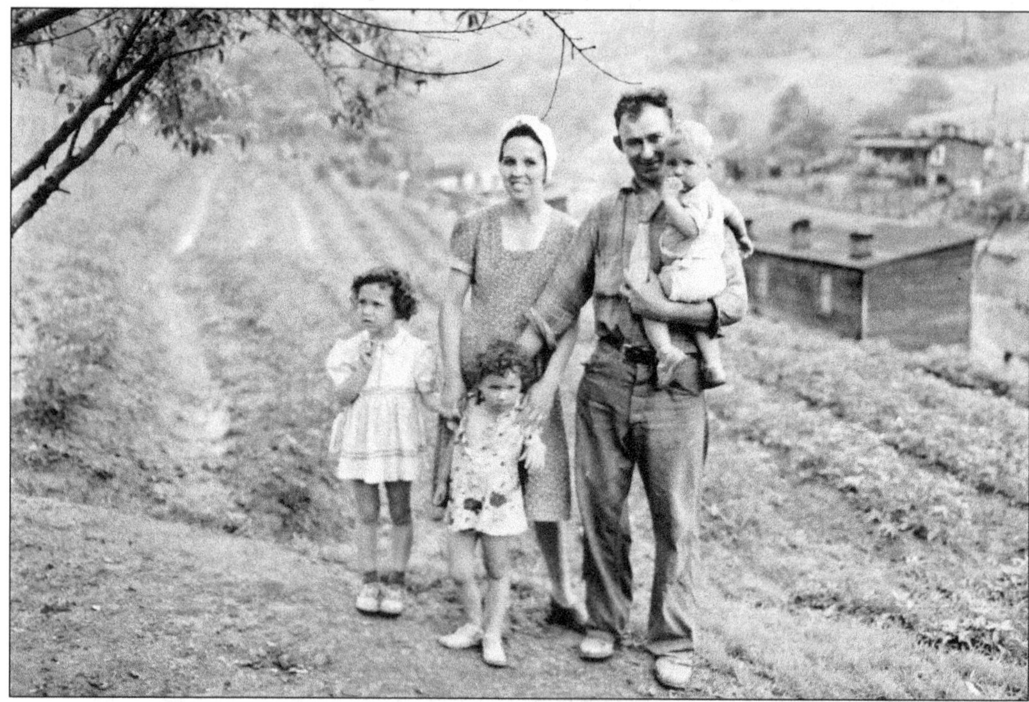

This coal miner and his family posed in front of their garden in Osage in 1946. Vegetable gardening was common in both town and country until the 1960s, but only a few families do it today. (National Archives.)

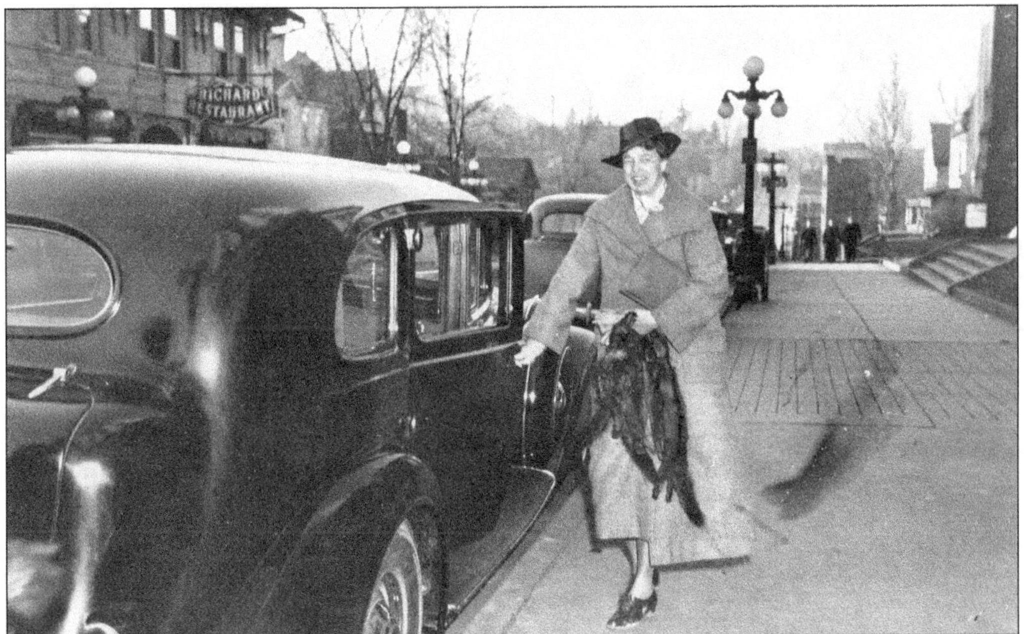

First Lady Eleanor Roosevelt was caught at the entrance to the Hotel Morgan. She was a frequent visitor to Morgantown between 1933 and 1940. One of her projects involved resettlement of unemployed miners from Scotts Run to a rural, light-industry community in Arthurdale. The industries never developed. Mrs. Roosevelt also visited local schools to speak at dedications and graduations. (West Virginia and Regional History Collection, West Virginia University Libraries.)

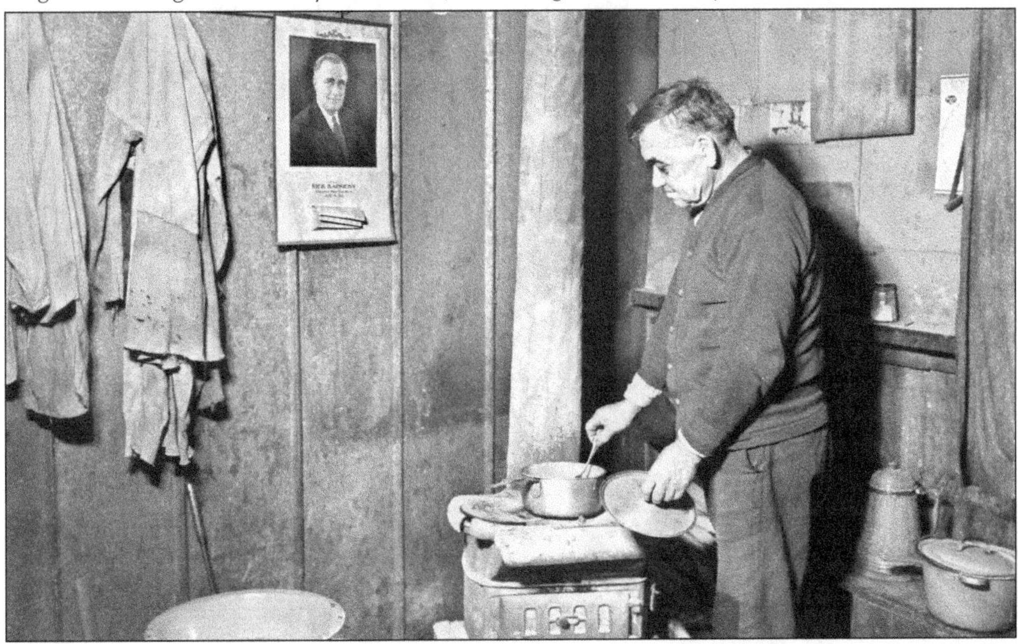

Many of the miners were immigrants living bachelor lives, although they might have had families to support in Europe. This man's shack is heated with a small coal range, which also serves as a cook stove. The WPA photographer interpreted the calendar with its picture of Pres. Franklin Roosevelt as a sign that the government was interested in his welfare. (National Archives.)

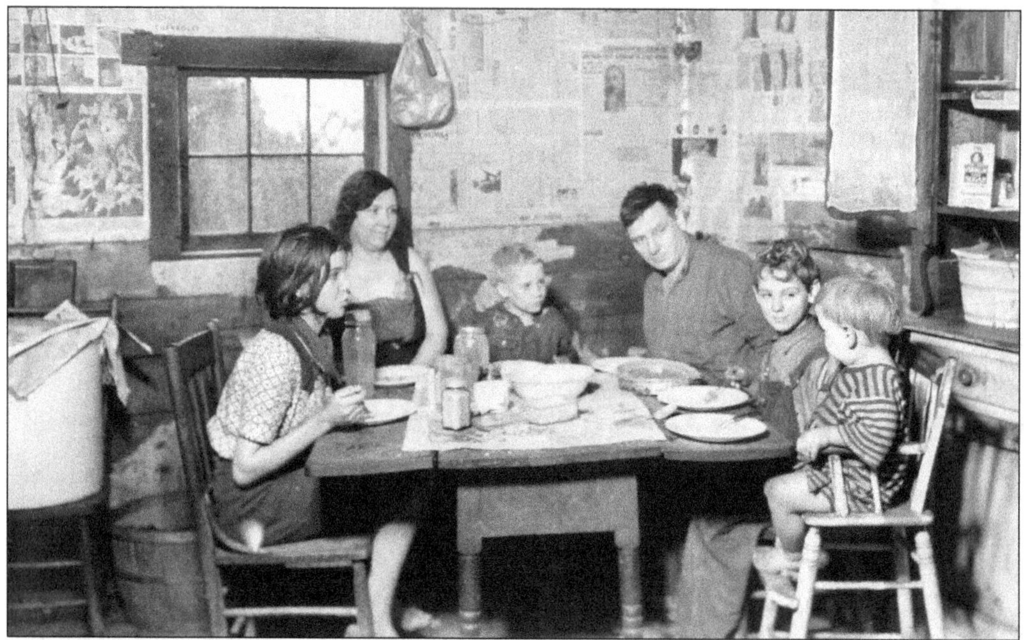

A photographic team from a Depression-era federal investigation visited this family in a company house on Sessa Hill in 1937. The man, a skilled mine mechanic, showed them six statements that he held in five different bankrupt mines on Scotts Run. He had not been paid his last pay in any bankruptcy. (National Archives.)

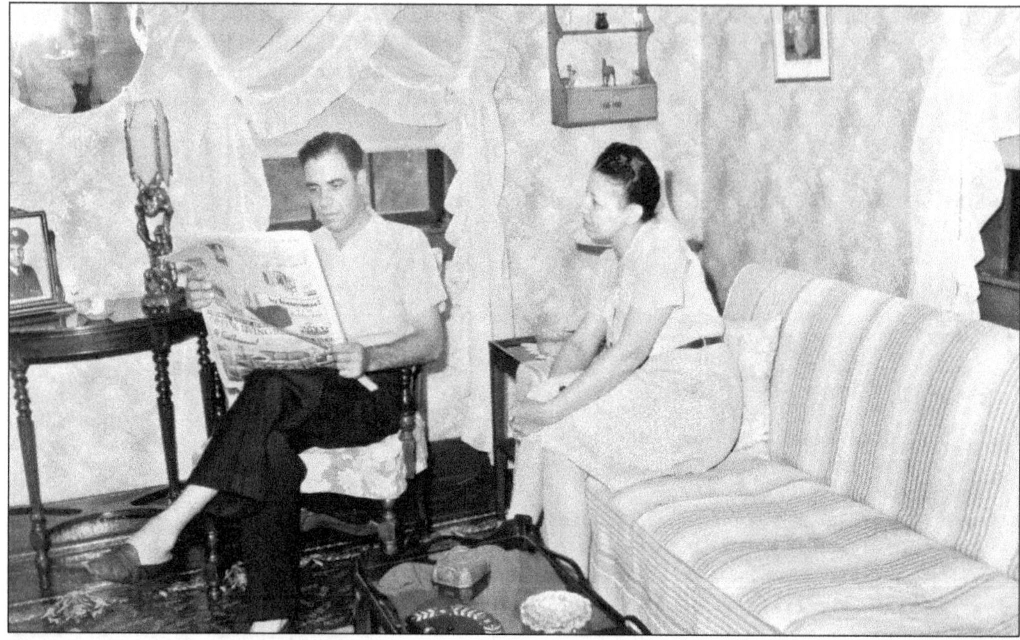

This miner and his wife lived in company housing built by the Christopher Coal Company in Osage. The photograph was taken in 1946, when the soldier in the picture on the table might still have been serving in uniform. While many mines were owned by out-of-state interests, the Christopher family lived in Morgantown. The Christopher mines later were sold to CONSOL. (National Archives.)

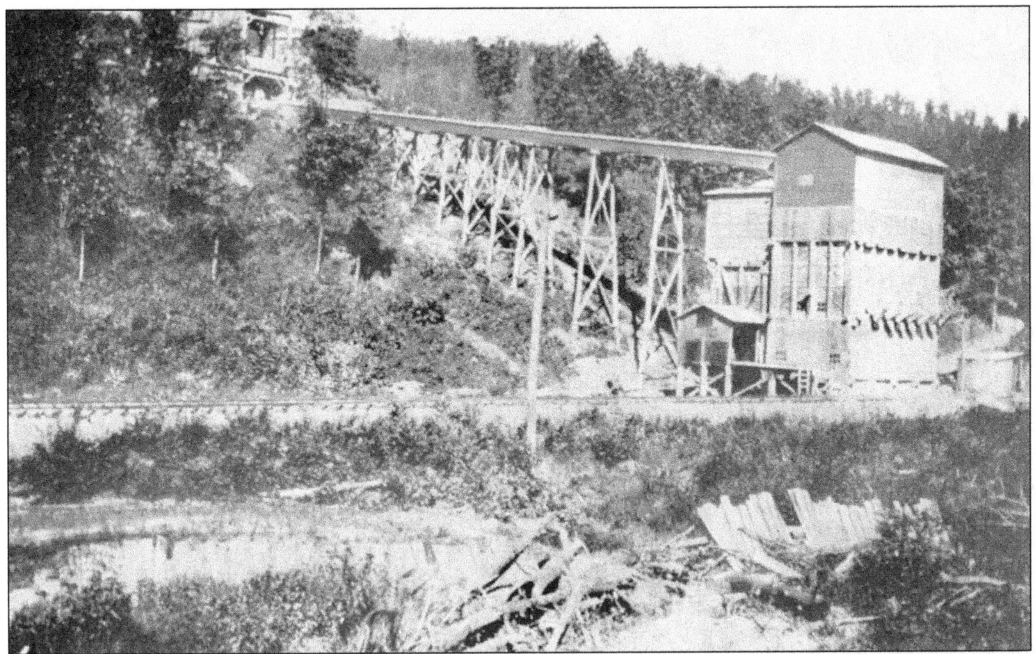

Although most mining activity around Morgantown involves coal, limestone mining is also important. The Greer limestone mine, shown here about 1902, provides sizes ranging from powder to bucket-sized rocks for use in agriculture, construction, and cement making. Some of this is marketed hundreds of miles from the mine.

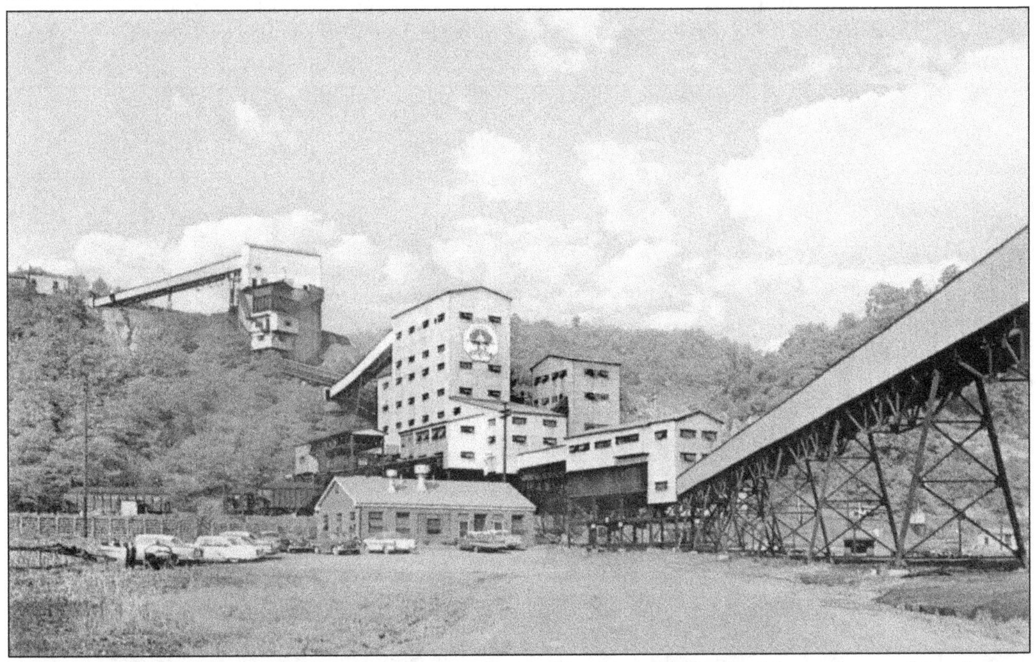

A postcard recorded the Arkwright mine in Granville about 1961. Coal from the working face as much as 10 miles away was conveyed here underground. The buildings at the center housed the cleaning and screening operations. Waste went up a set of conveyors to the top of the hill, while the conveyor on the right carried coal to barges for shipment locally or out of state.

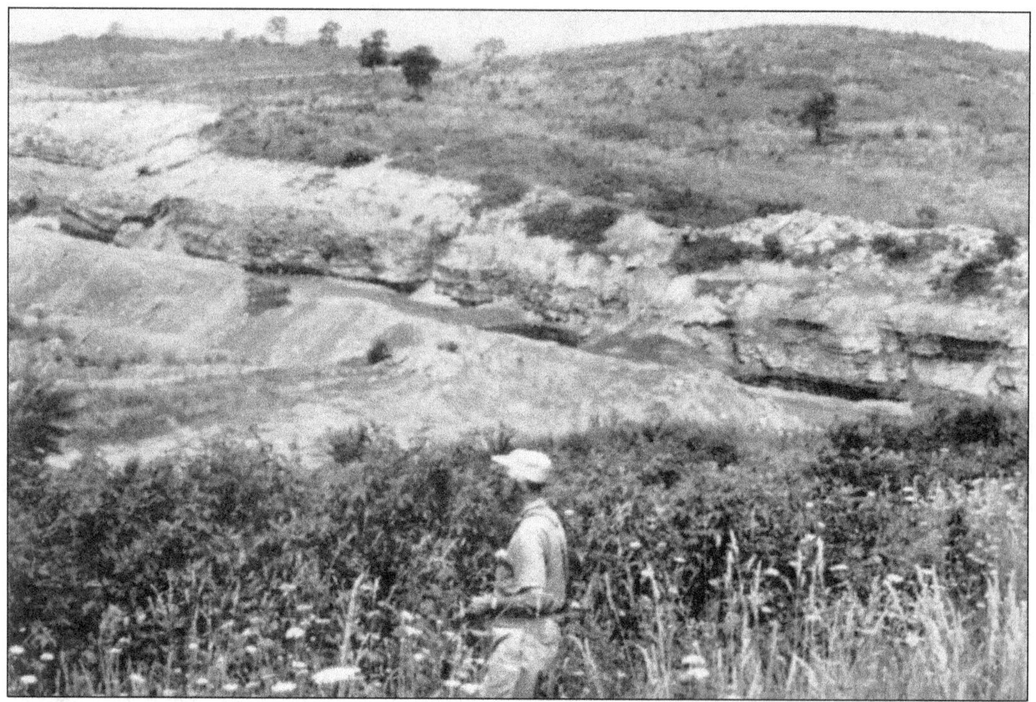

Surface, or strip, mining is done when coal seams are close to the surface. This 1960s photograph shows a mine after removing all soil and rock over the coal and digging the coal with excavating equipment. When mining ends, the edges have high walls, and little will grow on the exposed rock. Local companies have a pretty good record of regrading and planting vegetation tolerant of acid soil conditions.

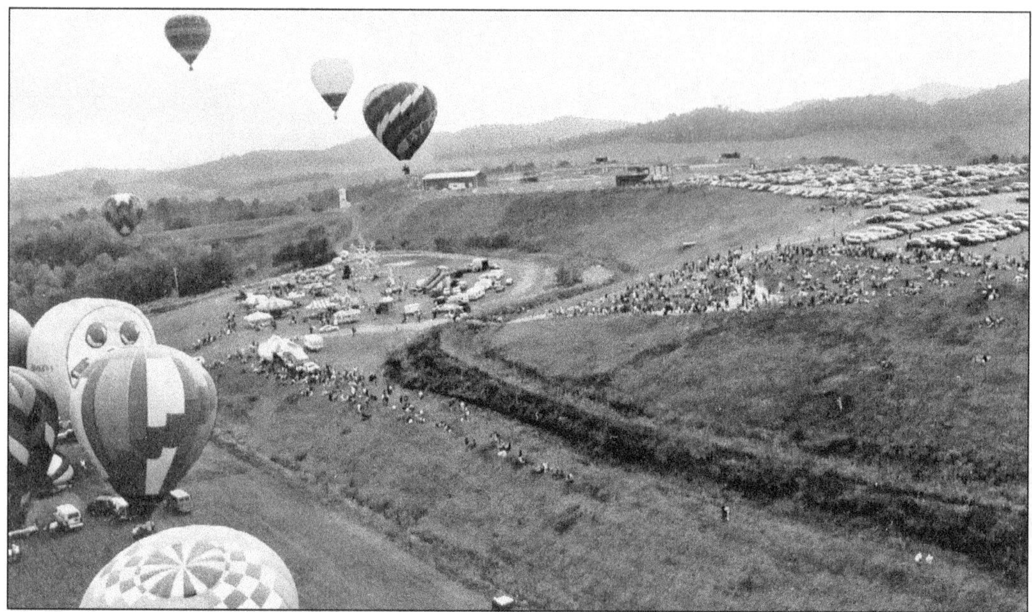

The Morgantown Balloon Festival began over 20 years ago as an activity at the Morgantown Airport. In 2002, it was moved to a new site at Mylan Park, a large recreational area on a reclaimed surface mine near Interstate 79 north of town. (University Motors Mountaineer Balloon Festival.)

Five

Oil, Gas, and Other Industry

Small-scale industrial operations were established in Morgantown at an early date. In addition to the iron industry previously mentioned, potteries were established before 1785 and operated at least through 1855. Nineteenth-century industries also included wool carding, a foundry, furniture and wagon making, lumber mills, and tanneries.

Most early production not for local use was dispatched by river. Boat building started after the American Revolution and continued for at least three-quarters of a century. Initially they built flatboats, which drifted down the Monongahela and then into the Ohio. Later wooden coal and cotton barges were constructed. Sometimes months would elapse between the time a boat was finished and the time when a sufficient rise in the river allowed the boat to leave.

In the 1880s, industry in the county changed rapidly. One driving force was the discovery of oil and gas. A second was the building of the first railroad line and river locks and dams.

By 1891, the Standard Oil Company had constructed an oil pipeline from the Ohio River to Philadelphia. A major pumping station in Morgantown pumped up to 60,000 barrels of oil per day by 1912. Local entrepreneurs were also piping natural gas into town.

Gas and railroad tracks provided the foundation needed for the establishment of metalworking industries employing over 1,000.

With the growth of coal mining, Morgantown became a center for the manufacture of mining equipment. During and after World War II, the area became involved in the production of coal-based chemical products.

While traditional manufacturing provides only a small percentage of local jobs today, several local industries operate in specialized global markets.

Morgantown has developed a major employment base in "knowledge-based industry." It has the primary facility of the country's largest drug maker and federal research laboratories working on energy questions and on health and safety. The university is constructing a research park for companies developing biotechnology products.

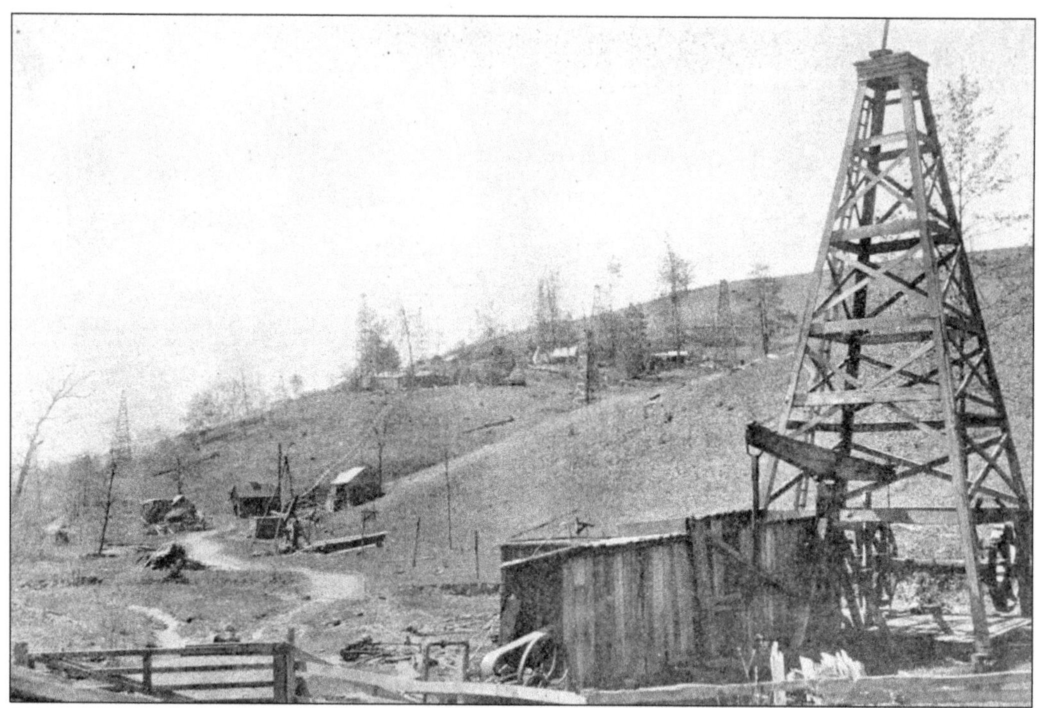

Around 1890, an oil field was developed northwest of Morgantown and provided a supply of natural gas. The new oil wealth also meant new houses with gas lights and an end to cooking on wood stoves for many families. Early oil derricks such as the one pictured were wood. Derricks and working wells were often seen here until the 1960s, although oil production peaked in the 1920s.

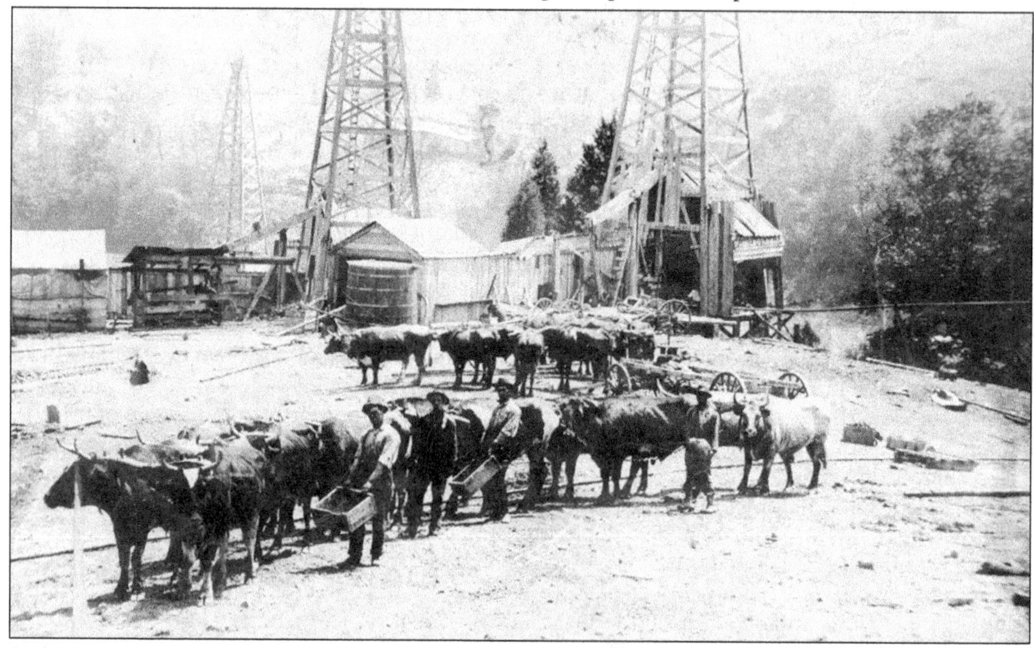

Before 1915, any heavy moving in the countryside was done with animal power. This shows two teams of oxen moving oil well equipment. Near the center of the picture is a wooden tank for oil storage. (Ron Rittenhouse.)

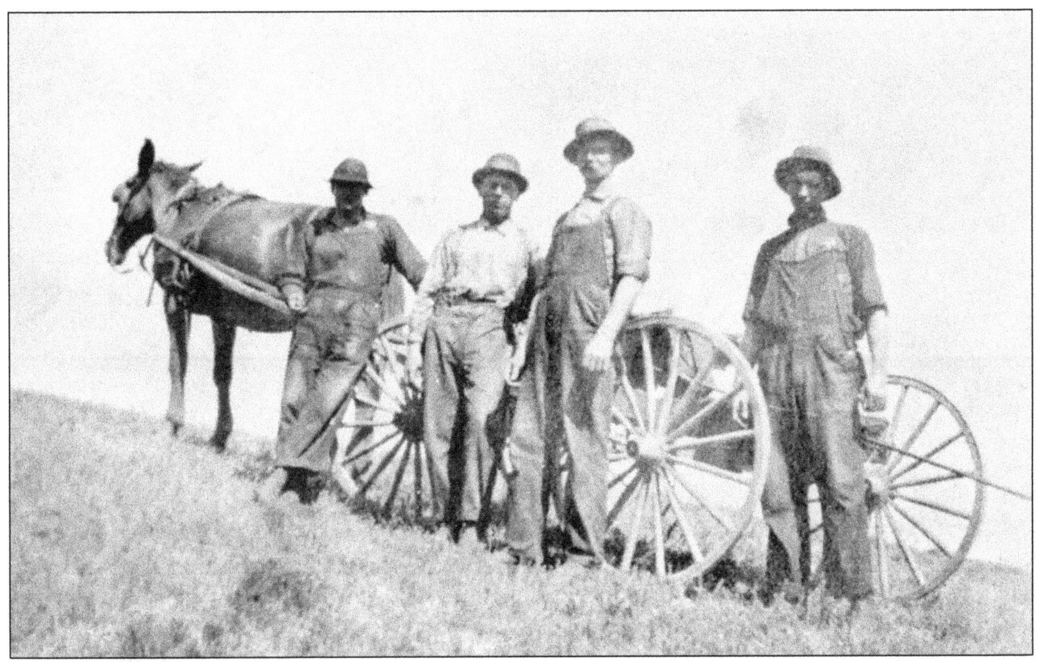

This oil field crew is hauling sucker rods—wooden rods that connected the pump at the bottom of the well to the walking beam on the surface. The oil boom, lasting from around 1890 to 1920, provided many jobs, including teamsters driving wagons and roustabouts working directly on the wells.

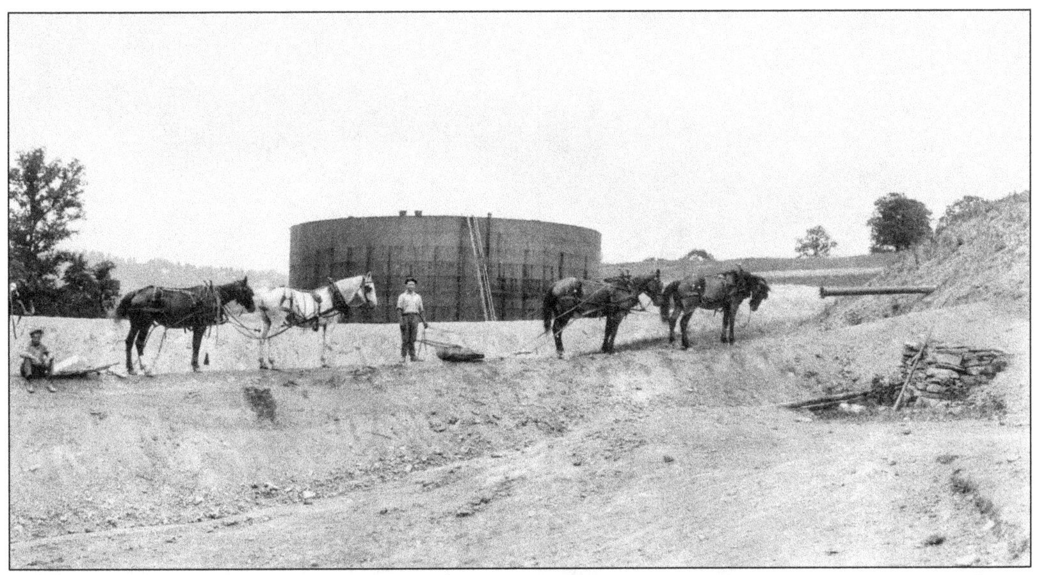

This shows one of the oil storage tanks in the Standard Oil tank field south of Morgantown. The date is around 1910. The horses, hitched in tandem, were being used to grade the site for additional tanks. (Morgantown Public Library.)

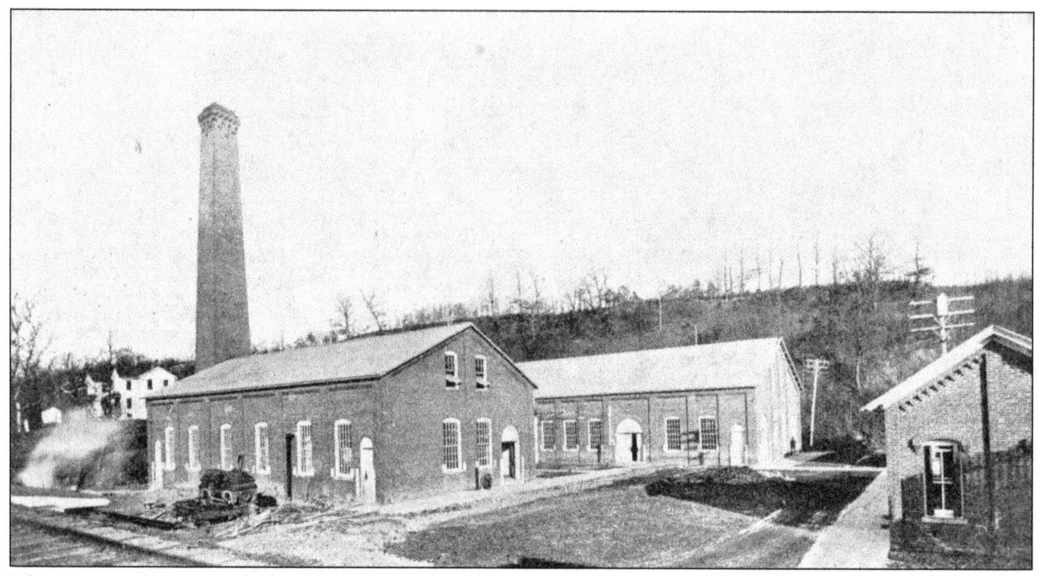

This shows the pump house in the Standard Oil plant. Oil from the wells in fields as far away as Parkersburg and Kentucky was pumped to a tank field on the south edge of Morgantown. From here, it was pumped through a pipeline to refineries in New Jersey. The pipeline was closed about 1940, but this building is still in use along Don Knotts Boulevard (South University Avenue).

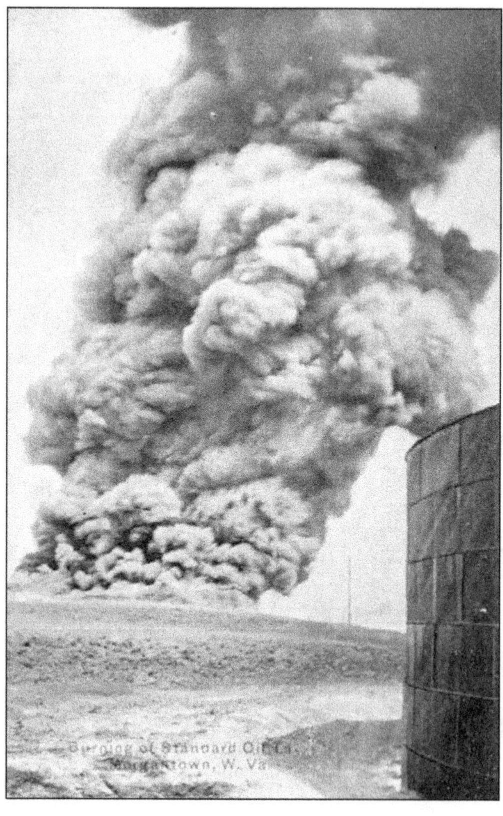

This postcard preserves a photograph of a fire in the oil tank field south of Morgantown. It is probably the 1916 fire, which was caused by lightning.

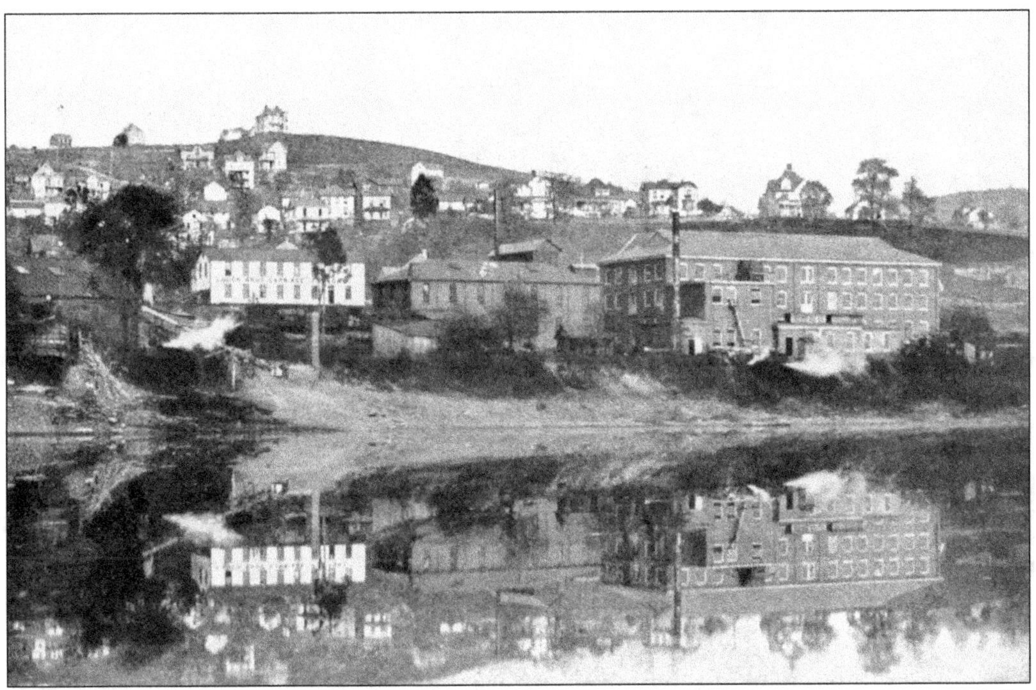

The manufacturing district, as captured in 1902, lay between the university campus and the Seneca glassworking community. The brick building on the right was Monongahela Textile Company, which made "fine woolens." It closed in 1903 after only a few years of operation. The white building to the left is the Lough Brothers Carriage Works. W. C. Lough and Brothers was established in 1880 in Cassville and moved into Morgantown about 1890.

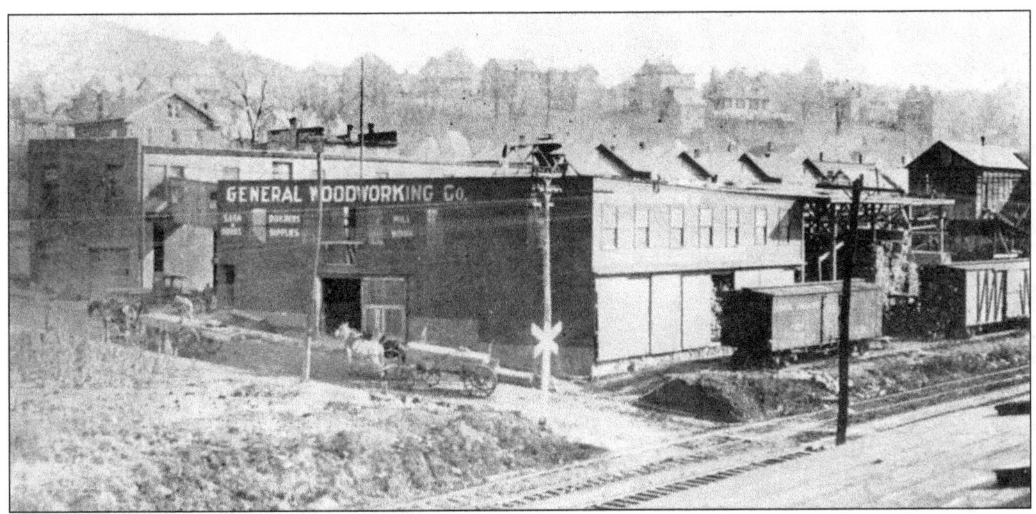

For nearly 100 years, the General Woodworking Company served Morgantown builders with custom millwork in addition to general building materials. This picture shows their plant in 1921, when they were located in Seneca at Beechurst Avenue and Fourth Street. The company moved to Westover in 1924. Owned and operated by the Thorn family, the business was terminated and the land sold in 2006.

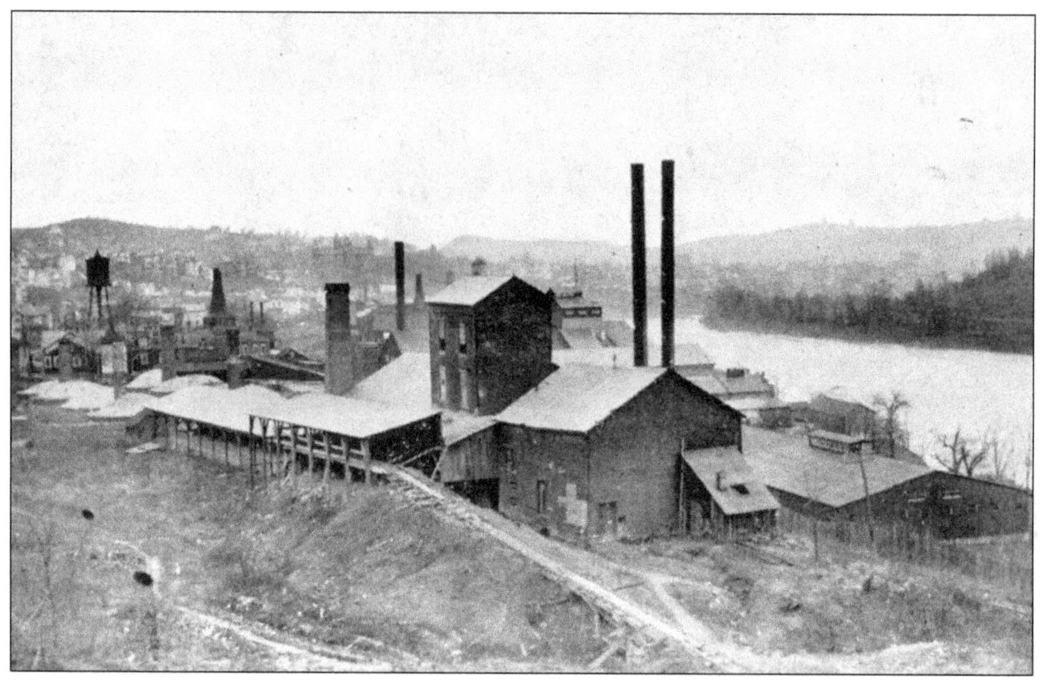

This picture shows the brick works of the Morgantown Brick Company in 1922. The large buildings housed the machinery used to shape the bricks and dry them before they were fired in the kilns. This is now the site of the Personal Rapid Transit System garage.

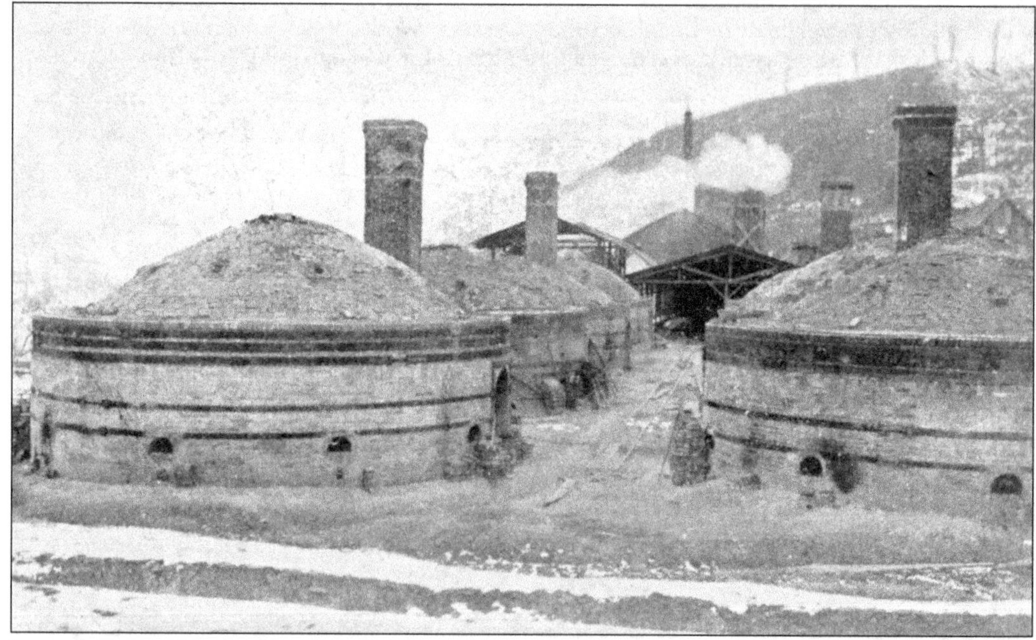

In early times, bricks for important structures were locally made on the building site. The Morgantown Brick Company began centralized production of several kinds of bricks in 1892. This picture shows their shale brick kilns in 1902. The plant produced 30,000 bricks a day. Local clay from the area now occupied by West Virginia University's Evansdale Campus was used in brick making.

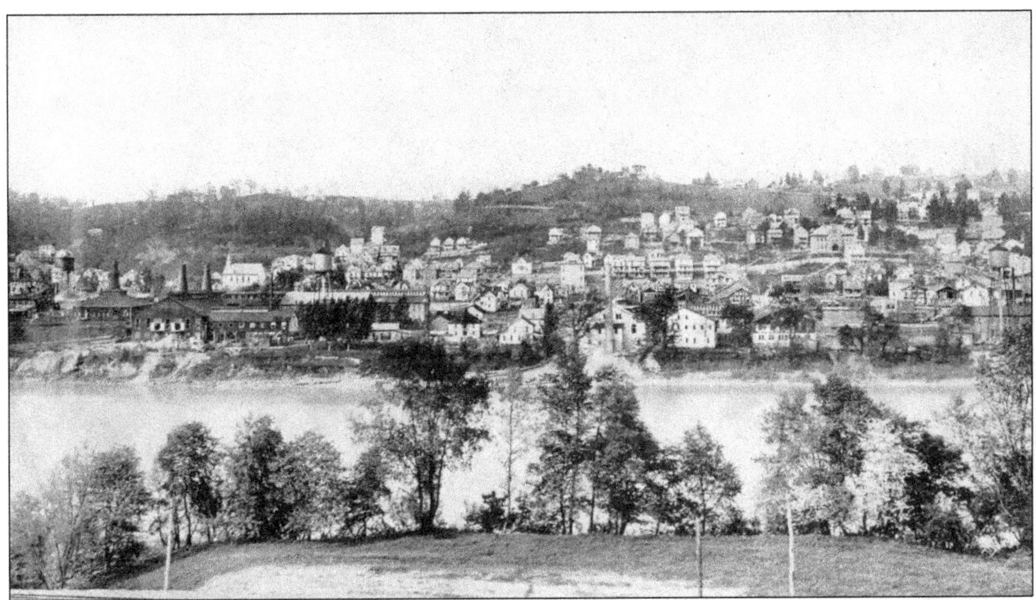

This is a view of the Seneca area in 1920. The Seneca and Morgantown Glass factories are on the left, with the white frame Catholic St. Francis de Sales Church just above them. The three-story building at the center is the Turn Verein club. The Seneca school, now an apartment building, is near the right side.

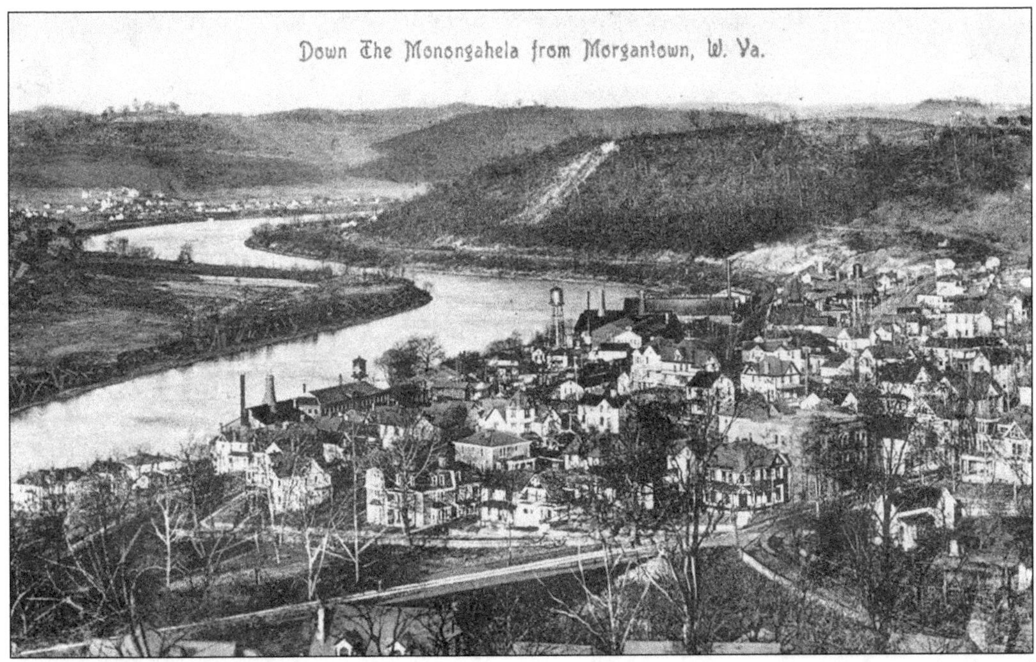

This postcard shows the town of Seneca in 1905, although by then it had become a political part of Morgantown. The area covered by this industrial community had been little more than a cow pasture 15 years earlier.

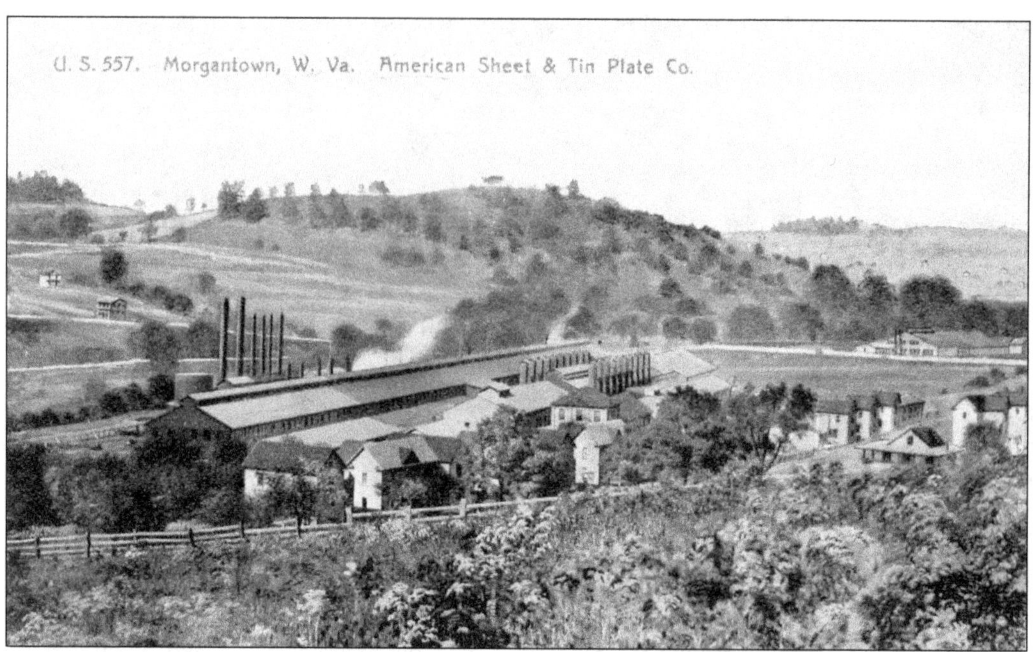

Construction of the tin mill in Sabraton began in 1902, with production starting in 1906. At its peak, the mill employed 1,000 workers and shipped 75 carloads of tin-plated steel sheet per week. Later the Sterling Faucet Company moved into the plant and became an important part of the local economy for 40 years.

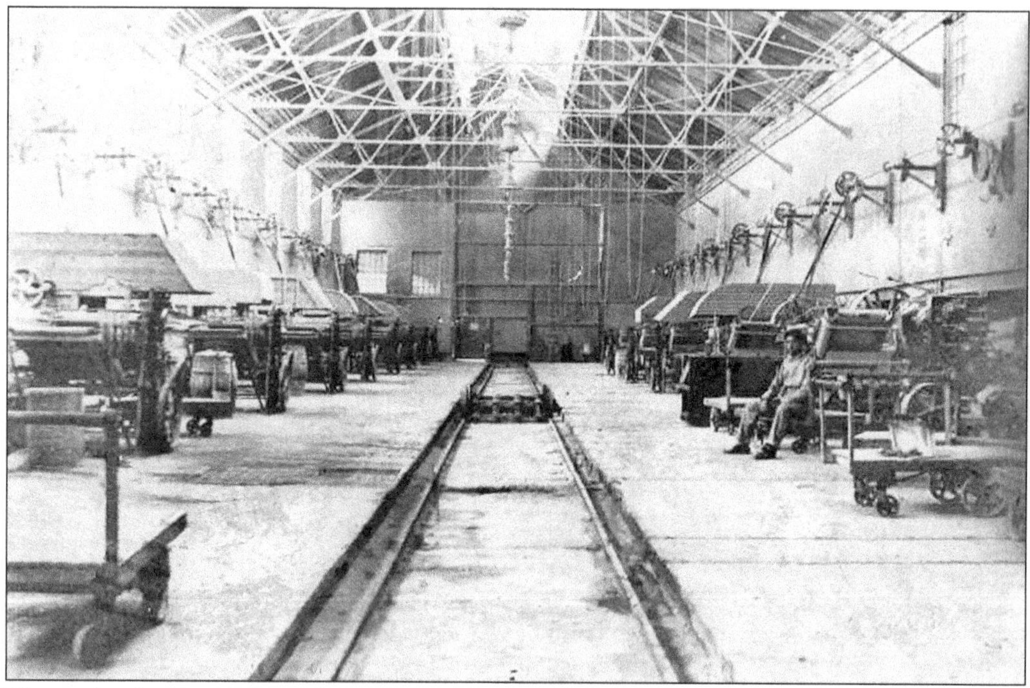

This undated postcard shows the interior of the tin mill. Under the American Sheet and Tin Plate Company, the mill employed as many as 1,000 men. Raw steel came from Pittsburgh. In 1909, it was reported that tin plate was being shipped to Hawaii for use in pineapple cans.

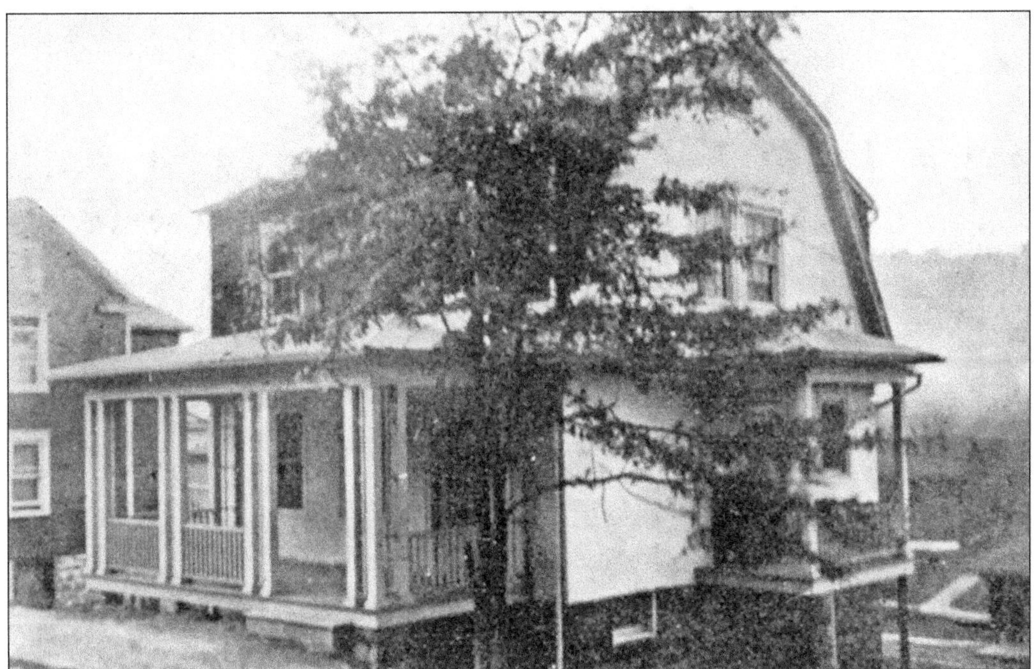

The tin mill brought Eastern European workers to the area. The mill was locally owned, and the Community House was part of efforts to help immigrants adapt to the American lifestyle. The mill itself was relatively short-lived, but there is still a Byzantine Catholic church within walking distance of the site.

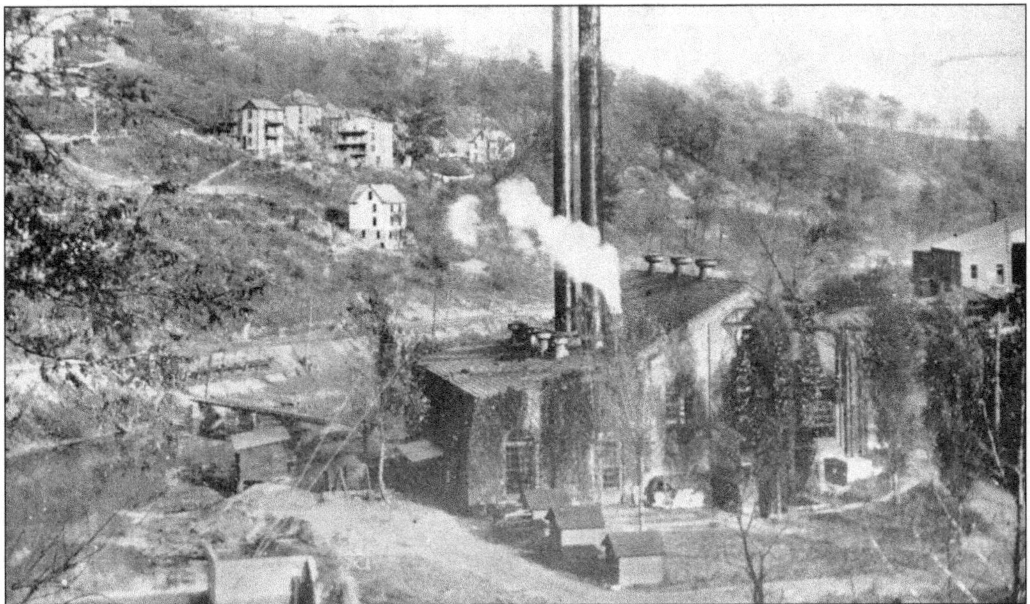

The West Virginia Utilities Company was established in the late 1880s to bring natural gas to Morgantown. By 1920, when this picture was taken, they supplied the town with gas, water, and electricity and operated seven miles of streetcar lines. The company's customers were transferred to other utility companies over the years, but the power plant building can still be seen from the Pleasant Street Bridge.

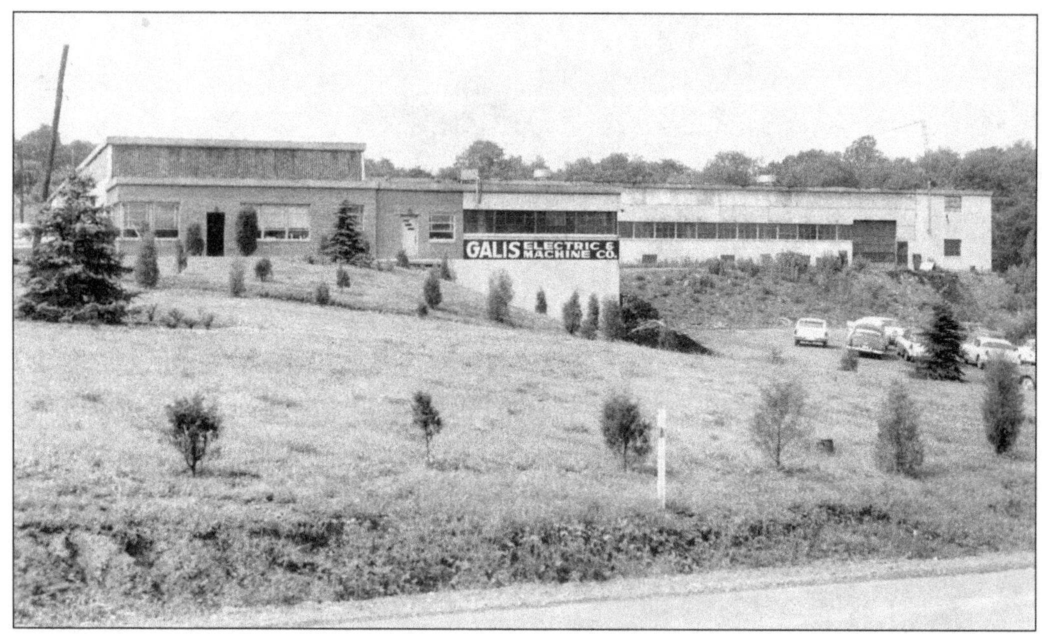

Morgantown has long been a center for the construction and repair of mining machinery. This photograph shows the Galis Electric and Machine Company in Westover in 1961. Company founder Alex Galis invented machines for cutting coal, transporting coal underground, and roof bolting. Galis Electric became a division of the FMC Corporation in 1972. (West Virginia and Regional History Collection, West Virginia University Libraries.)

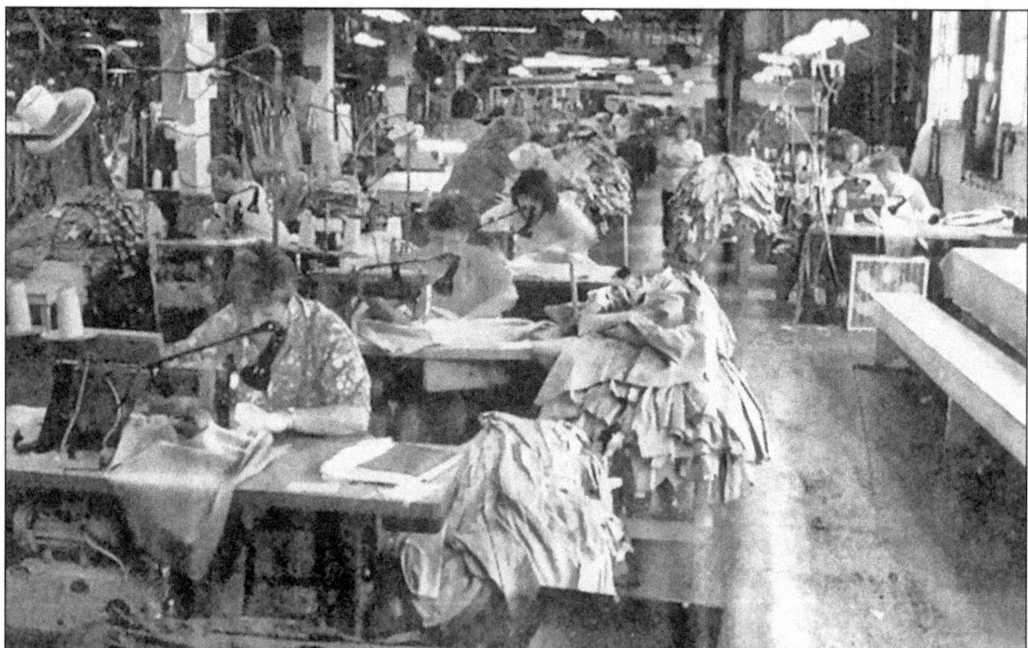

Women employed there generally considered the Morgan Shirt Company a good place to work. It was established as an operation of the Raritan Shirt Company in 1937 and employed over 200 people. The company was well-known for making high-quality shirts, but it also produced war materials in 1943 and pajamas at other times. This shows the sewing room in 1995.

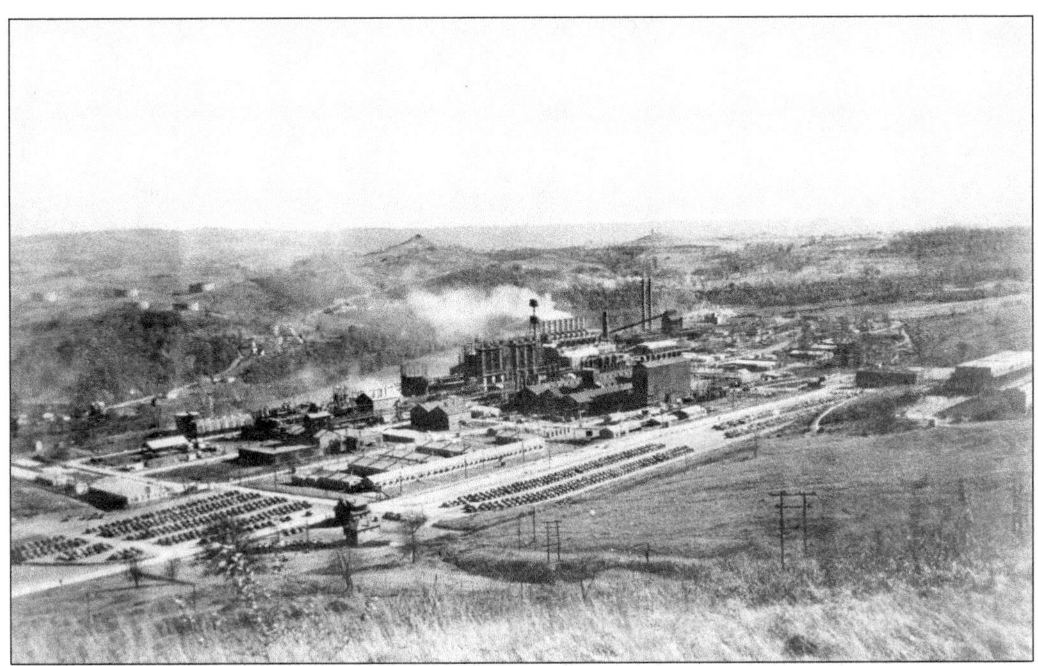

The Morgantown Ordnance Works was built to supply chemicals based on coal for World War II. It was operated by the Dupont Chemical Company. This aerial view shows the plant in 1950. It was generally known that the plant produced formaldehyde, hexamine, methanol, light oil, ammonia, coke, catalysts, and caustics. The plant also made heavy water for the Manhattan Project. (West Virginia and Regional History Collection, West Virginia University Libraries.)

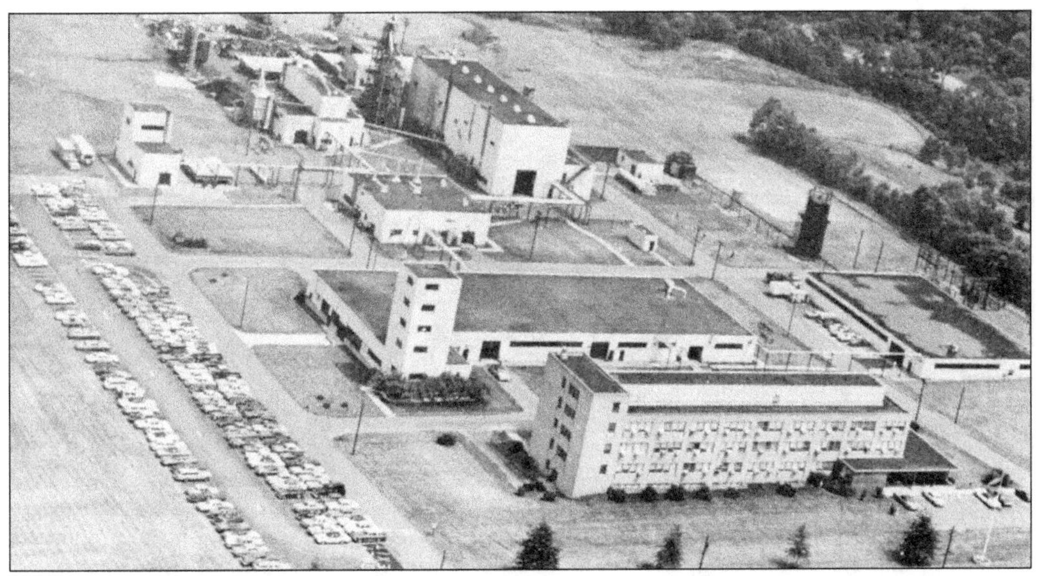

This photograph shows the Morgantown Energy Research Center of the U.S. Bureau of Mines in about 1970. Over the years, the name of the center has changed, but it has always focused on research on uses for coal and efficient and clean coal combustion and conversion processes.

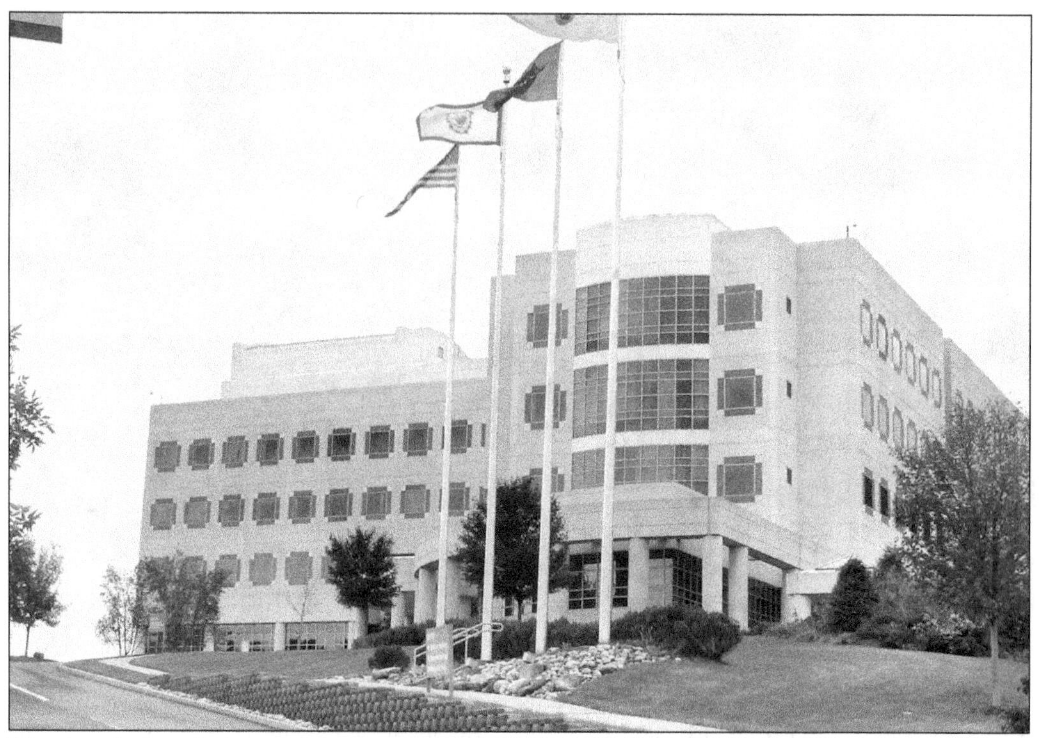

The Appalachian Laboratory for Occupation Health and Safety of the Centers for Disease Control, U.S. Public Health Service, is home to about 300 professionals working at preventing industrial diseases and injuries. It was built in 1996. There were earlier Public Health Service activities in conjunction with the West Virginia University Medical Center.

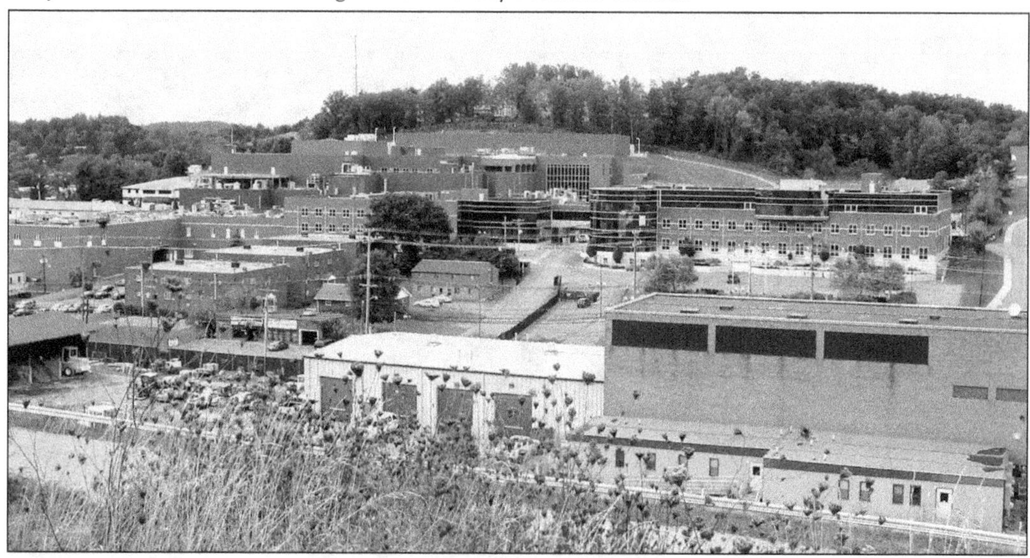

This is a recent photograph of Mylan Pharmaceuticals' one-million-square-foot campus on Chestnut Ridge Road. The company was founded in southern West Virginia in 1961 but moved its principal operations to Morgantown in 1965. The Morgantown plant is primarily focused on solid oral-dose generic pharmaceutical products. In 1995, Mylan became the most dispensed line of pharmaceuticals in America, branded or generic.

Six

West Virginia University

When the western counties separated themselves from Virginia in 1863, one of their first acts was to establish a land-grant university. Morgantown won the right to be home to the West Virginia Agricultural College in part because it committed major local resources to the new institution. The directors of the Monongalia Academy (founded in 1814), the Morgantown Female Academy (established in 1831), and the Woodburn Female Seminary (started in 1858) all donated their facilities. These institutions were formally "high schools" but essentially acted as regional colleges.

The faculty was actually more interested in the "learned professions" than agriculture, and the name was quickly changed to West Virginia University.

Initial enrollment in the university was limited to white males, although at about the same time, the state legislature established normal schools admitting women and a college for blacks. The faculty voted to admit women to the university in 1889. Restrictions on black enrollment ended in 1954, although a few had been specially admitted to some programs at earlier dates.

As a land-grant university, West Virginia has always had a commitment to teaching practical, as well as literary, disciplines. Today it has professional programs in almost every area except veterinary medicine and architecture.

Intercollegiate football started in 1891, and athletic activities at the university are followed enthusiastically statewide. WVU teams, students, and fans are known as Mountaineers. At one time, the mascot might have been mistaken for a "hillbilly" by his dress, but today he or she is a buckskin-clad frontiersman.

In 1946, military veterans under the G.I. Bill swelled the student body to over 6,000.

During the 1960s, the university underwent a sudden expansion, creating two new campuses on the outskirts of the city. The Evansdale Campus became home to engineering, agriculture and forestry, education, athletics, and fine and performing arts. A nearby hilltop became the site for medicine, dentistry, and related health professions. At that time, the university increased its commitment to doctoral level degrees and research, and enrollment passed 15,000.

Today enrollment has passed 25,000 and is still increasing.

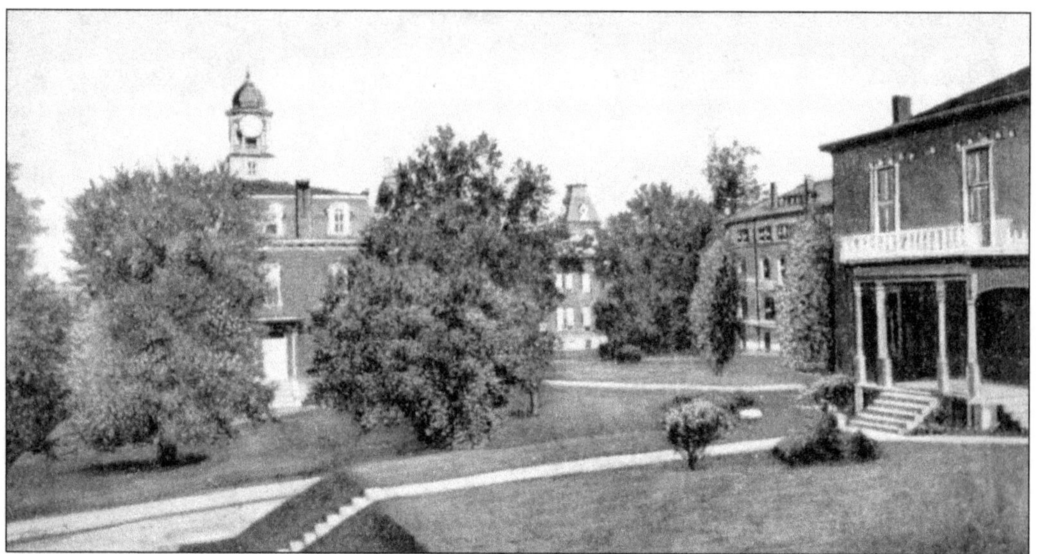

This is Woodburn Circle, the original WVU campus, as it appeared in 1910. Only the structure on the right is gone; it was the Agricultural Experiment Station, built in 1899. The other three buildings, although remodeled and renamed several times, still remain and house programs in liberal arts and journalism. The quadrangle is still a center for outdoor events.

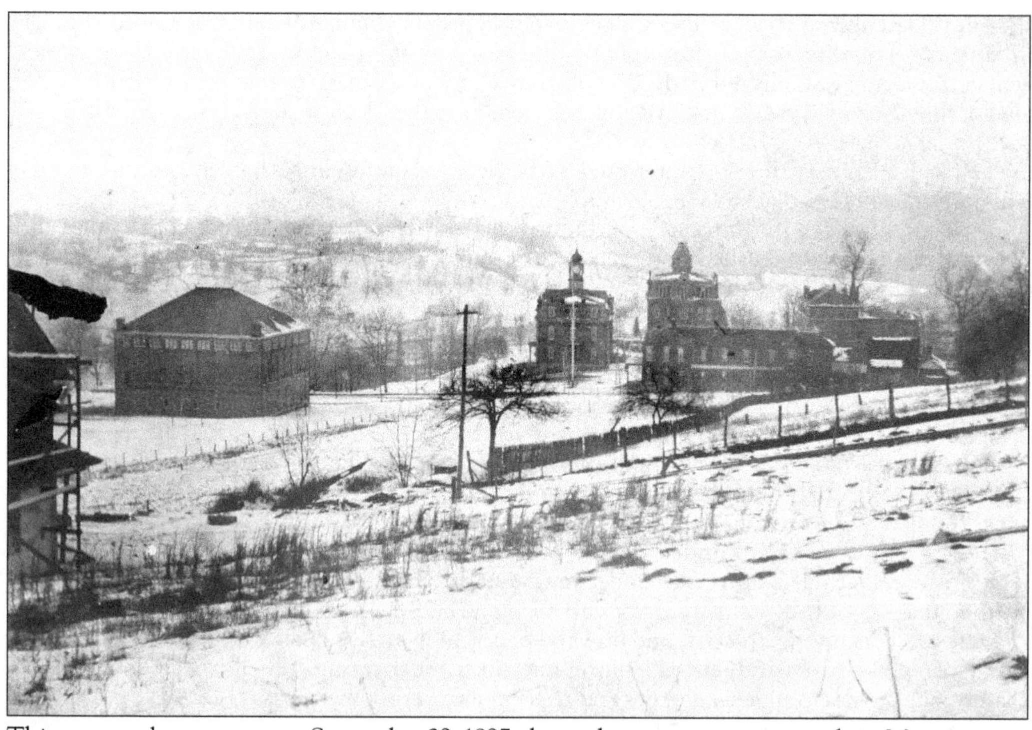

This scene, taken on campus September 29, 1897, shows that snow can come early in Morgantown. Woodburn Circle is on the right, and Commencement Hall is on the left.

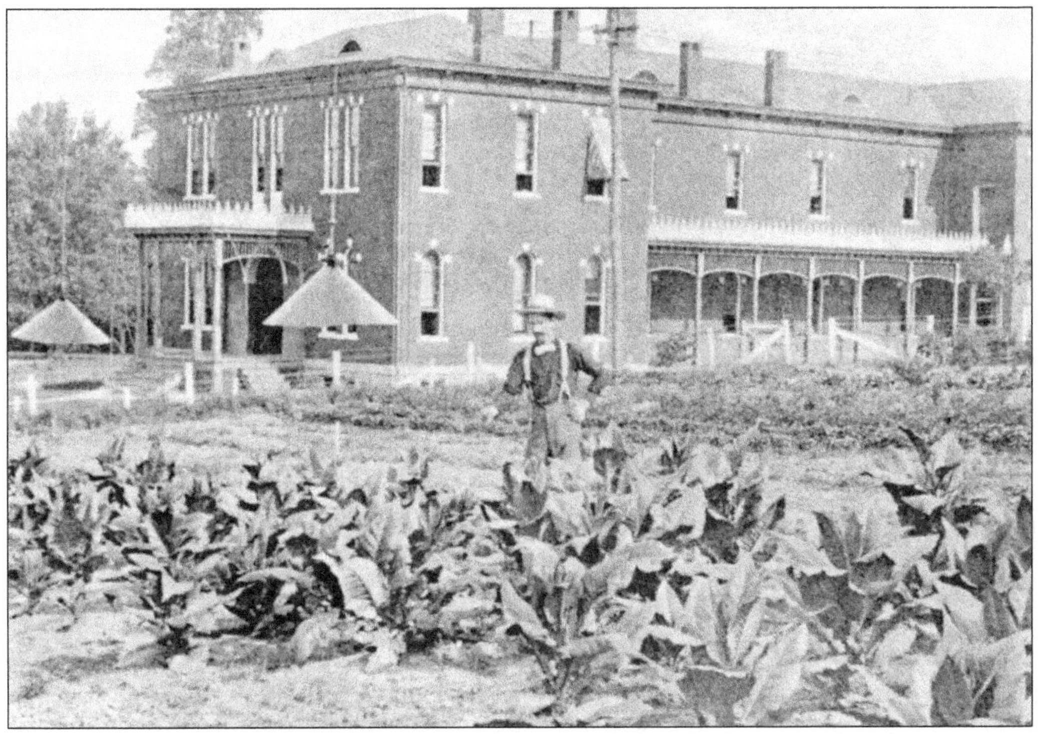

This photograph shows an experimental tobacco patch beside the Agricultural Experiment Station in 1900. Other experimental vegetable plots can be seen behind the workman. The first Experiment Station was remodeled from an older armory in 1888–1889 and expanded in 1893. The site was near Woodburn Circle and is crossed by present-day University Avenue.

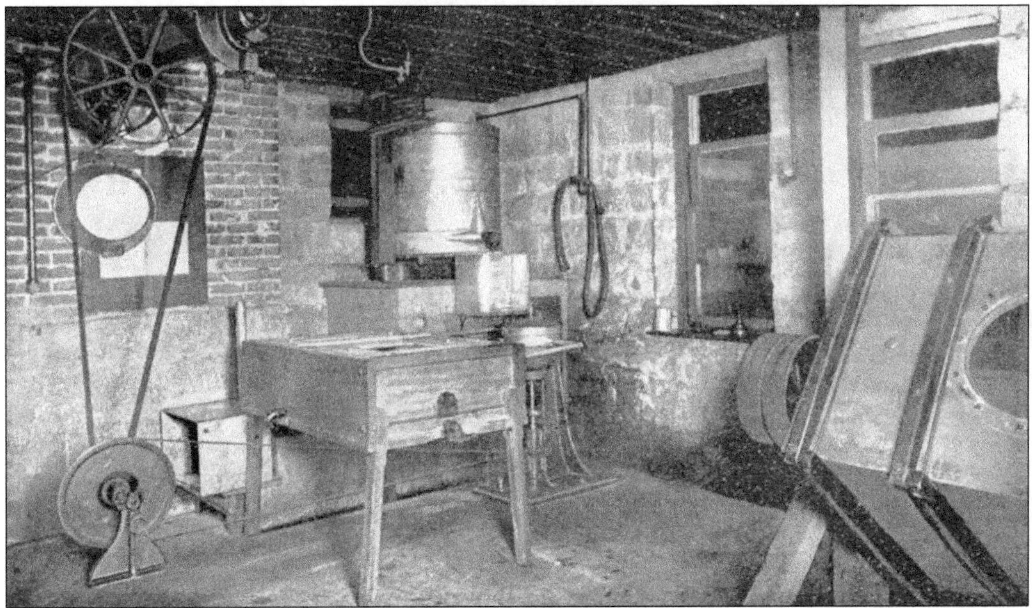

The state-of-the-art research creamery in the agricultural research station in 1889 had the latest equipment and outstanding cleanliness and did research on butter-making methods adapted to Southern farms. Unfortunately local consumers did not like the slightly different taste.

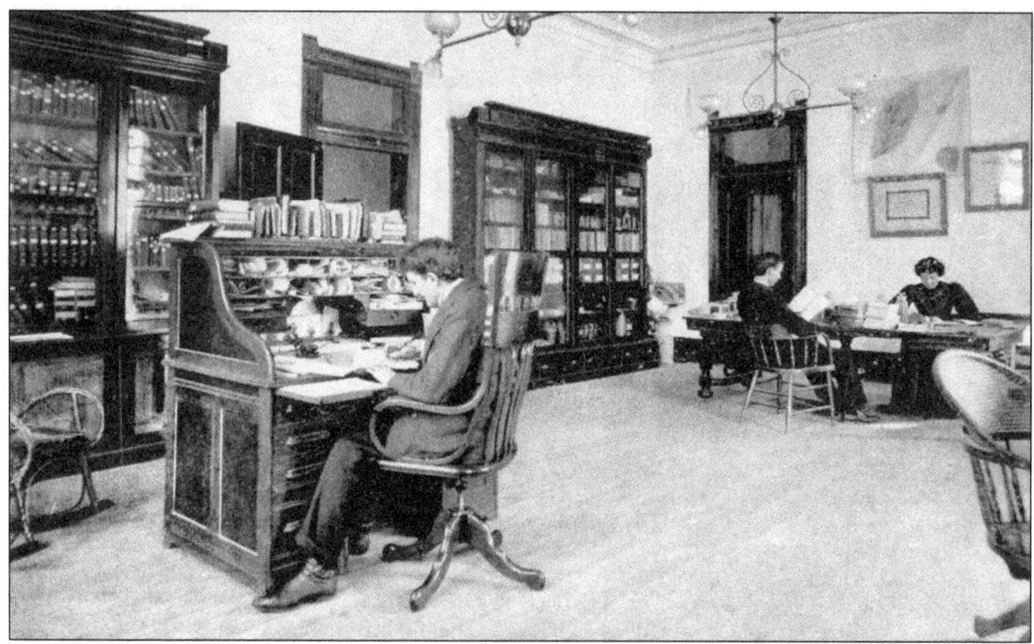

The 1896 edition of the *Monticola*, the WVU yearbook, included this picture of a research office in the Agricultural Experiment Station. Built in 1889, the building had modern gas lighting, which allowed employees to work without candles or oil lamps. This was a modern high-tech research facility for the times. Research in agriculture is still a part of WVU. (Morgantown Public Library.)

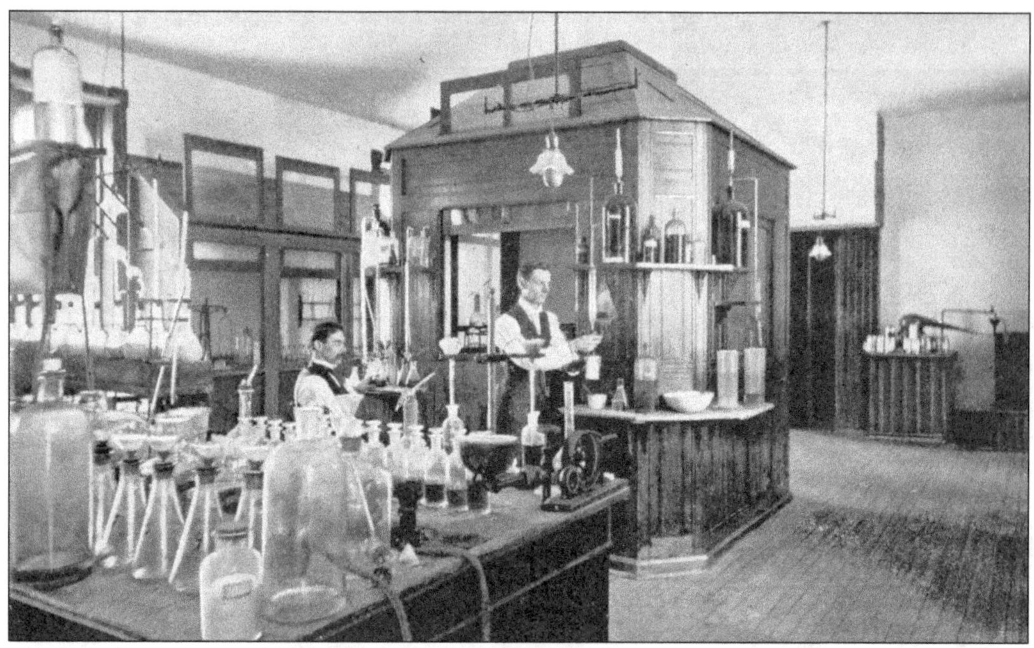

Pictures in the 1896 *Monticola* also included this chemical laboratory in the research station. By then, electrical lighting was in use on campus. Among other activities, the early station research included the testing of chemical fertilizers, which were just coming on the market and were often of dubious quality. (Morgantown Public Library.)

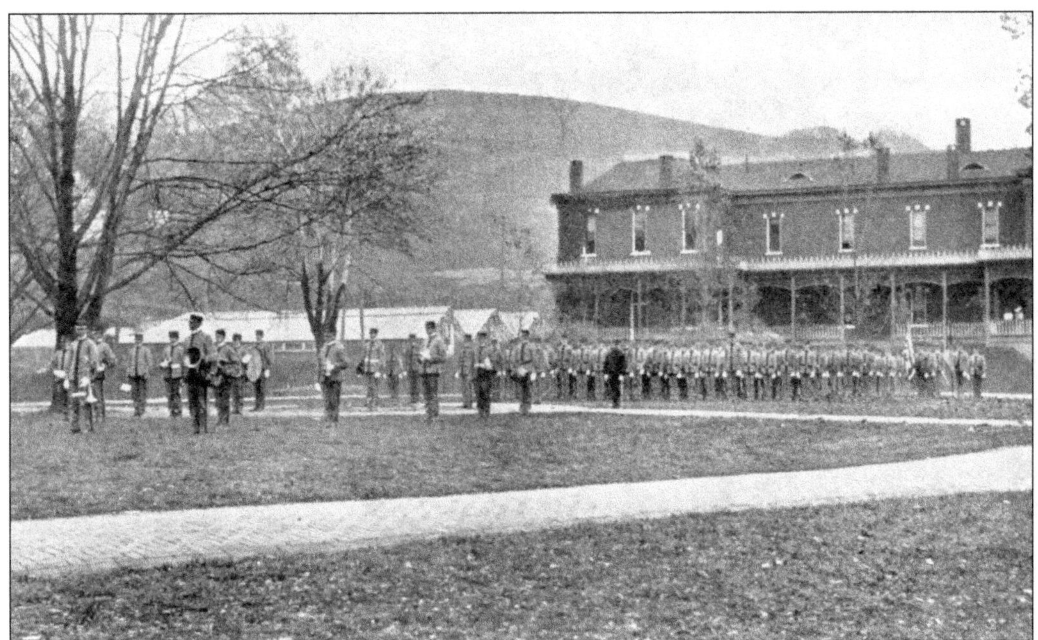

Led by the military band, these West Virginia University cadets were drilling in Woodburn Circle about 1900. For its first century, WVU required all men to participate in ROTC for two years. The hilltop now capped by University High School was bare farmland. The photograph also shows that the Experiment Station had extensive greenhouses in which to conduct research.

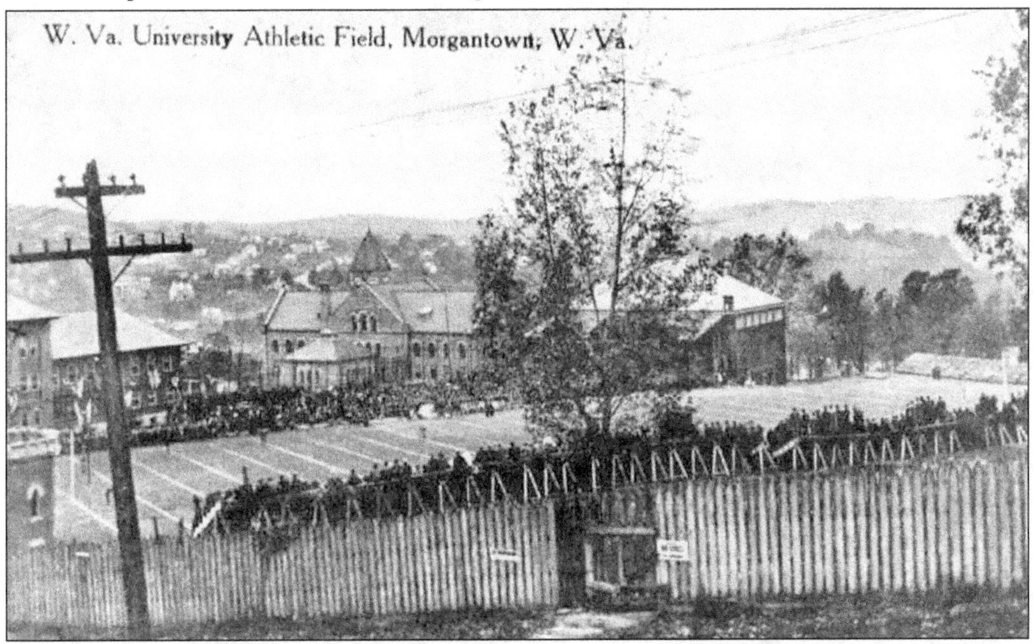

This was the drill and athletic field about 1913. It appears that a football game is in progress. This area is now the Mountainlair parking garage and plaza. Behind the tree are the library and Commencement Hall. Behind the telephone pole is Mechanical Hall, then home of the engineering school. The window and turret at the lower left are part of the armory, which housed the ROTC program.

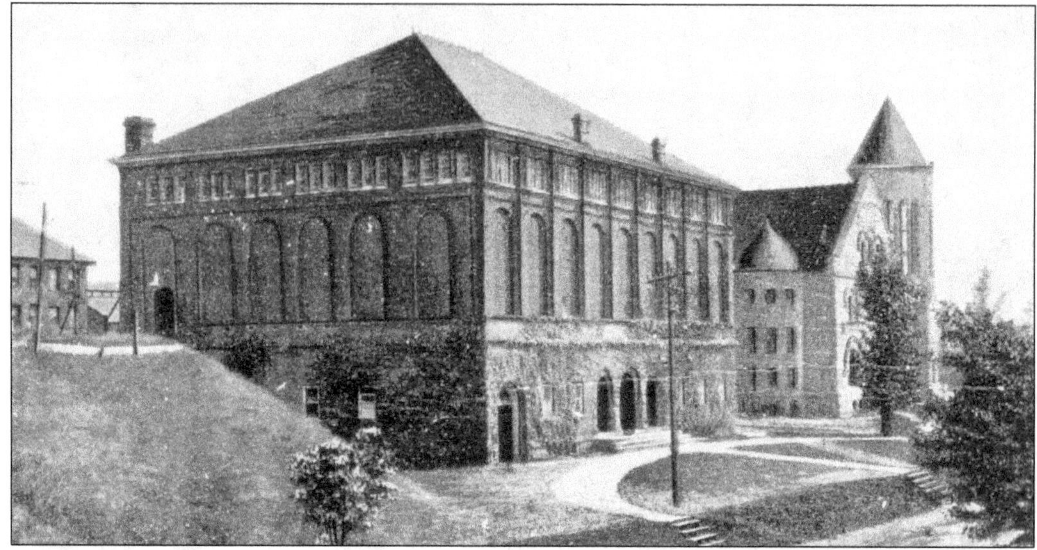

Commencement Hall, built in 1892, was used for many activities open to the entire community, including plays, concerts, and lectures. Commencement Hall was torn down in 1965 to make way for the new student union, the Mountainlair. The ornate library building, on the right, was built in 1900. It became Stewart Hall and is now used as an administrative center.

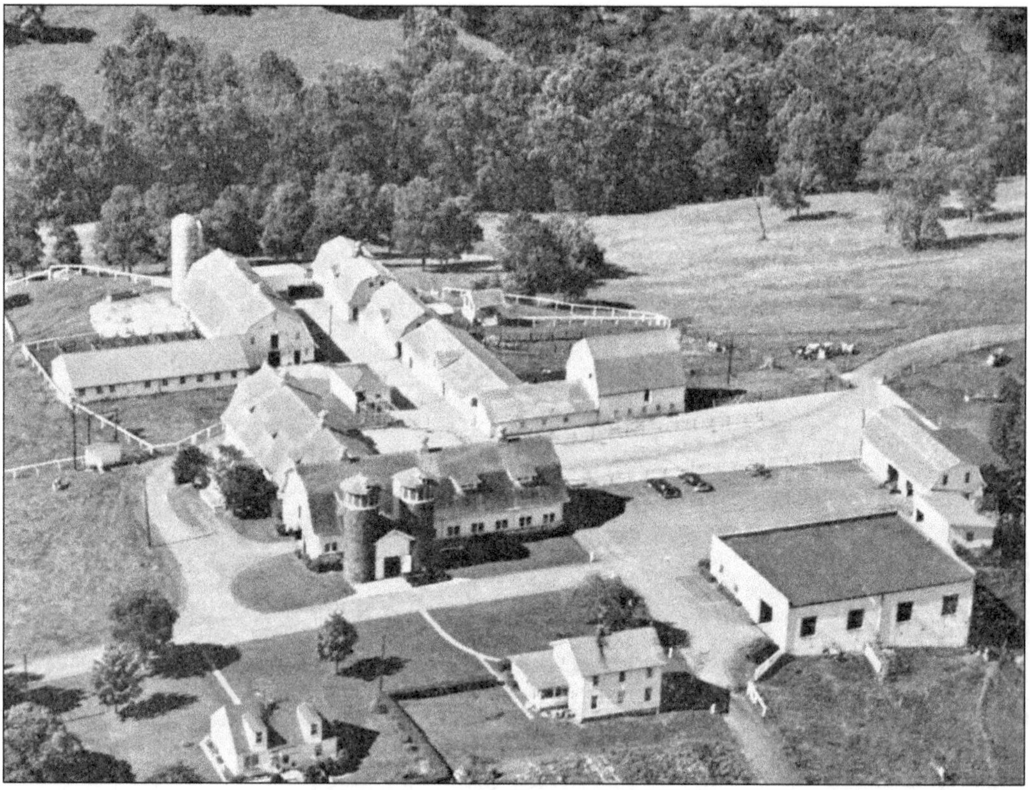

The WVU Dairy Farm was built for research and instruction. It also hosts open houses where Morgantown "city kids" have an opportunity to see and touch animals. The facility is still in use and is located on the Stewartstown Road. The large barn was destroyed by an arsonist in 1974.

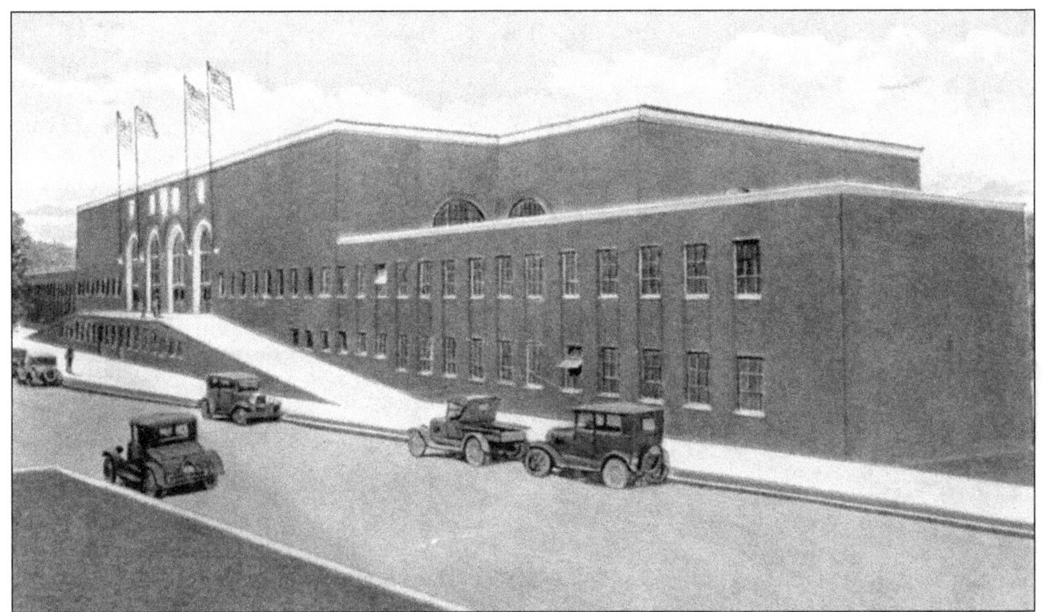

The Field House, built in 1929 and shown here in 1931, is located on Beechurst Avenue. It was the home for basketball and other indoor sports for over 20 years. Older alumni will recall standing in long lines here to enroll in courses and pay fees during semester registration. It was renamed Stansbury Hall, and today it houses ROTC and the English department.

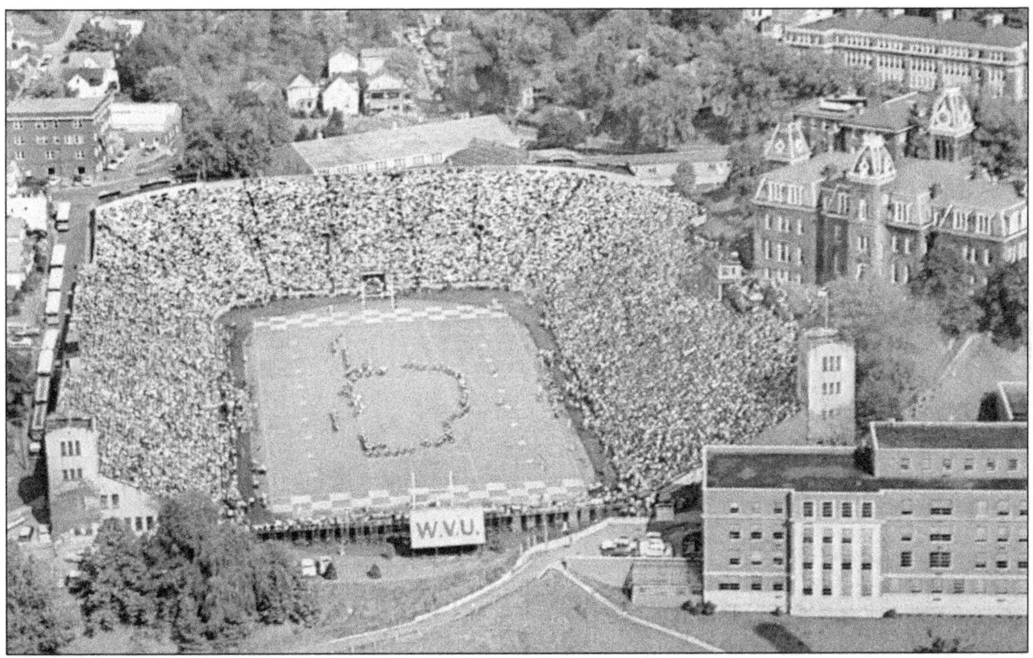

Old Mountaineer Field, built in 1924, was the scene of action for many football games. Woodburn Hall with the pointed towers is in the background, and Brooks Hall is to the right. A new Mountaineer Stadium was built in 1980.

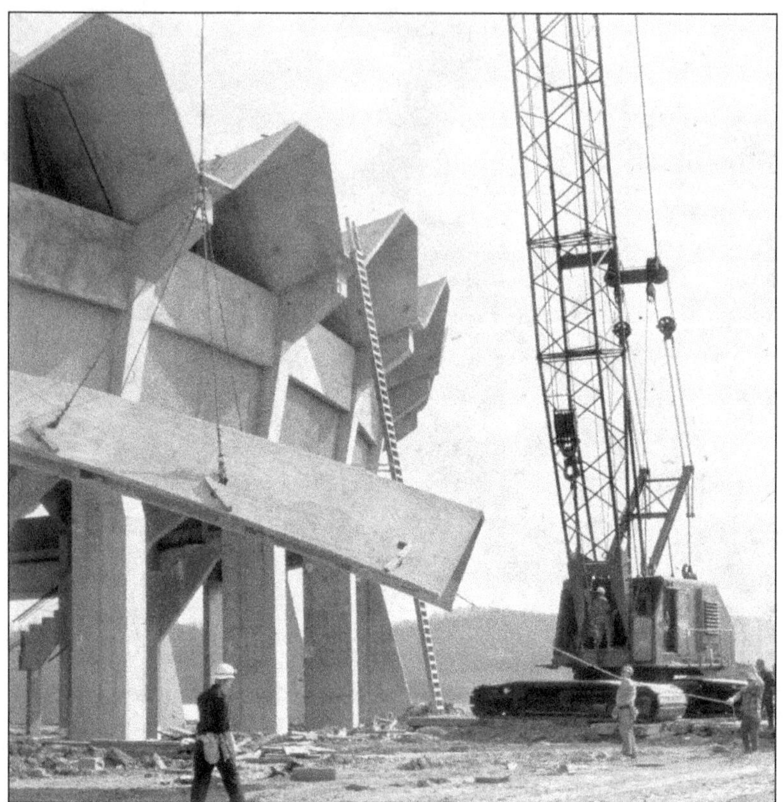

Construction of the West Virginia University Coliseum began in 1968. This photograph shows a concrete roof panel being lifted into place. Panels were cast on-site on shaped earth forms. Usually basements are dug before roof construction starts, but in this case, the excavation for the playing floor did not start until the roof had been completed.

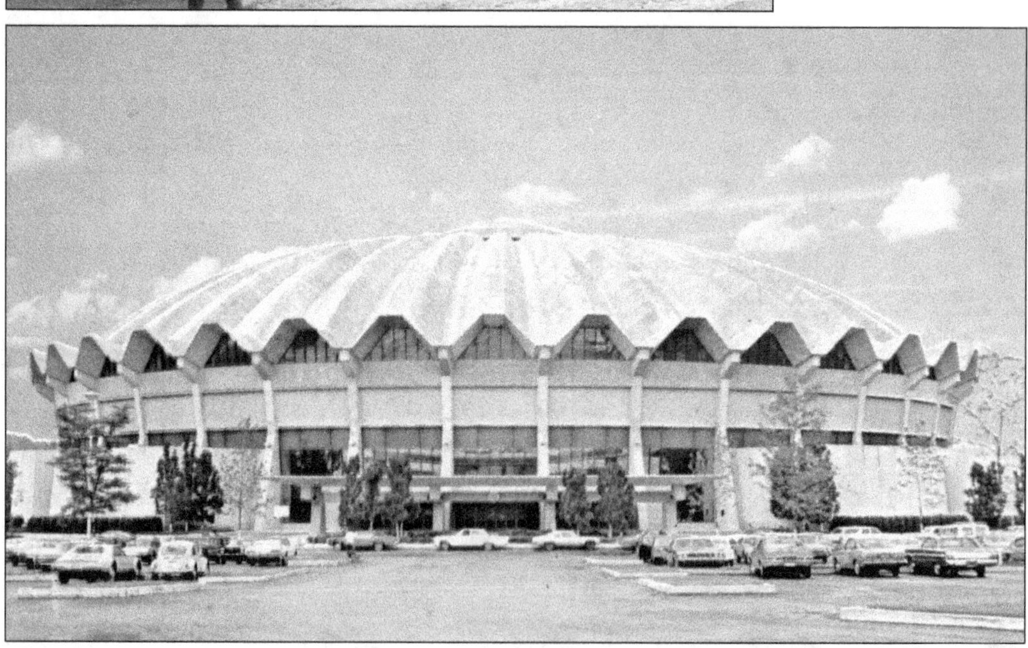

The West Virginia University Coliseum was finished in 1970. The dome houses the basketball court and physical education offices. In addition to athletic events, it has hosted events ranging from circuses and concerts to graduation. The building's circular outer hallway is also used by many Morgantown residents for indoor walking.

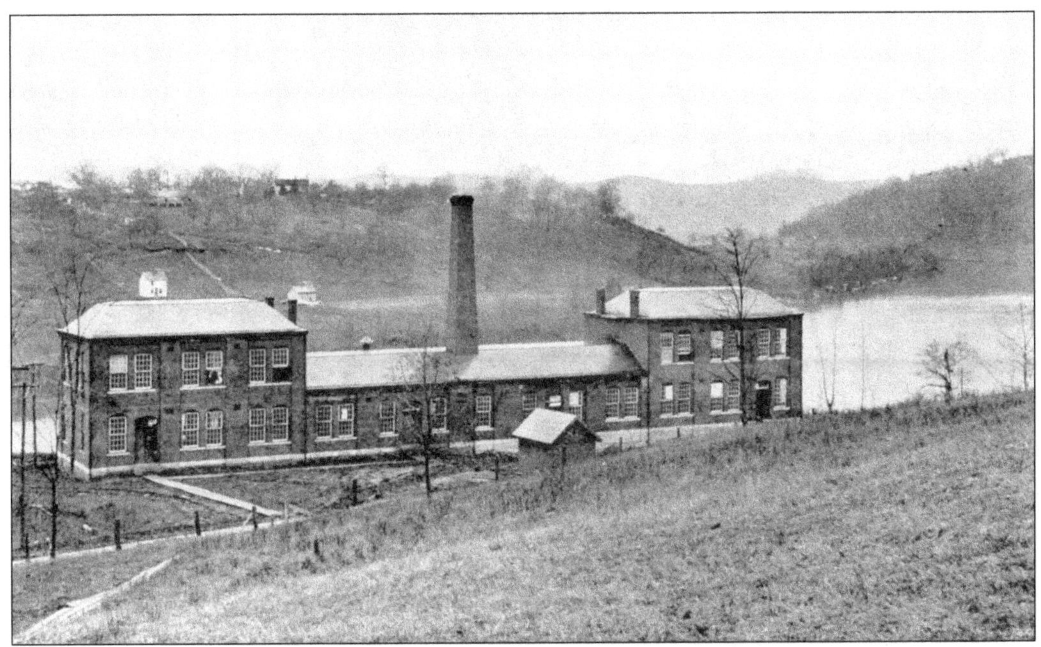

The old Mechanical Building was built in 1894 alongside the Monongahela River. It housed laboratories for studies of electricity and machinery and workshops where engineering students developed hands-on skills. The building burned in 1899.

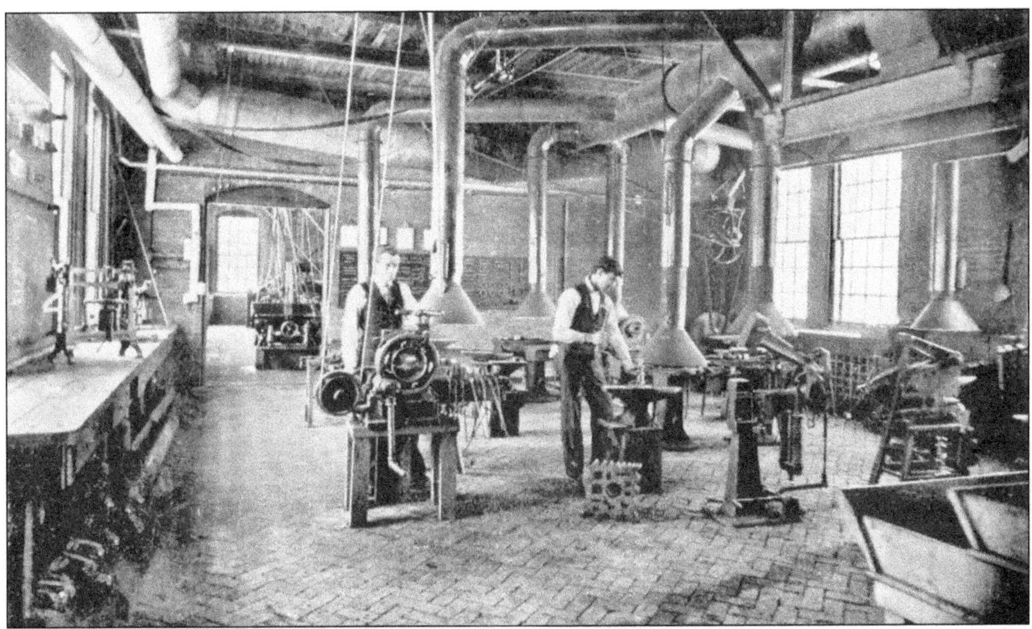

This photograph shows a blacksmith shop about 1896. Here students would learn to forge items in iron, not with the aim of making them blacksmiths, but so they could develop an understanding of what they could expect from craftsmen. It was probably located in the Mechanical Building. (Morgantown Public Library.)

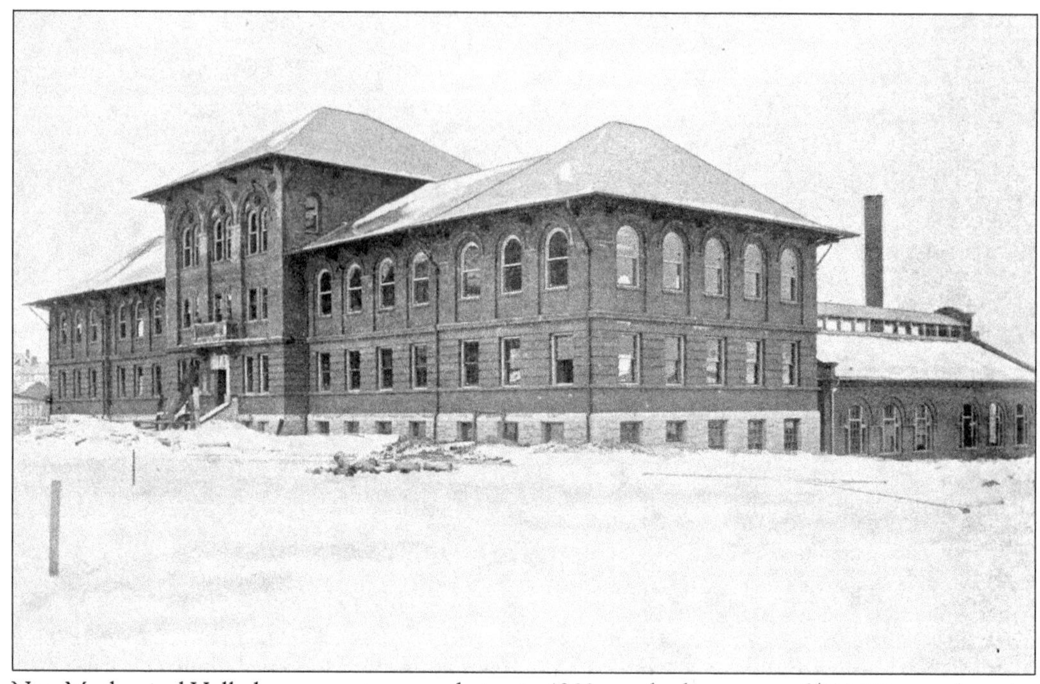

New Mechanical Hall, shown nearing completion in 1902, was built at a cost of $55,000 to replace the old Mechanical Building. This building was located on the present Mountainlair Plaza. It housed the College of Engineering's classrooms, offices, and laboratories. (Morgantown Public Library.)

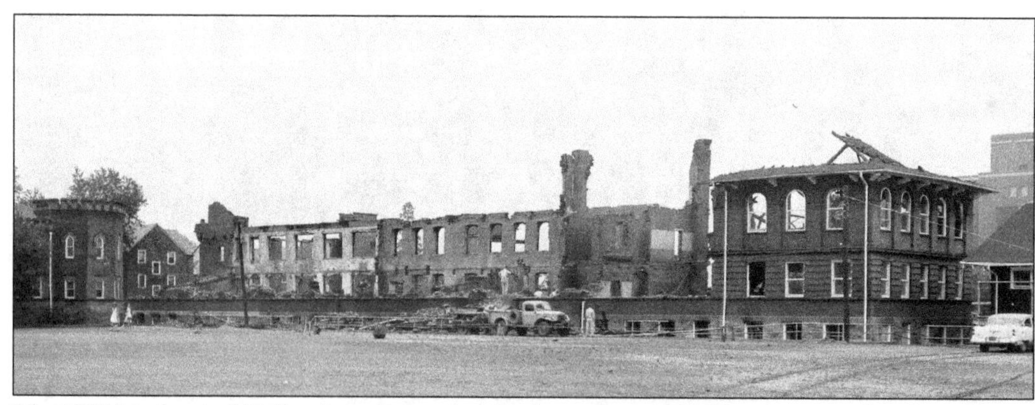

The 1902 Mechanical Hall is shown here after the fire in June 1956. Planning was already underway for a new engineering building in Evansdale, and Dean Chester Arents would later recall telling people throughout the state "the old firetrap could burn any day." (Thomas Long.)

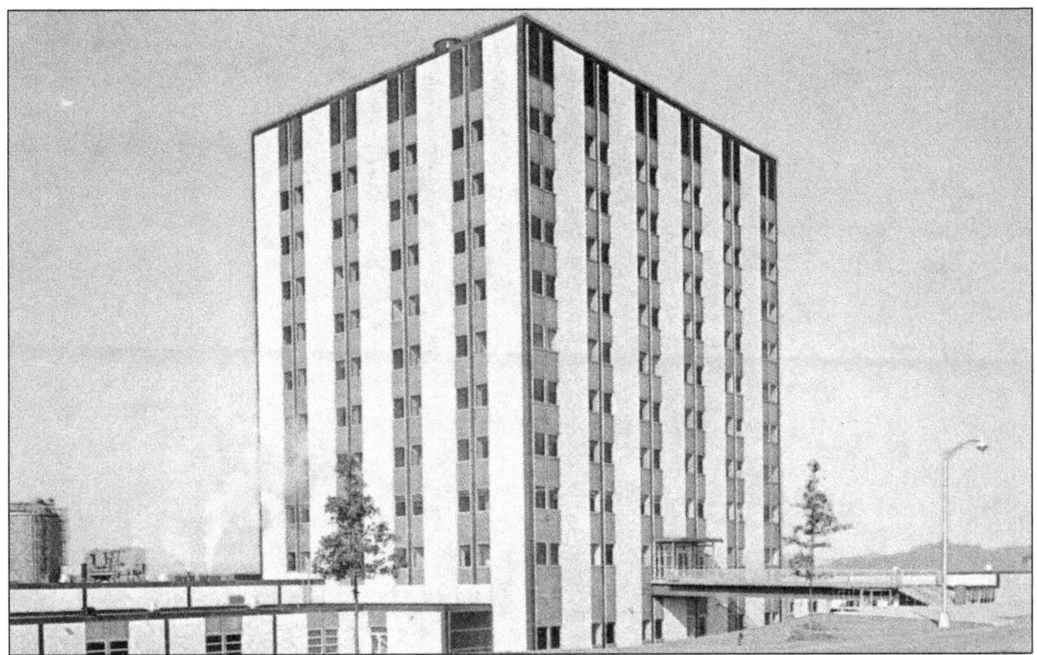

This shows the current Engineering Sciences Building on the Evansdale Campus. In 1959, contracts were awarded for the building's construction. The building was completed in 1961.

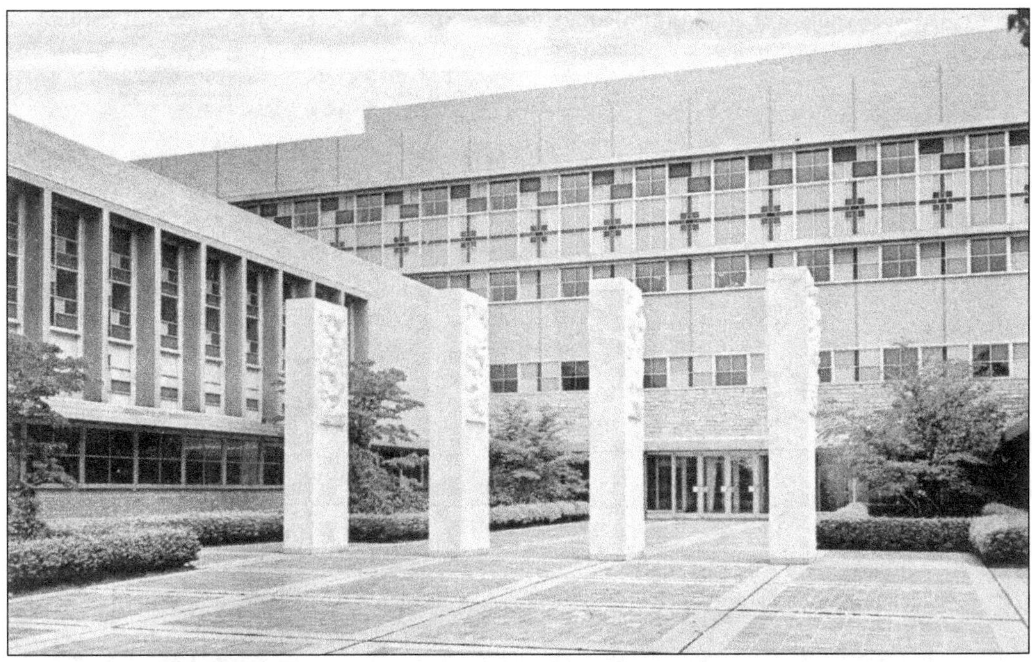

The pylon sculptures mark the entrance to the health professions teaching facilities at the Basic Sciences Building, built 1957. They depict traditions in the healing arts. In recent renovations, the entrance to the building has been extended to cover them, and the pylons are now protected from the weather. The adjacent Medical Center housing the hospital and clinics was not completed until 1961.

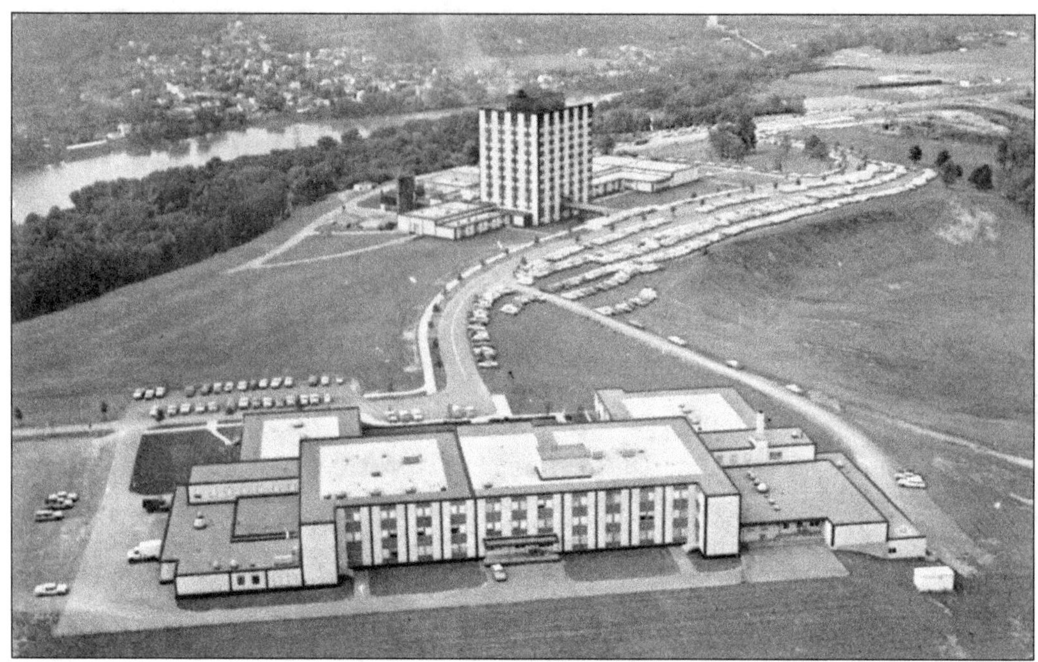

This is West Virginia University's Evansdale Campus in the early 1960s. The Agricultural Sciences Building is in front, and the Engineering Sciences Building in back. Today this campus is also home to the Towers residential complex, the forestry and education buildings, the Creative Arts Center, the Coliseum and Natatorium, and the large Student Recreation Center. It is linked to the other campuses by the Personal Rapid Transit System.

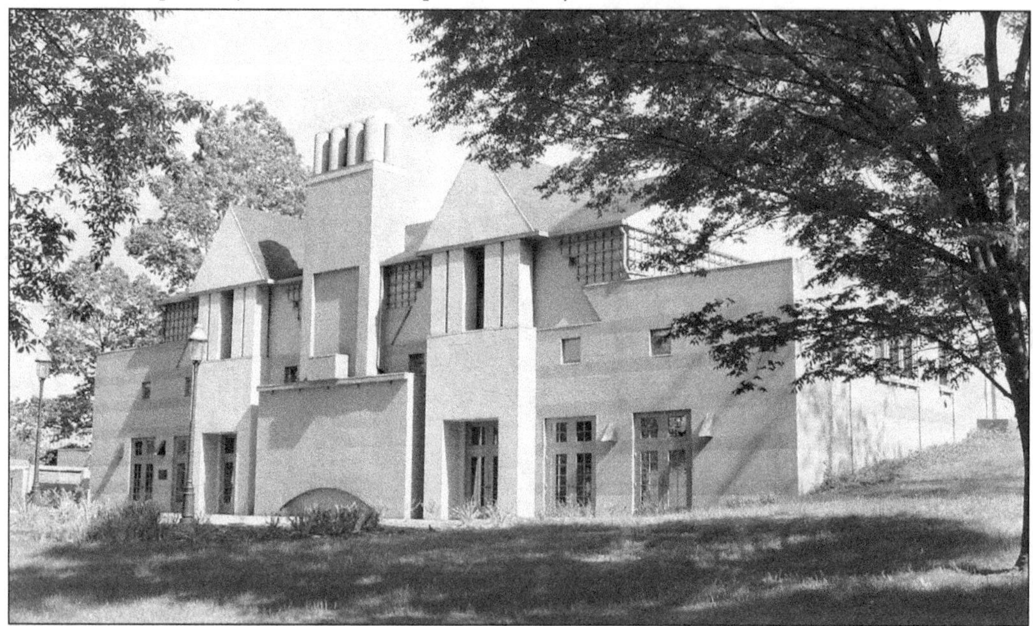

The Ericson Center is home to the West Virginia University Alumni Association. It is located on the Evansdale Campus. The building may be the most architecturally significant structure in Morgantown. It was designed by Michael Graves, often referred to as "the dean of the Postmodern School of Architecture."

Seven

Around the Town

While Morgantown is expanding at a dizzying rate today, most area residents have reasons to go downtown. The central business district is still vibrant. In part, this is due to the way in which the area's topography has limited building sites and restricted transportation.

Activities and services at the courthouse encourage lawyers, financial service providers, and insurance agents to remain in town.

The university's central operations base and the student union are on the original campus, which abuts the central business district. This brings students to town at night to eat, see movies, and drink, and registration fees for university students include unlimited use of public transportation.

Until recently, the malls were located where they were hard for car-less students to reach, although recent aggressive improvements in public transportation are changing that. Road congestion makes a visit to a mall or shopping plaza across town more of a challenge for all residents.

South Park and adjacent neighborhoods are still considered prime places to live. This is an area where children can still walk to school, the library, and recreational facilities. The tree-lined streets provide a pleasant route to walk to work either downtown or at the university.

Historically the central district was the location for churches, and several of the community's most important churches are still downtown.

While the biggest commercial developments are in malls and plazas on the periphery of the metropolitan area, local developers are building a new mixed-use commercial, residential, and recreational area along the river adjacent to the city center.

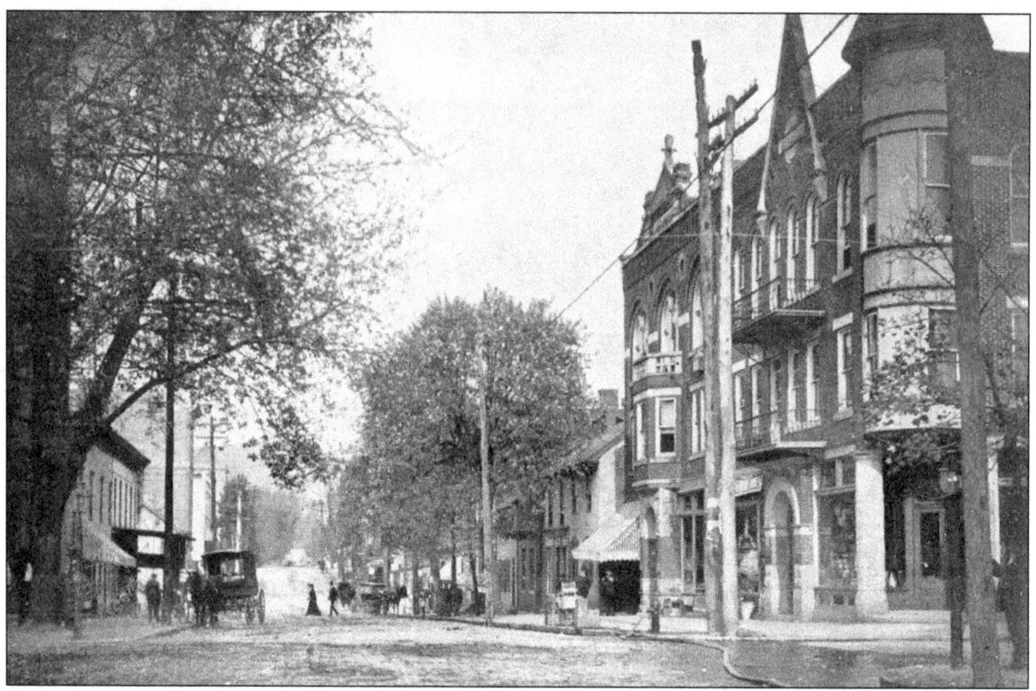

This shows the corner of Pleasant and Main (now High) Streets in 1902. The building on the right is still in use, although the upper decorations and spire have been removed.

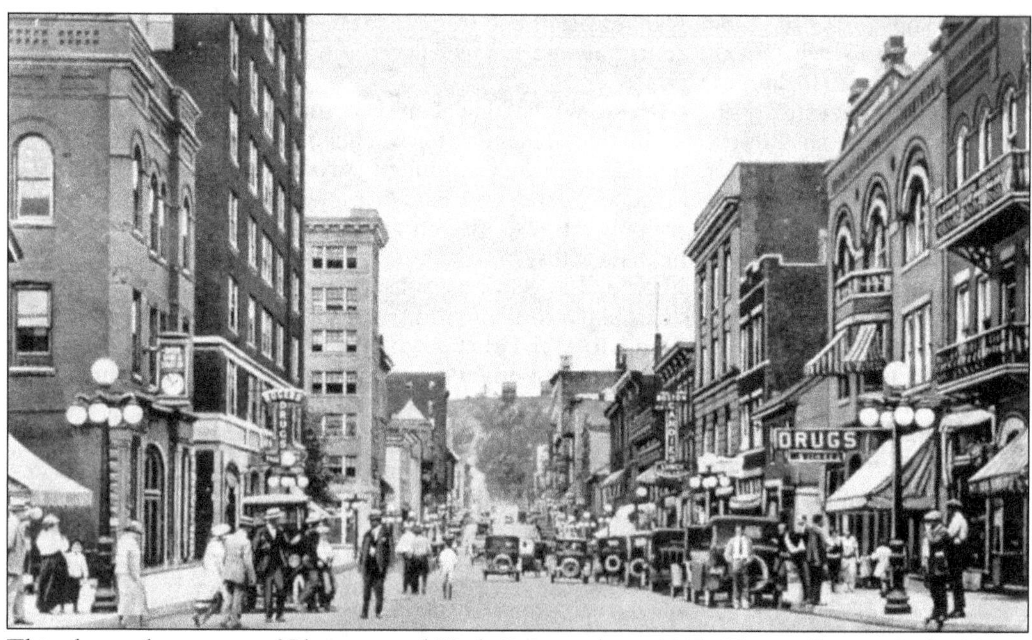

This shows the corner of Pleasant and High Streets about 1925. The trolley tracks had been removed. Although many of the buildings have been remodeled, the scene has changed little if we disregard the cars and clothes.

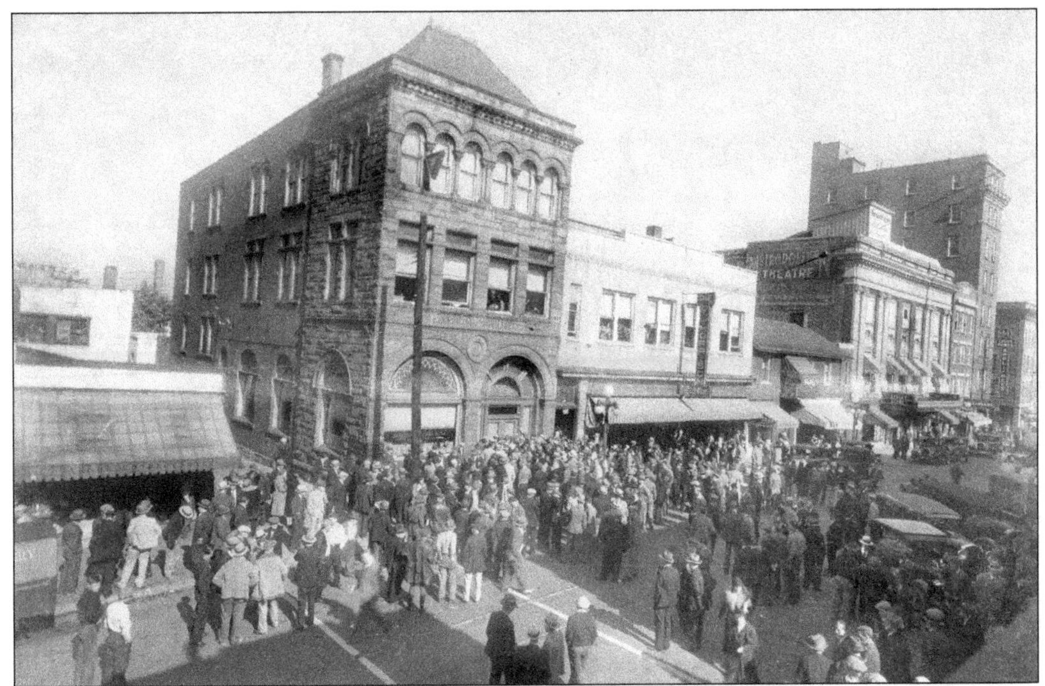

A photographer caught the crowd making a run on the Second National Bank on October 12, 1931, during the Depression. The bank closed permanently. The other banks had been closed earlier, and for about a month, the county had no banking facilities. The building was built in 1894. It has housed radio station WCLG for many years. (West Virginia and Regional History Collection, West Virginia University Libraries.)

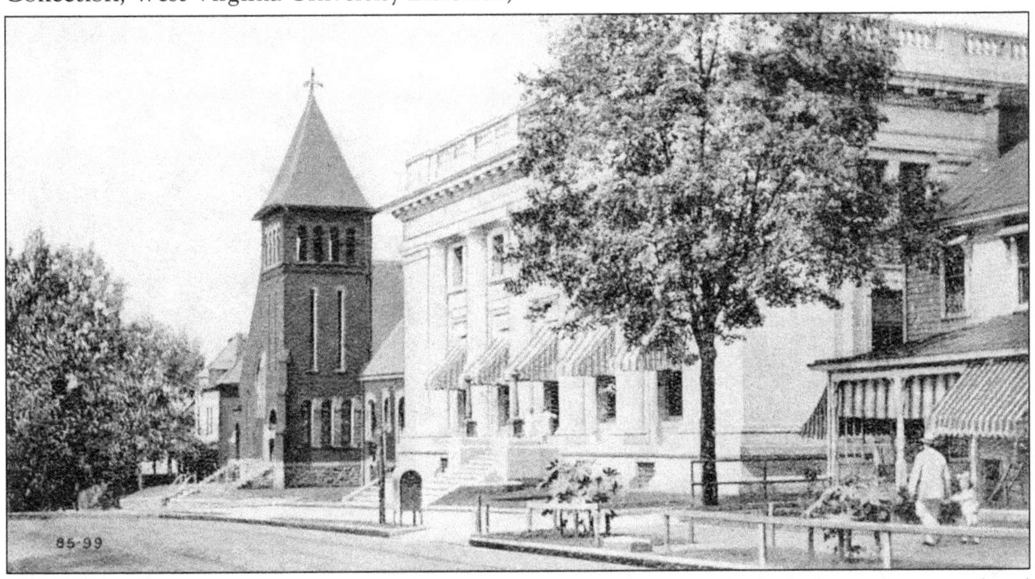

The Morgantown Post Office on High Street, at center, is shown as it looked when it was completed in 1915. Morgantown's first federal building, it features a neoclassical style. On market day, the hitching rail would have been filled with farm wagons. A new post office was built in 1973, and since 1977, the old post office has been the Monongalia Arts Center, which houses art exhibits, art classes, and a theater.

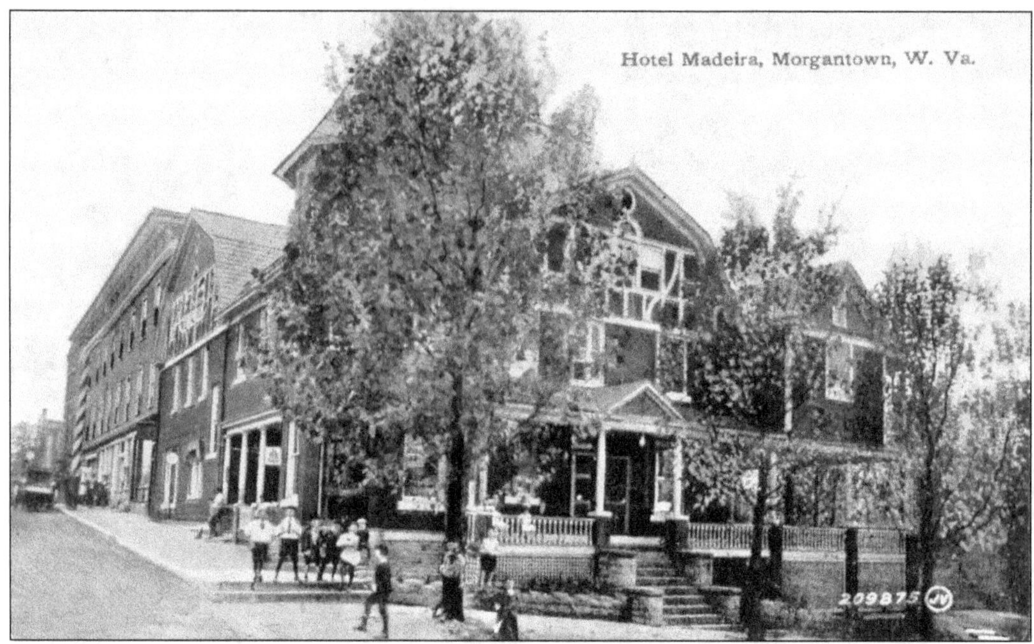

The Hotel Madeira offered its own electrical lighting plant, water from a 620-foot-deep well, and rooms with bath and telephone and touted its location near the boat landing and railroad depot. The hotel is seen here in 1911. Morgantown civic leaders meeting at the Hotel Madeira organized a local Kiwanis Club in 1920.

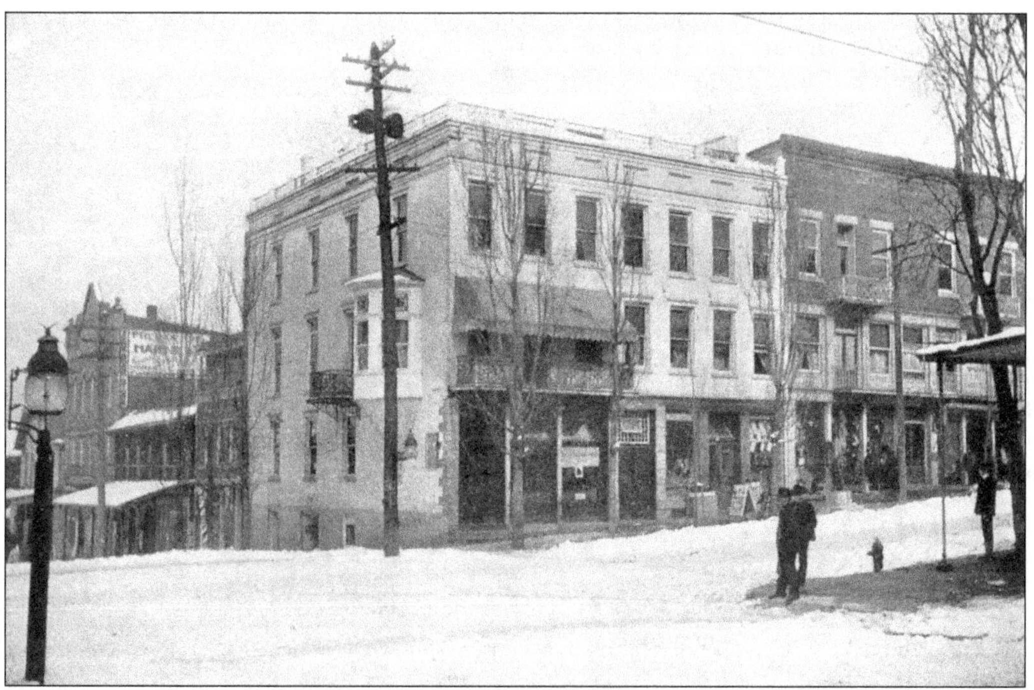

In 1902, the Citizens Bank was on the opposite corner of High and Walnut Streets from its current site. The building is still in use. A gas streetlight, electrical power and telephone lines, and a fire hydrant can be seen in the picture.

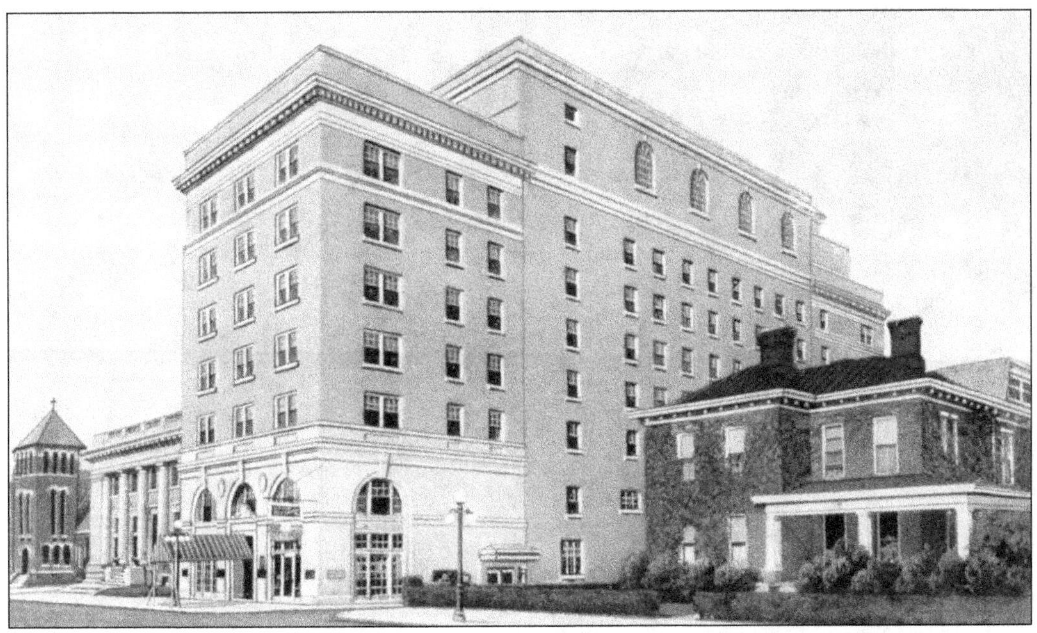

The Hotel Morgan on High Street was built in 1925. When it opened, the hotel featured 150 rooms, a governor's suite, barbershop, and club dining room. Noted guests included Eleanor Roosevelt and John F. Kennedy when he had an office here during his presidential campaign in West Virginia. It is still a hotel today. The home on the right was replaced by the Warner Theater in 1931.

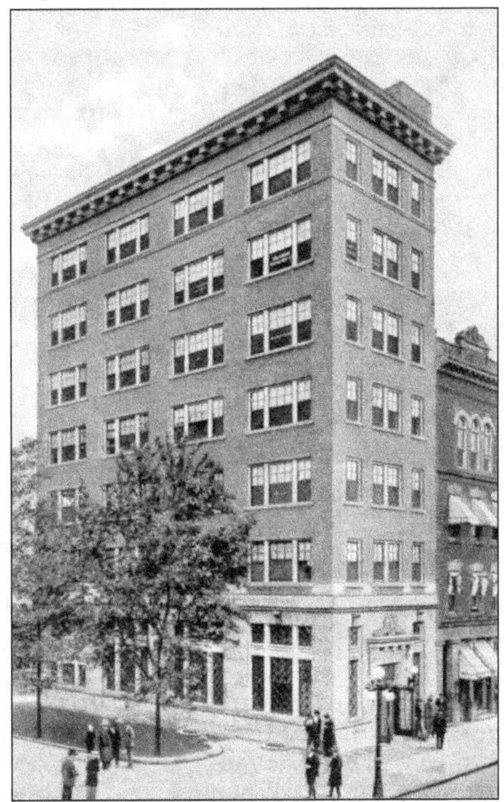

This building on the side of the Courthouse Square was built in 1921. It has served Morgantown as a bank and office for almost 90 years. Today it houses Citizens Bank, a rarity in having only one office, no drive-in, and only one ATM.

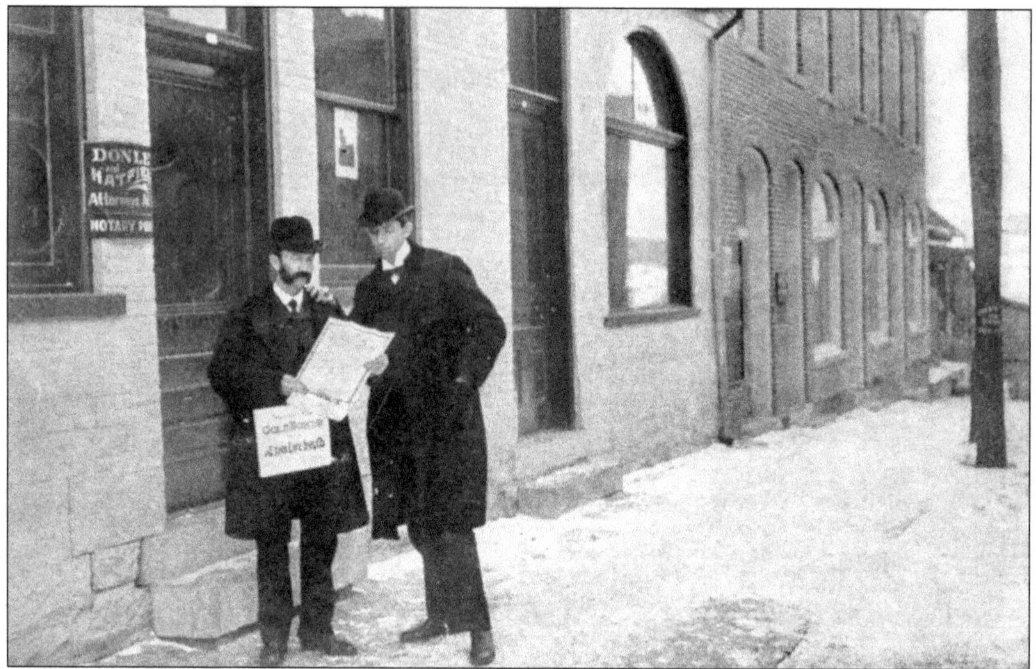

Chancery Row is directly across from the courthouse on a street originally known as Court Alley. The Chancery Row buildings are built of brick and have distinctive arched transoms over their windows. The buildings were constructed between 1852 and 1881 and have traditionally housed legal offices.

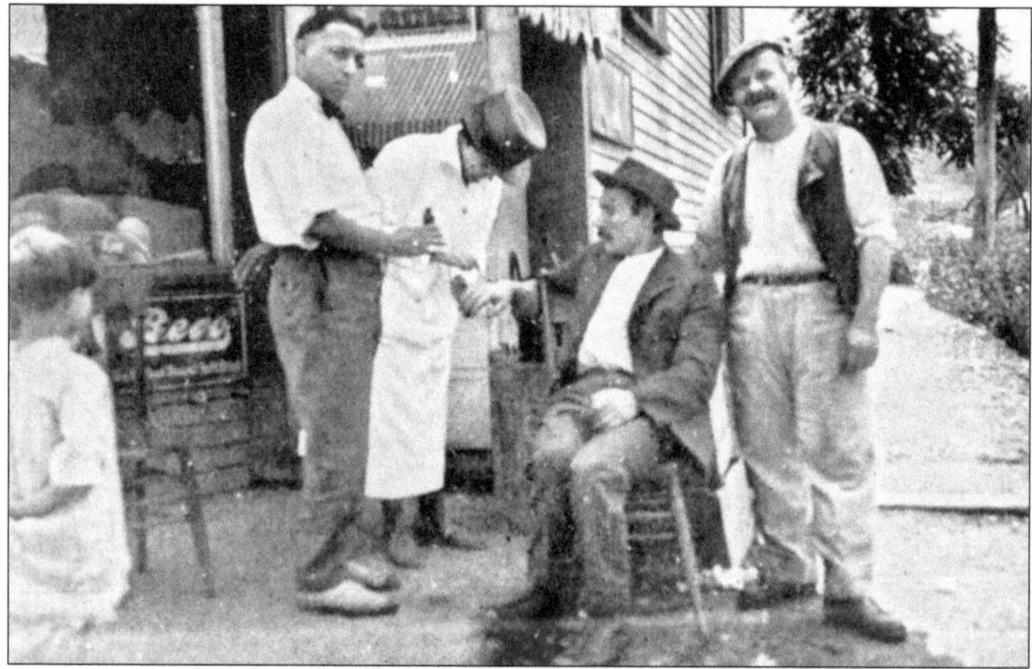

In 1922, the chamber of commerce promoted the idea that Morgantown cared for all its citizens. This photograph shows an immigrant worker being treated for an injury by the nurse from the tin mill. His friends do not seem to be making him feel any better.

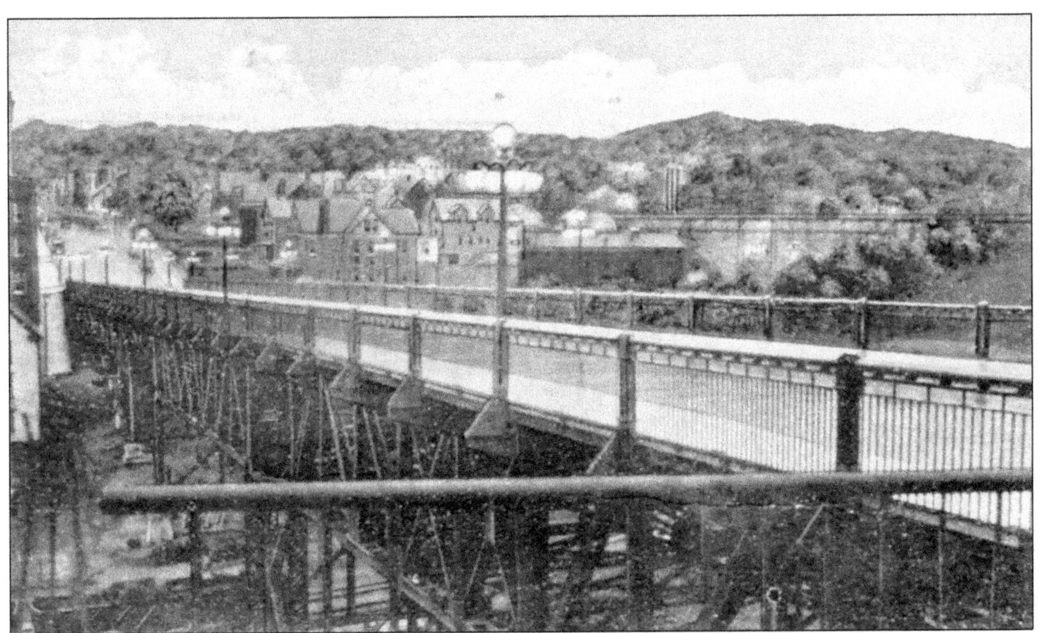

The High Street Bridge, shown in 1939, crosses Deckers Creek. This view is looking north towards the shopping district.

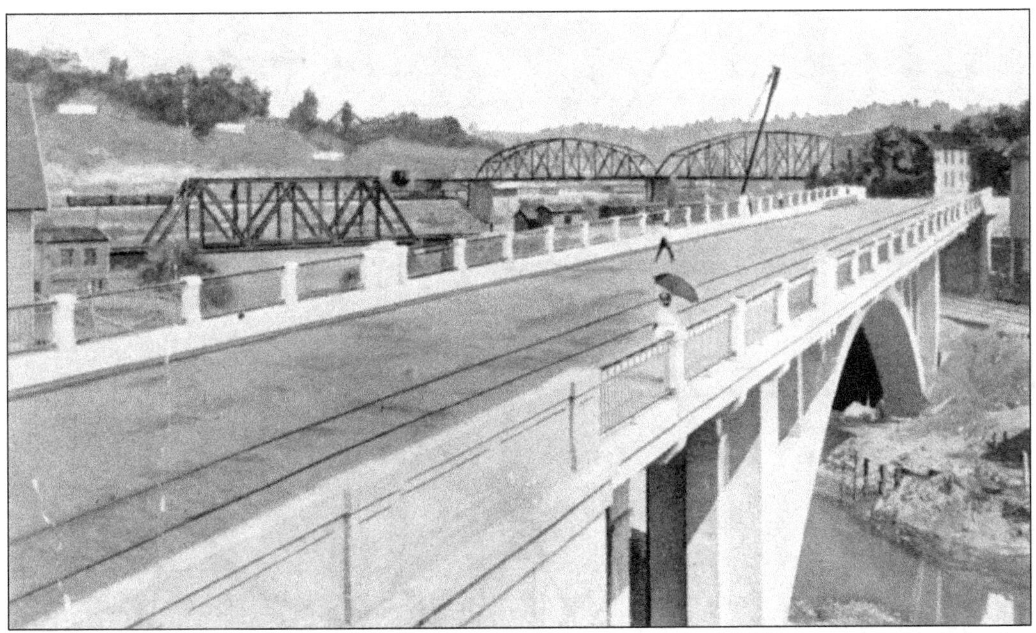

Once called Bridge Street Bridge, this is now University Avenue. The concrete-arch bridge crosses Deckers Creek. The Westover Bridge in the background was torn down to make way for a new bridge. The railroad truss bridge on the left is still standing and is part of the Rails-to-Trails System. This postcard is based on a photograph taken during construction in 1915.

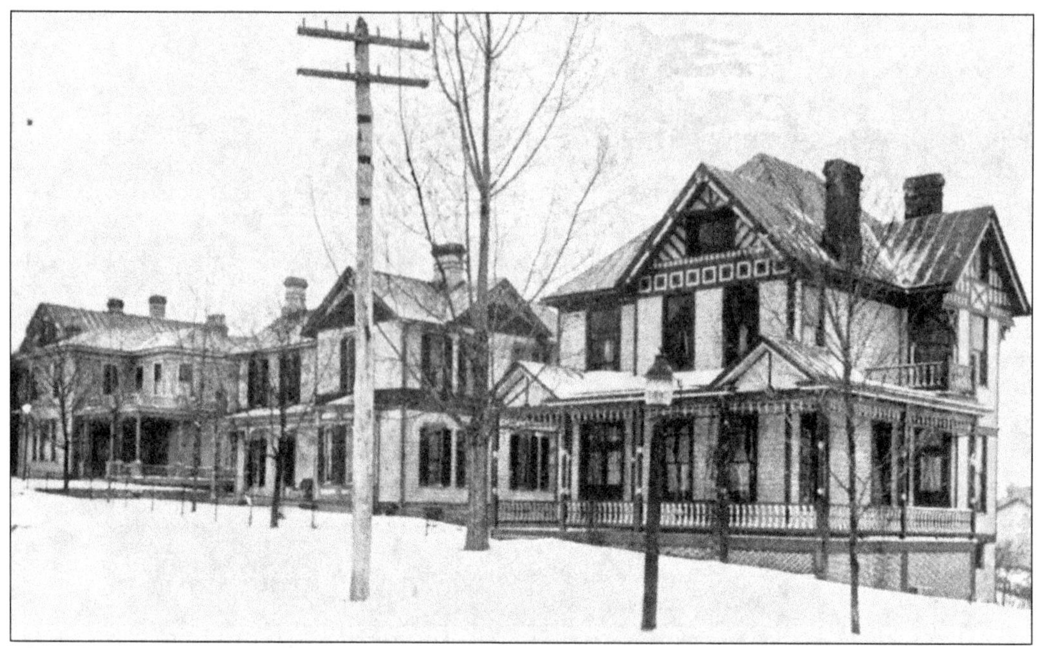

These homes on Willey Street were known as Professor's Row in 1902.

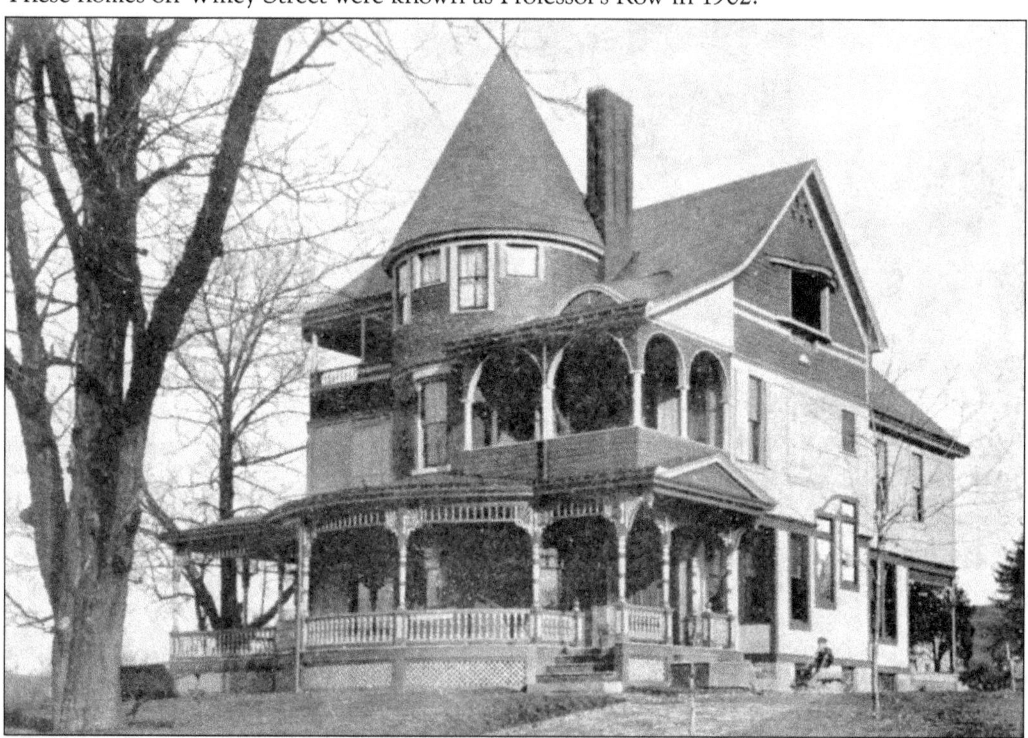

Cherryhurst was the home of Dr. I. C. White, West Virginia's first state geologist. Born in 1848 in Monongahela County, he was one of the first students to enter West Virginia University. Dr. White was famous as an oil and gas geologist as well as a savvy investor. Cherryhurst was located where the Mineral Industries Building now stands. The building was renamed White Hall in his honor.

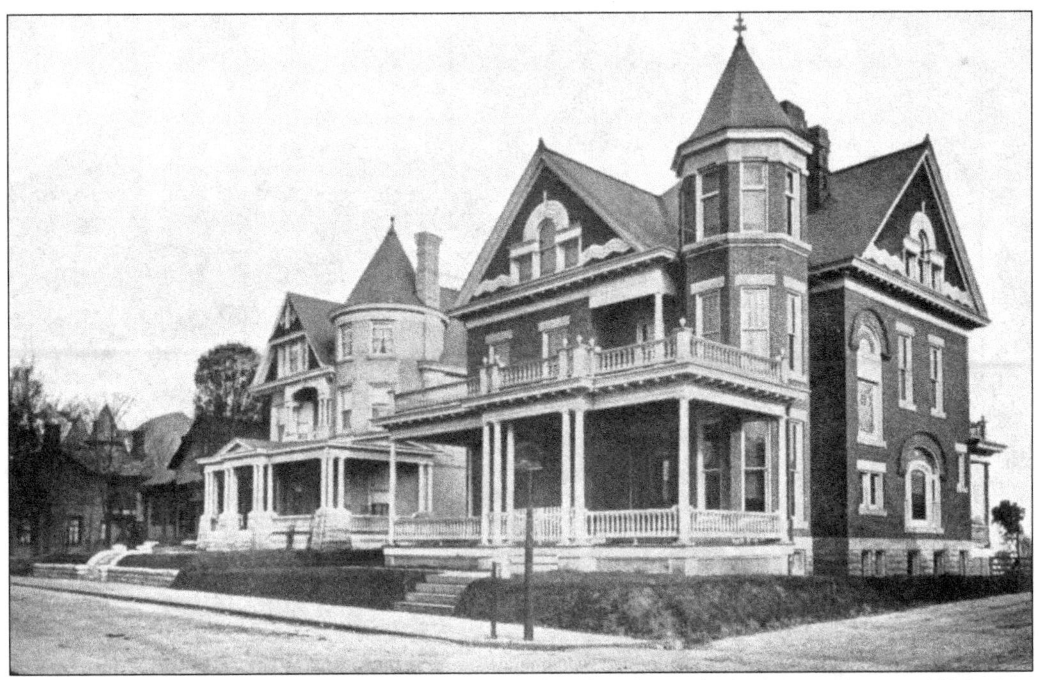

This picture of the residences of William Moorehead and Frank Cox was taken in 1920. Cox served as a judge on the West Virginia Supreme Court. The Cox home on the corner of Pleasant and Spruce Streets was designed by Morgantown architect Elmer Jacobs, and today it houses a real estate office.

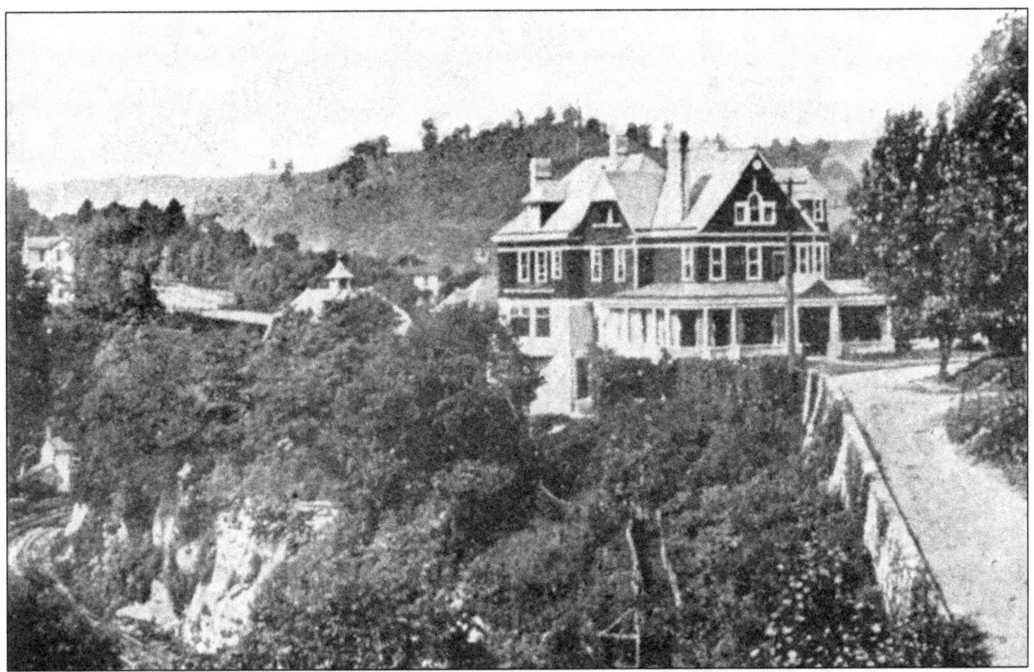

The residence of Joseph H. McDermott was on Walnut Street overlooking Deckers Creek. McDermott served in the West Virginia State Senate from 1905 to 1907 and gave a 500-volume library to West Virginia University in 1917.

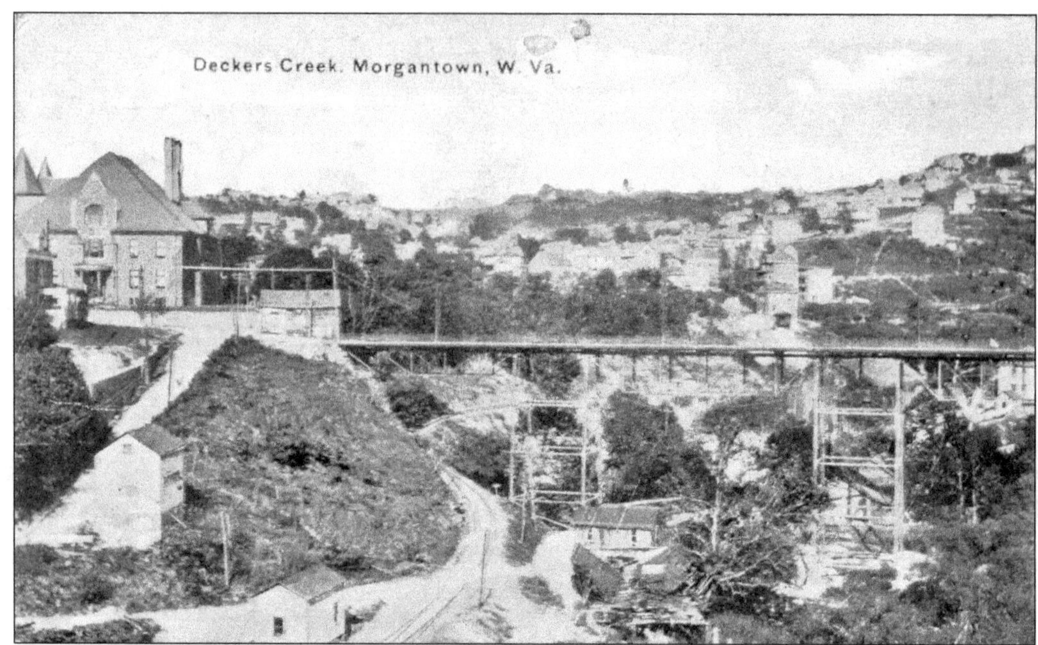

Before 1900, Morgantown's most elegant houses were in the downtown area. Expansion of the city's residential areas required construction of bridges across creeks and ravines. This new bridge connected Pleasant Street to South Park.

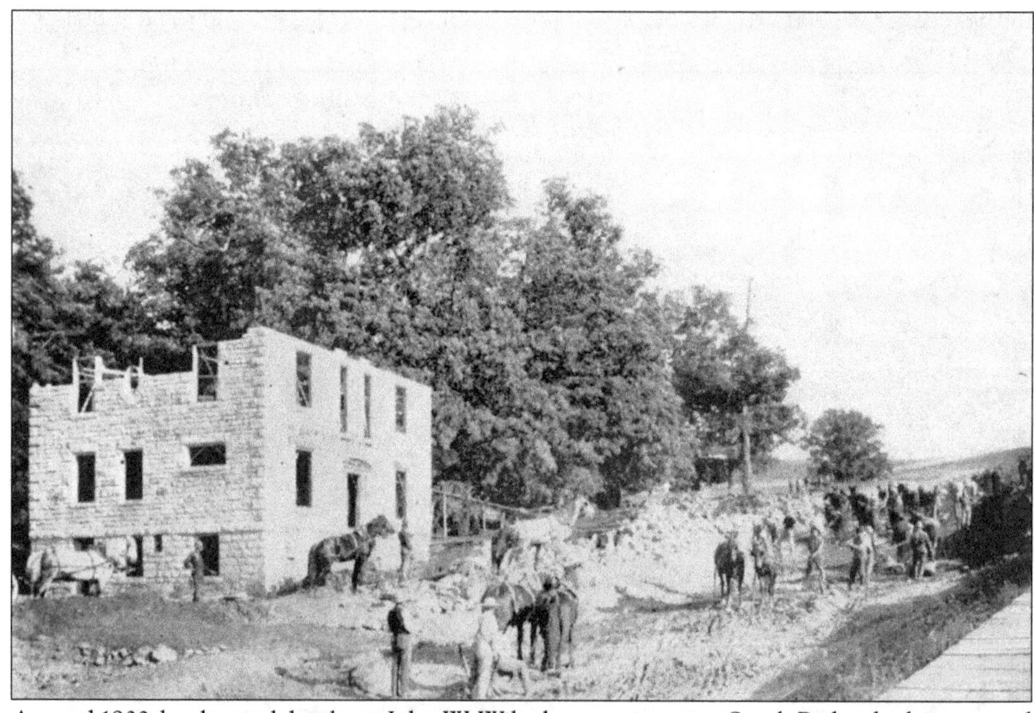

Around 1900, banker and developer John W. Wiles began promoting South Park, which contained hundreds of lots. Properties were on paved streets with city water and sewers. This picture shows a crew grading Grand Street. Today the city has several historic districts to encourage the preservation and appreciation of period houses.

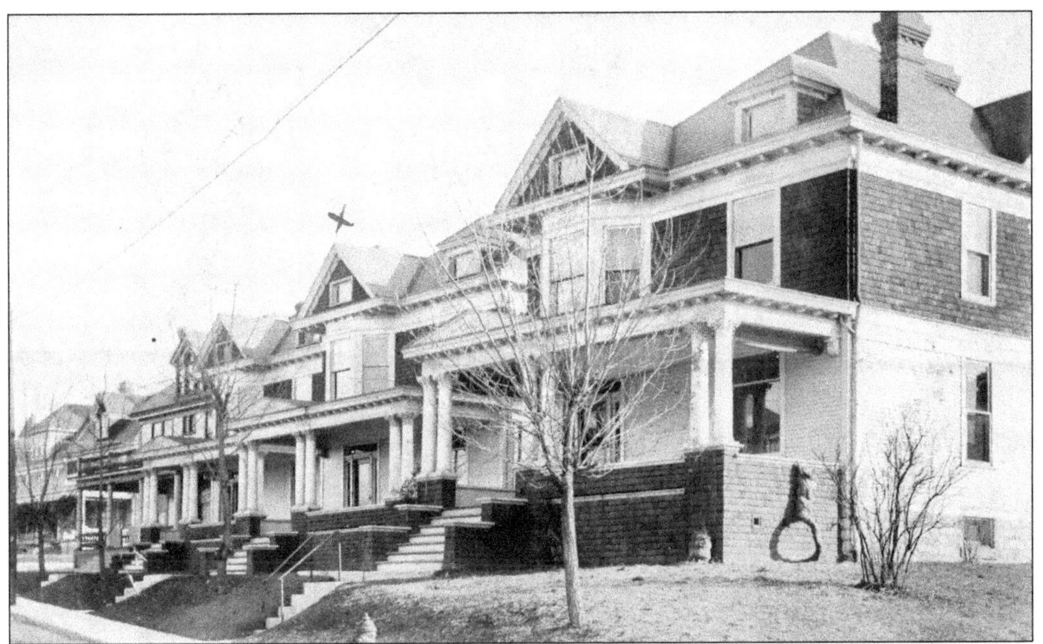

This was a personal photo postcard mailed in 1910. It shows typical houses on an unnamed street in the South Park neighborhood.

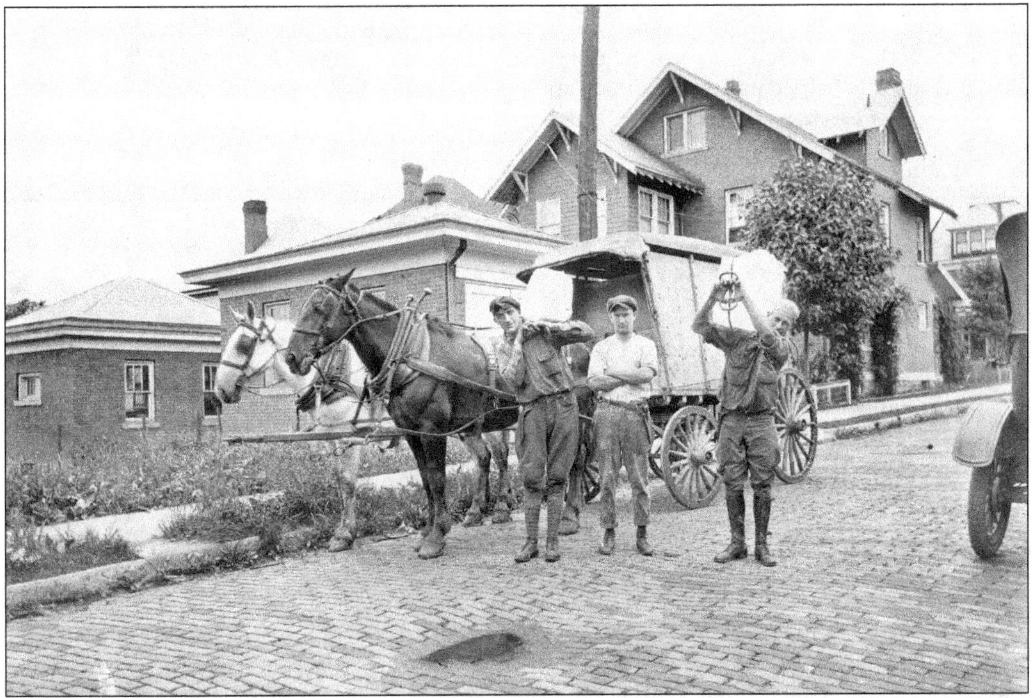

Well into the 1940s, household items such as baked goods and milk were delivered daily to homes by horse and wagon. This ice delivery crew and wagon was photographed by Scott Gibson about 1915. The street is brick paved, which made travel easier for both automobiles and wagons but also made life harder for horses. (West Virginia and Regional History Collection, West Virginia University Libraries.)

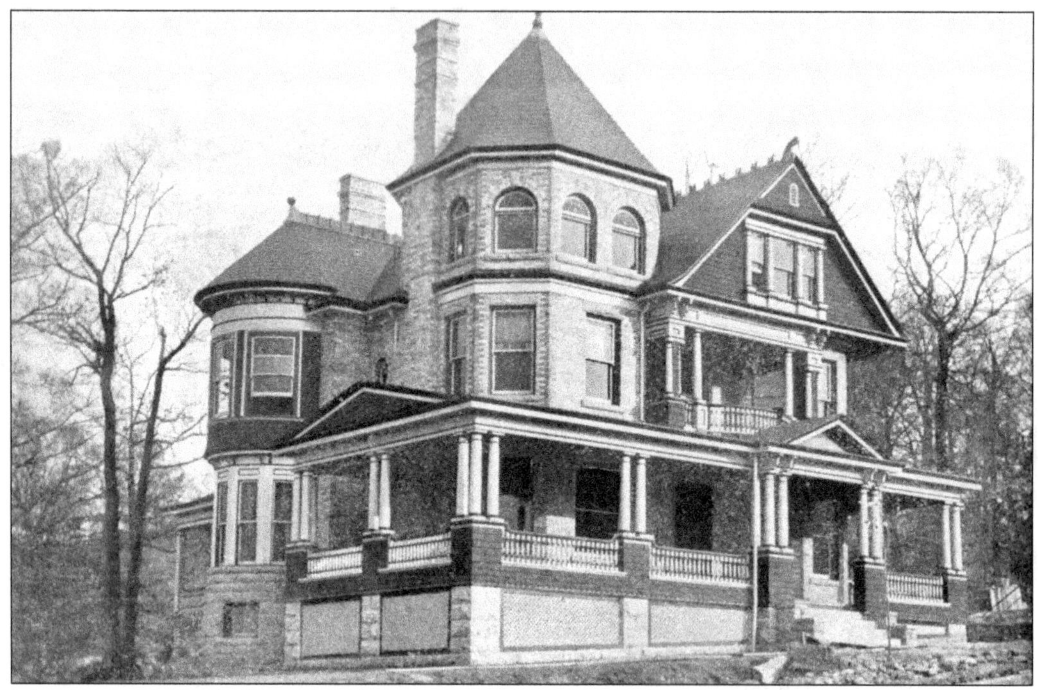

This home is typical of the many fine residences in South Park. It was constructed as the residence of Isaac Grant Lazelle. Lazelle graduated from West Virginia University in 1884 and, from 1897 to 1921, practiced law in Morgantown, and then he became a circuit court judge. He was active in real estate and helped establish South Park.

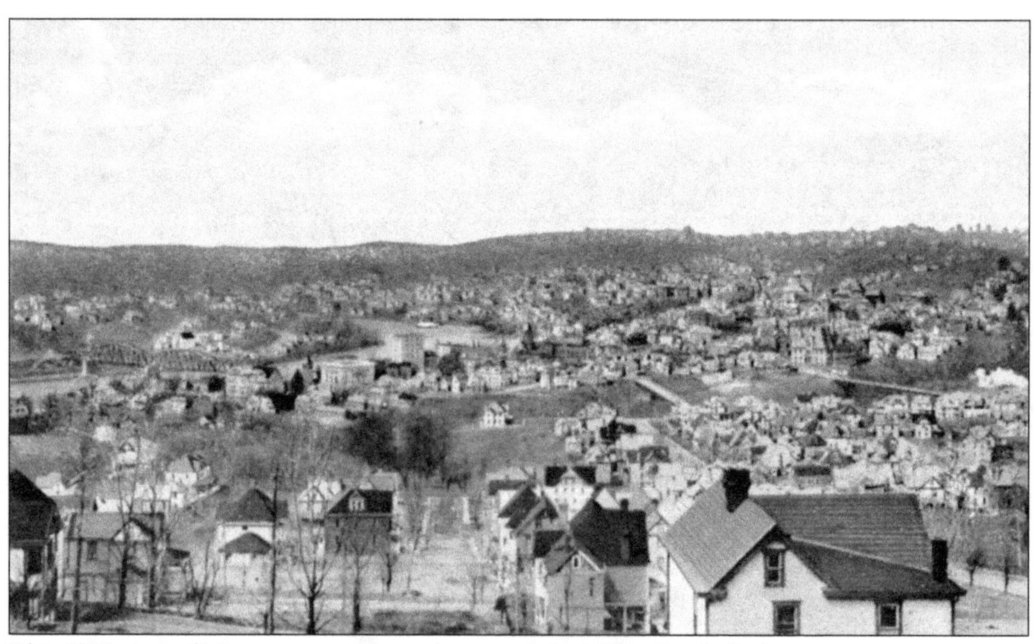

This 1916 view of Morgantown is from the top of the hill in South Park.

The Methodist Protestant Church stood on Walnut Street between High and Spruce Streets. It was built in 1885. Later it was rented for use as a courtroom during the building of a new county courthouse in 1891. This photograph was taken shortly before the congregation voted to build a new, larger church in 1903.

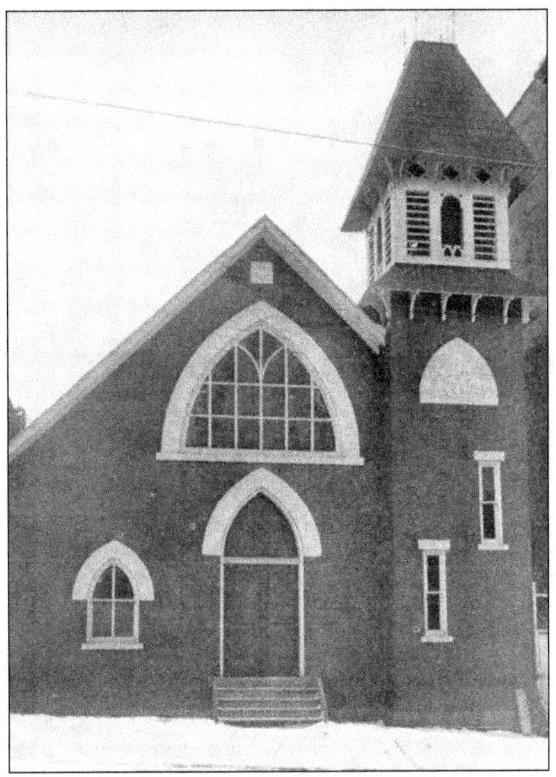

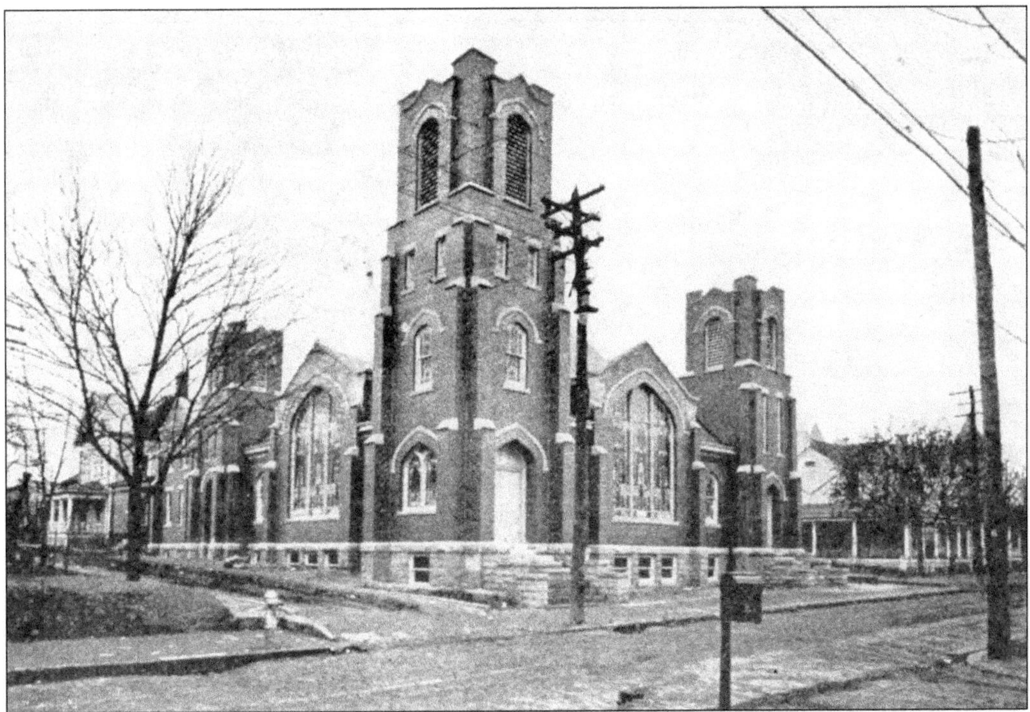

First Methodist Protestant Church, built in 1910 on Spruce Street, was designed by Elmer Jacobs. Today it is known as the Spruce Street Methodist Church.

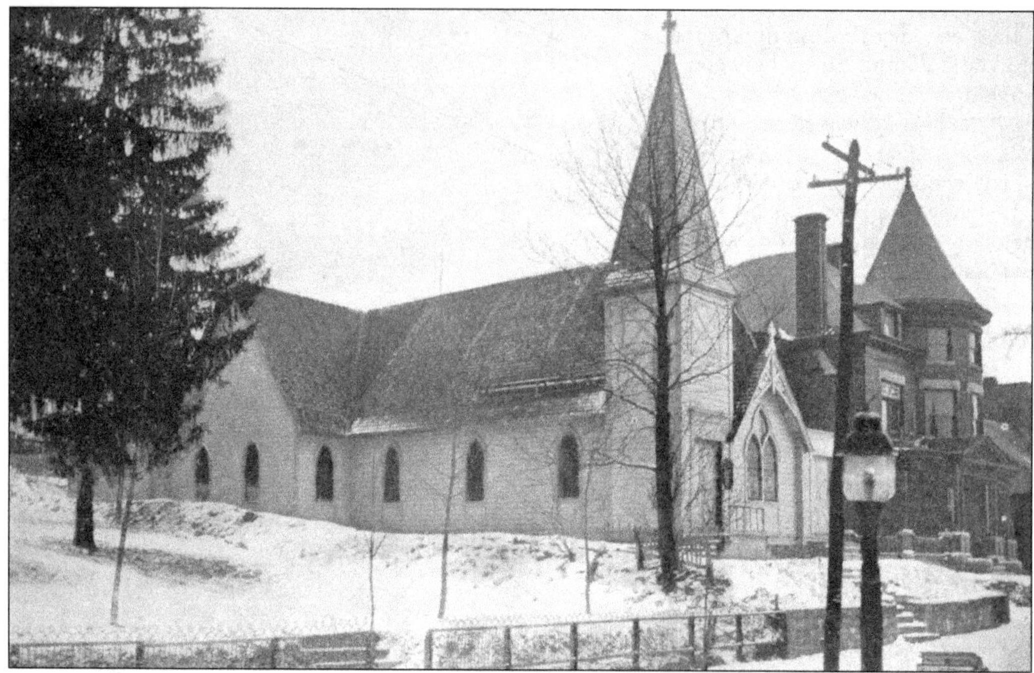

The Trinity Episcopal Church on Wiley Street was built in 1900, replacing the first small frame Episcopal church built on High Street in 1886. In 1952, the current stone Trinity Episcopal was built a few doors away. Lumber from the old church was used in the construction of Grant Methodist Church in Grant District.

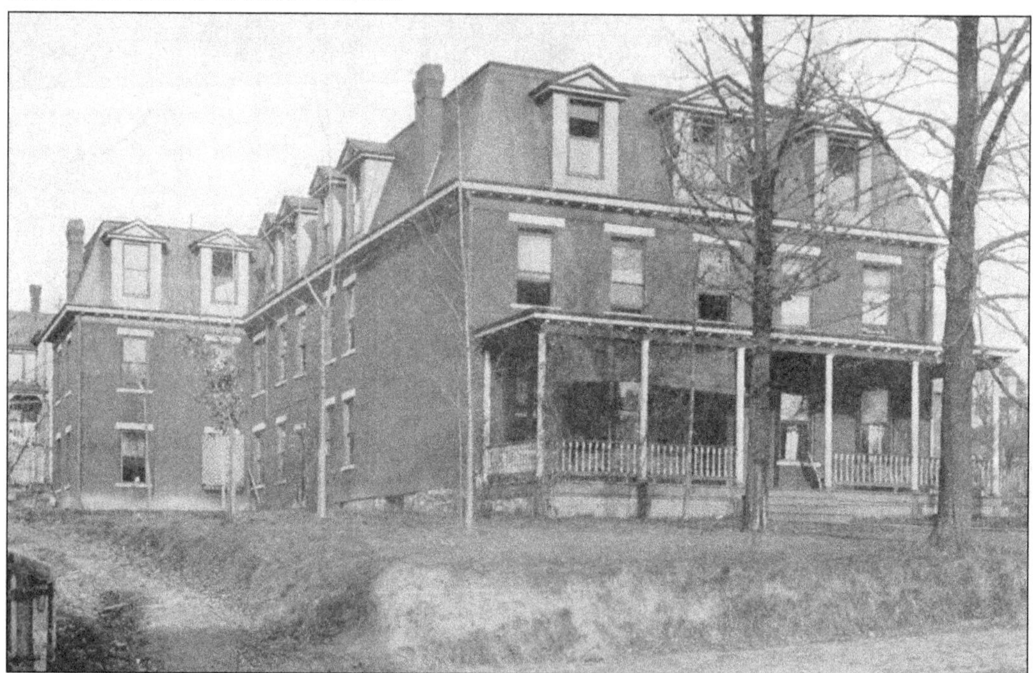

Episcopal Hall was built on Wiley Street as a student residence center by the West Virginia Episcopalian diocese. It opened in 1896 and had a library, steam heat, electric lights, and bathrooms. In 1907, it became Woman's Hall and served as a women's dormitory through 1927.

When this building was constructed, it was known as the German Lutheran Church. It was on University Avenue where the University Lutheran Student Chapel stands today. It was built soon after the congregation was established 1901. The congregation moved to a new building on Baldwin Street in Suncrest in 1962, and the building was razed in 1967. The new building is called St. Paul's Lutheran Church.

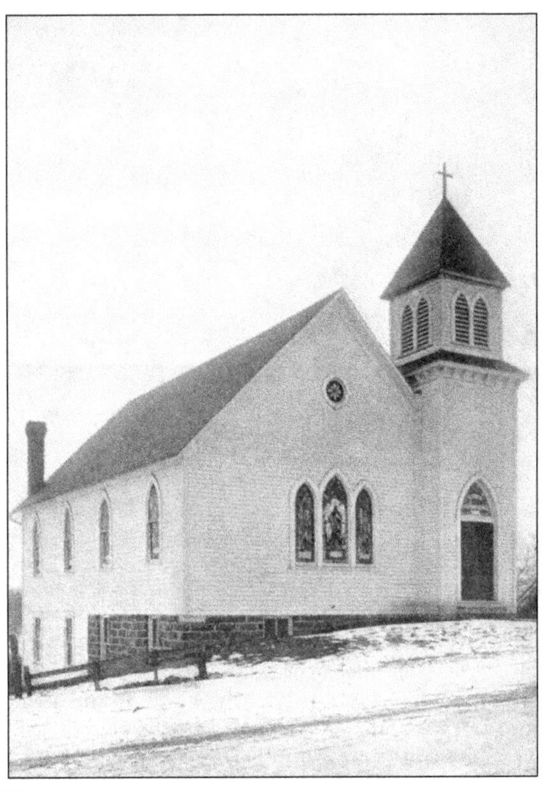

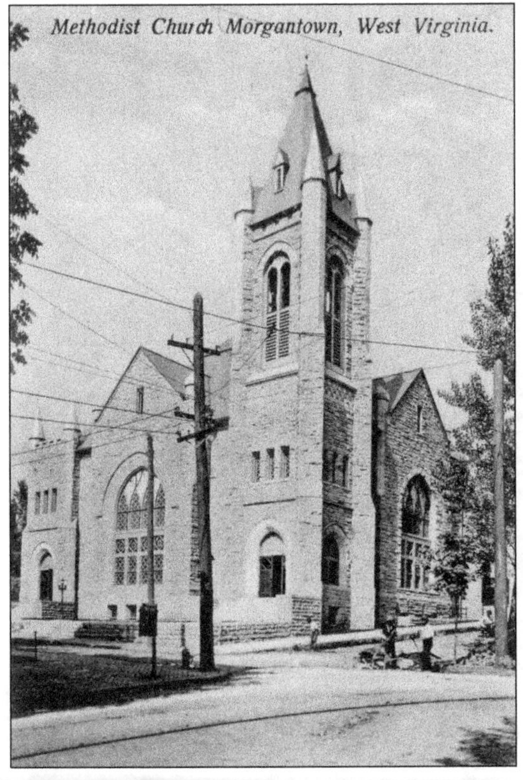

First Methodist Episcopal on Wiley Street was built in 1904. It replaced an 1850 building on Pleasant Street. It is known today as the Wesley United Methodist Church.

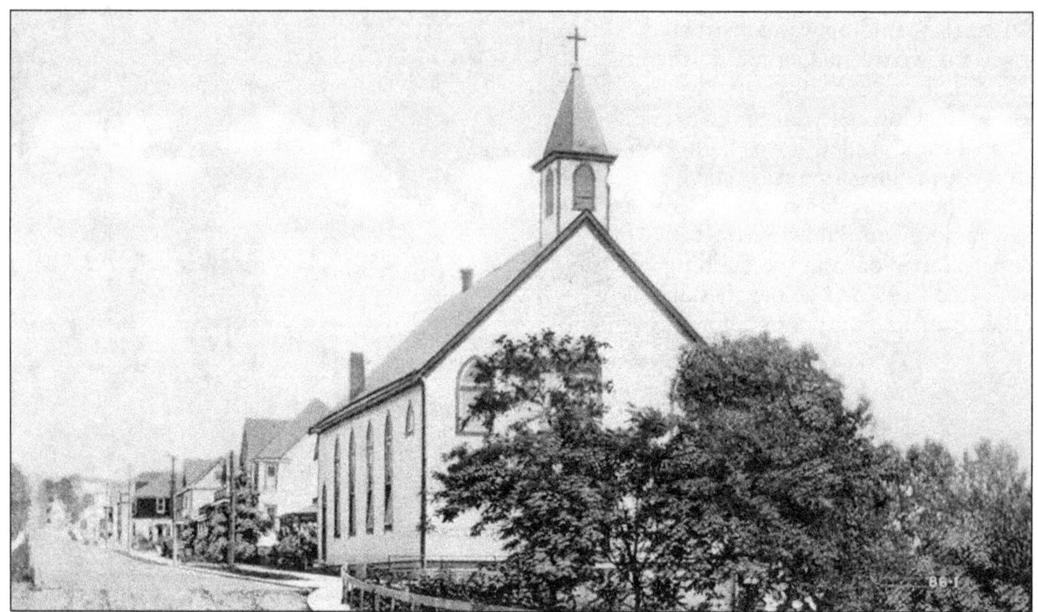

This modest frame building on McClane Avenue was Morgantown's first Catholic church. Named St. Francis de Sales, it was built in 1897 by Seneca Glass Company workers. Until 1901, services were conducted by a priest who came from Fairmont by train. In 1924, the congregation moved into a newly completed chapel over the classrooms in the St. Francis de Sales School. The building was used as a gymnasium before being destroyed by a tornado in 1929.

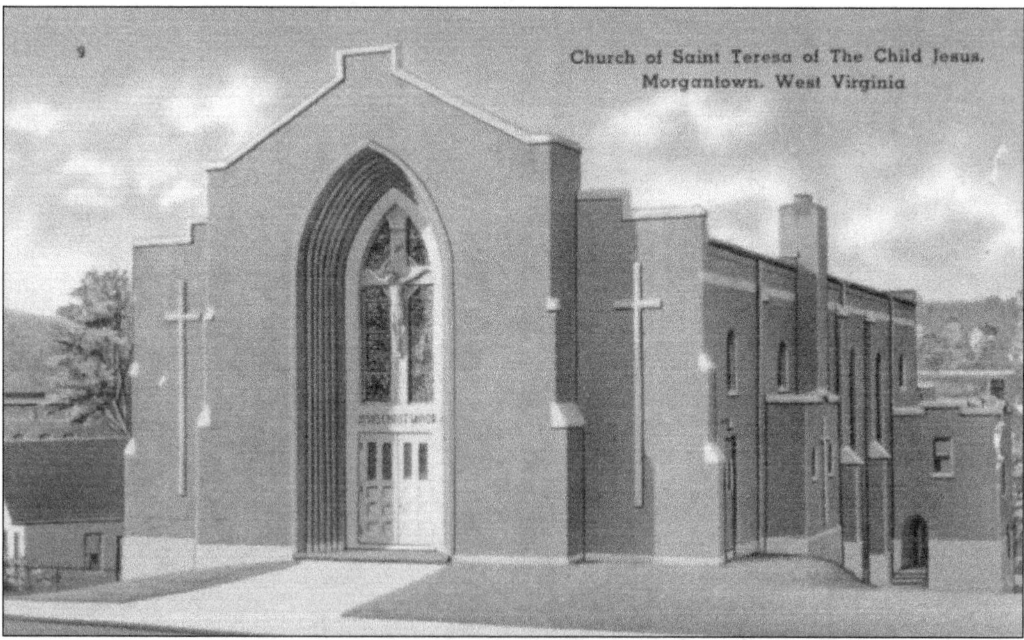

In 1918, the St. Francis de Sales parochial school moved into a new building on Beechurst Avenue. In 1924, the Church of St. Teresa of the Child Jesus was constructed over the classrooms with its front on University Avenue. The chapel accommodated 450, and three masses were said each Sunday. The parish was recently relocated to a site on Grafton Road, where it occupies an award-winning modern structure.

The First Baptist Church was built on High Street in 1897. The auditorium is still in use, sandwiched between a 1951 educational building in back and a stone facade dating from 1956. It replaced an earlier Baptist church on the corner of Long Alley (Chestnut Street) and Bumbo Lane (Fayette Street) that had been constructed in 1846.

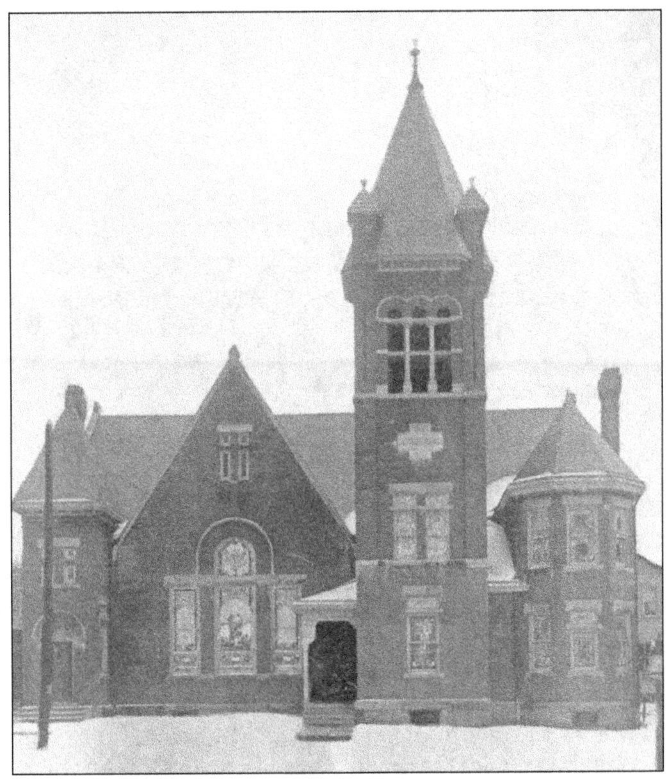

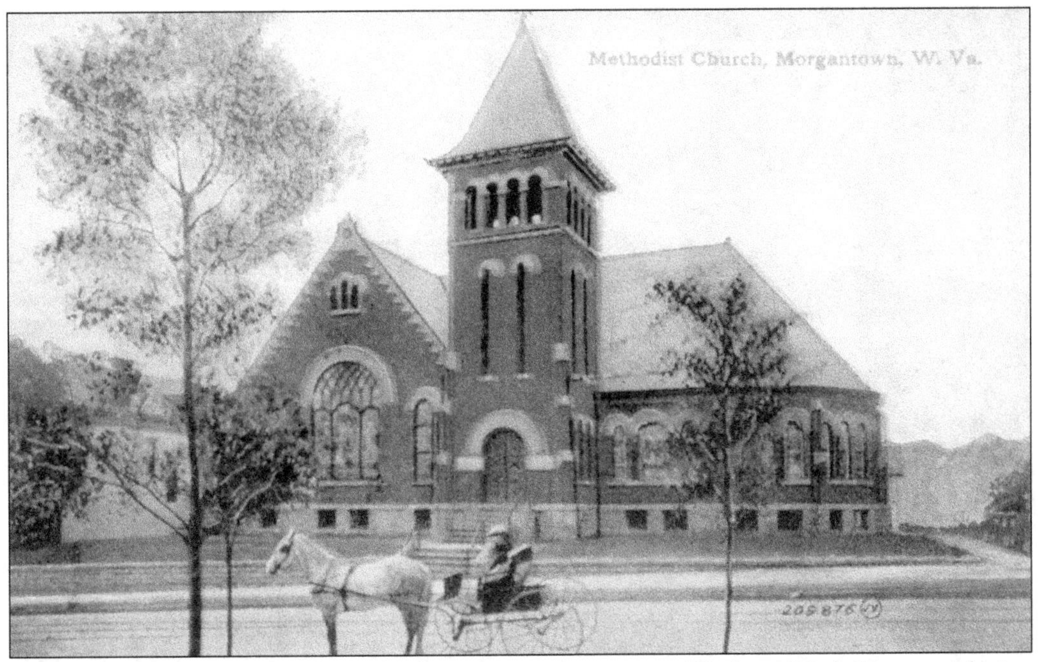

The First Presbyterian Church was built in 1910 on the corner of High and Kirk Streets, replacing one built in 1868. As early as 1924, the congregation was discussing plans to sell this property and erect a larger building on their old cemetery lot on Spruce Street, but this did not happen until 1953. The publisher of this postcard used an incorrect caption.

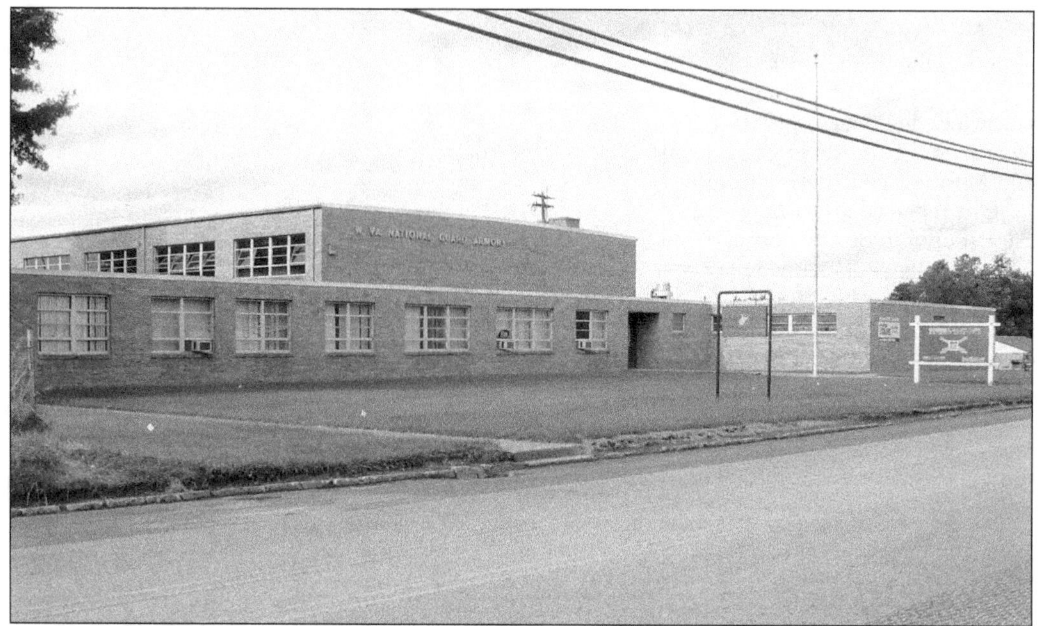

The West Virginia National Guard Armory on the Mileground is home to Battery B of the 201st Infantry Field Artillery and the 249th Army Band. One of the oldest active military units, the 201st has fought or trained men for every conflict involving the United States. This unit traces its origins to Capt. Morgan Morgan, who formed the company in 1735. It served in General Washington's militia in Gen. Edward Braddock's 1755 campaign.

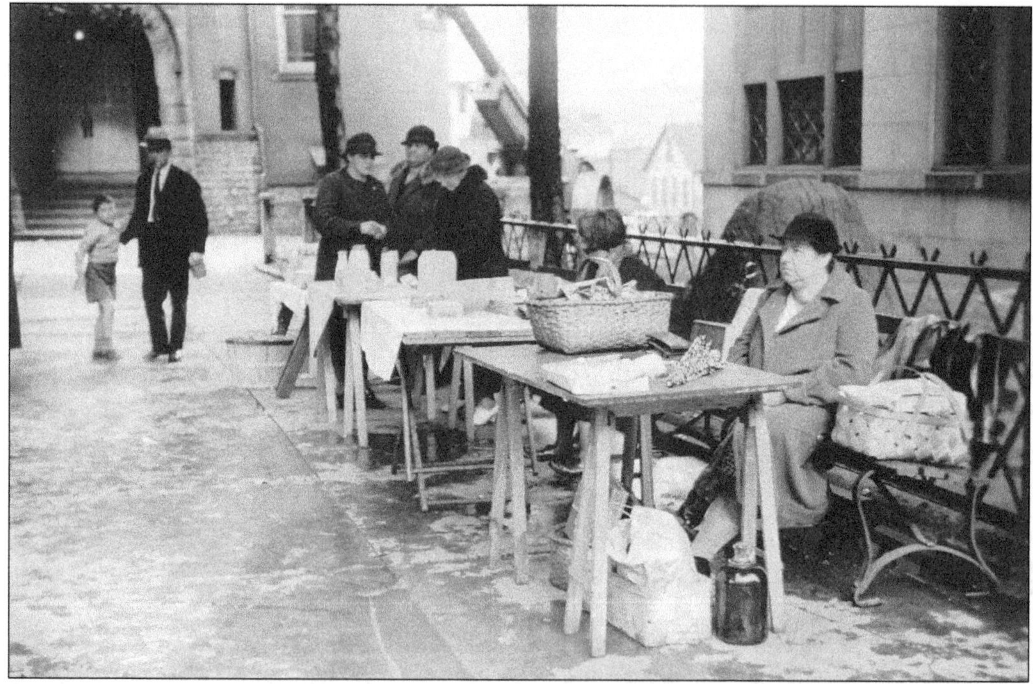

A Depression-era photographer recording coal miners' lives stopped on the Court House Square to take this picture of farm women selling produce. Local produce is still offered for sale here but only occasionally. (National Archives.)

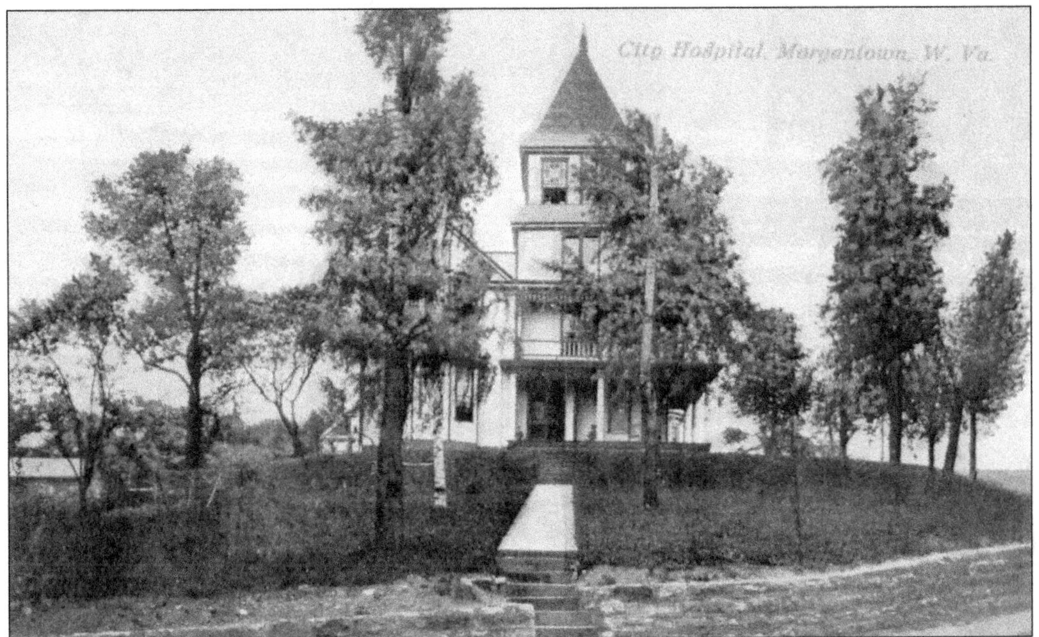

In 1913, Brock and Wade's Institution was incorporated as City Hospital and Training School for nurses. It was located on the Purinton property at the corner of Willey and Prospect Streets. It offered a three-year training program for nurses as well as patient care.

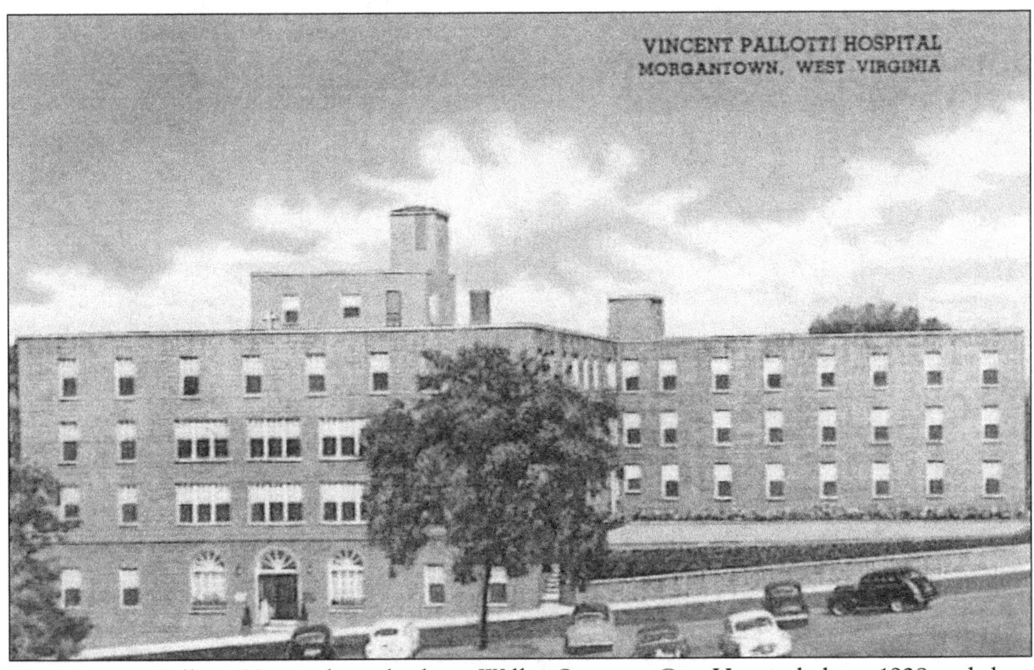

The Vincent Pallotti Hospital was built on Willey Street as City Hospital about 1928 and then renamed Heiskell Memorial Hospital in 1943. It was purchased and renamed by the Pallotine Missionary Sisters in 1950. The hospital operations were incorporated into a new Monongahela General Hospital. Today the building survives as an apartment building.

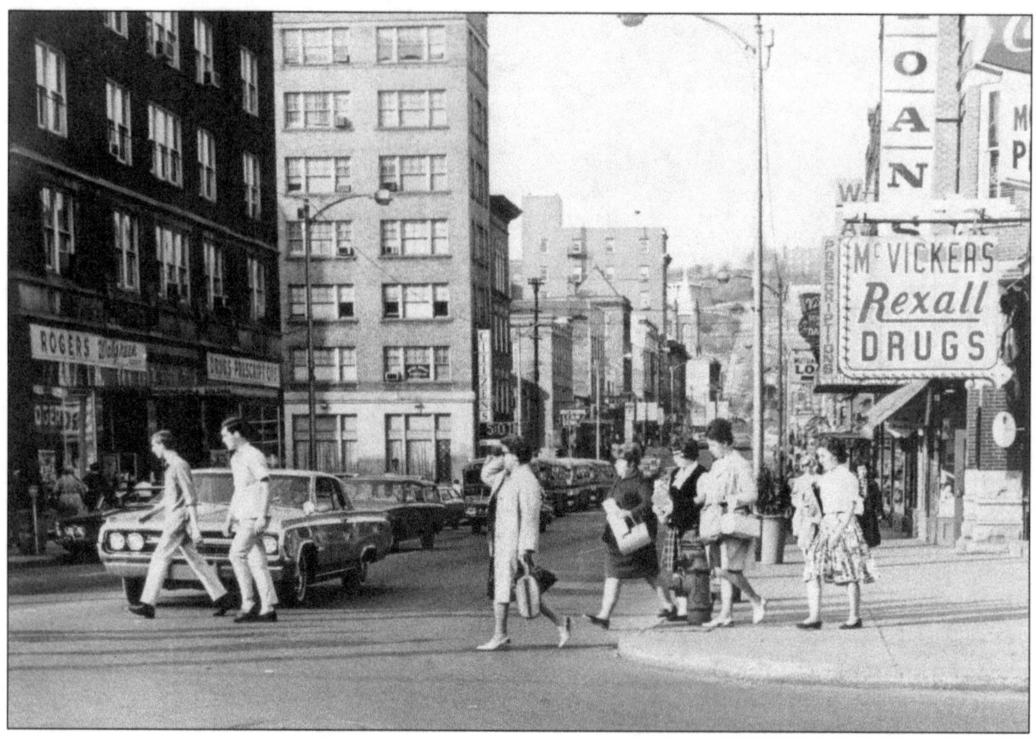

This view looking north on High Street from Pleasant Street was taken about 1960.

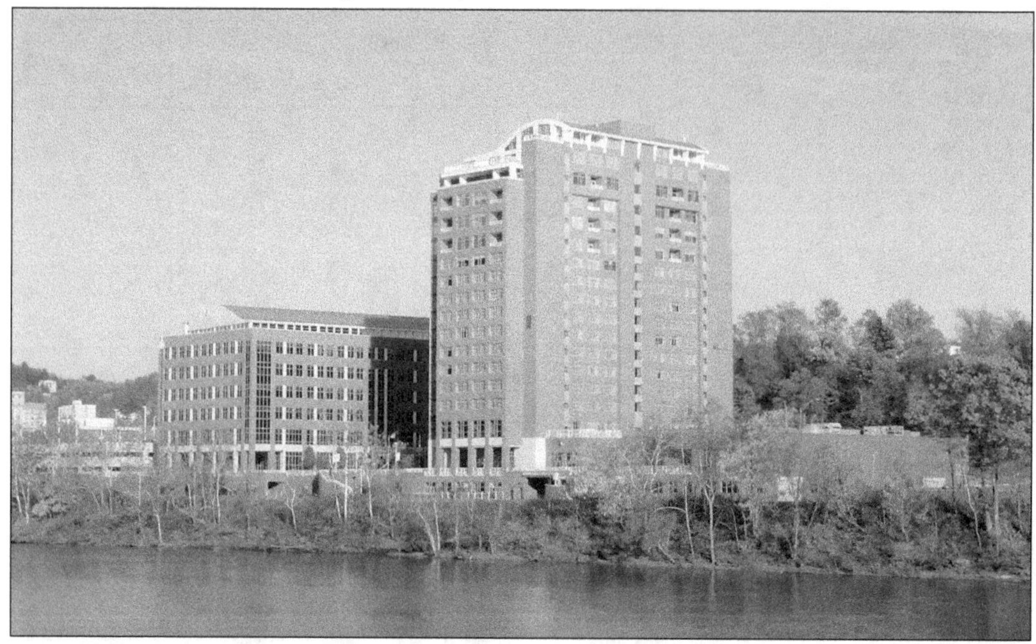
Since 2000, Morgantown has been developing an expanded central business district in the old Durbannah–South Morgantown area along the river south of Deckers Creek. The taller of these buildings is the Waterfront Place Hotel, which has both overnight and conference rooms and residential suites. The other houses the university's visitor center and human resources activities and the West Virginia University Foundation.

Eight

SCHOOLS

Early residents placed a high value on education. By 1803, Morgantown had a brick school building. In 1814, a private circulating library and an academy paid by survey taxes and tuition were introduced. In 1832, a "female academy" was established.

In 1818, Virginia established public funding for indigent students in privately run subscription schools for free whites, and by 1830, the county had 80 schools, a number that would change little until bus transportation and consolidation were introduced over a century later.

In 1863, the academy properties were donated to help found the new university. In 1868, a newly established Morgantown School District repurchased the old Morgantown Academy building from the university and established the Morgantown Graded School, which had a term of 10 months and 151 pupils in 12 grades.

Records show that the county had two free black children in school in 1850. In 1863, the state legislature provided for schooling of free blacks, and in 1870, the county provided a school for blacks that was housed in the African Methodist Episcopal church.

In 1874, Alexander Wade, Monongalia County superintendent of schools, introduced the requirements of specific objectives, examinations, and diplomas into public education. These had previously only been used in private academies and colleges. Wade's "Graduating System" may be Morgantown's greatest contribution to American education.

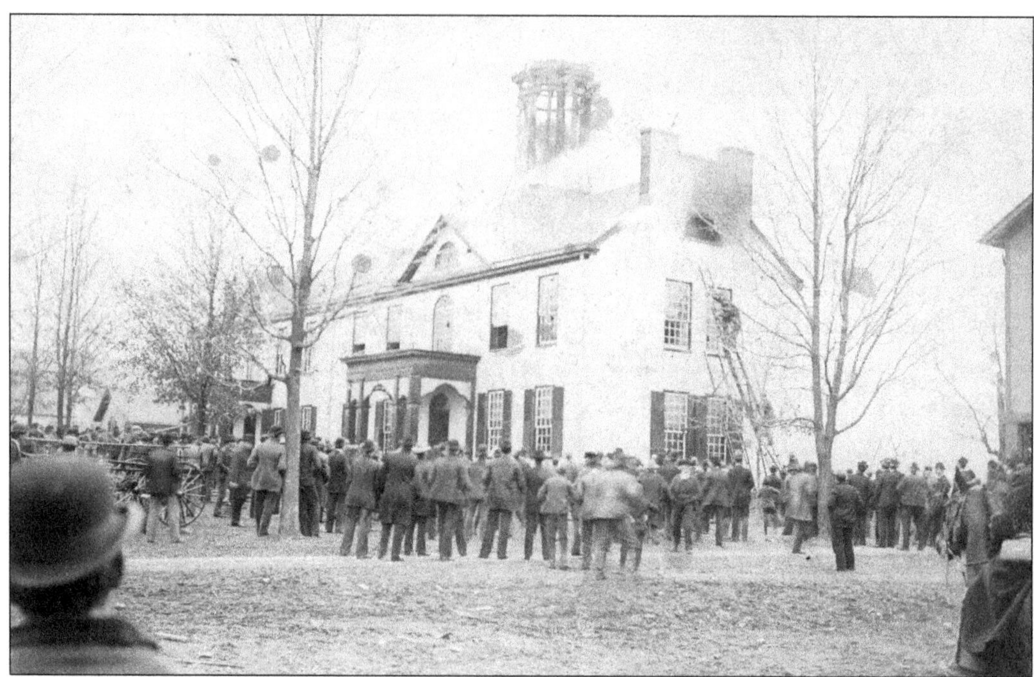

The Monongahela Academy was built in 1829. In addition to classical studies, the academy offered science, surveying, and navigation. New students were required to have basic reading and writing skills, but these were given further attention in the early classes. The building was given to West Virginia University, then repurchased in 1868 and used as the Central Graded School. It was destroyed by this fire in 1897. (Morgantown Public Library.)

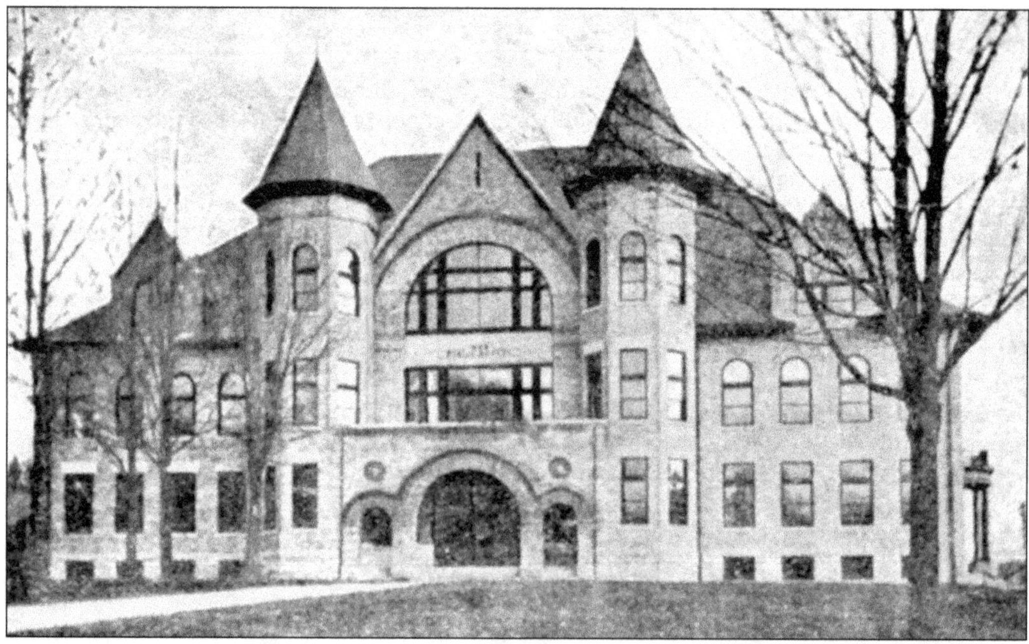

After the fire in the academy building, Morgantown constructed this new public school building, which included all 12 grades. It opened in 1899. The building became Central Grade School when a larger high school was built on an adjoining lot on Spruce Street.

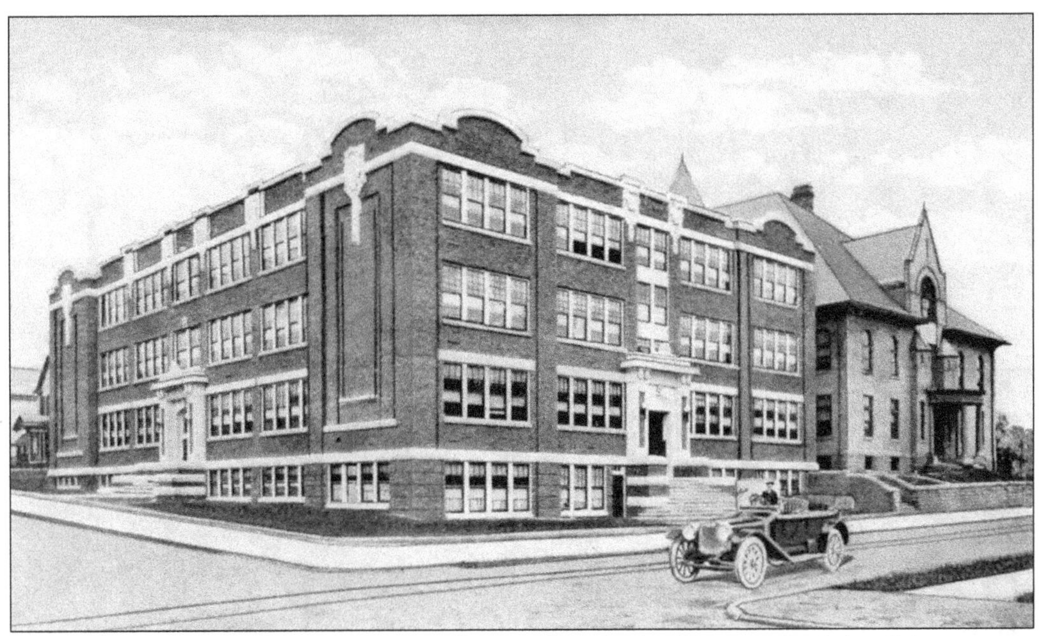

Many older residents of Morgantown will remember the building on the left as Morgantown Junior High on Spruce Street. When it was built in 1915, it was the high school. The Public Safety Building now occupies the site.

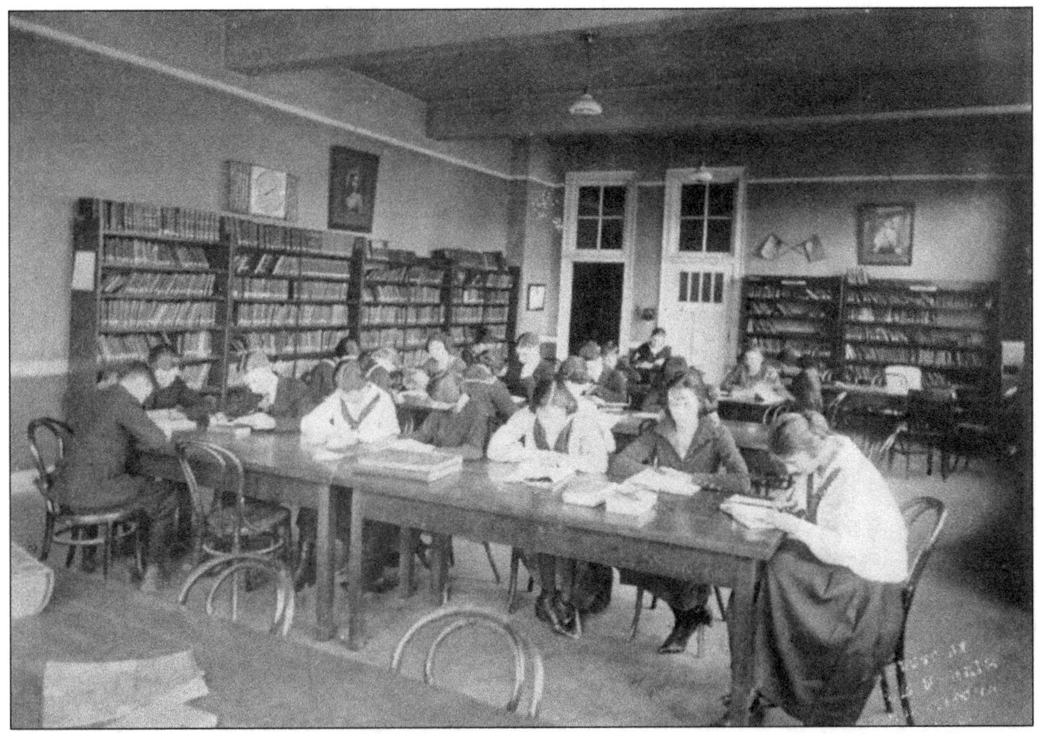

This picture shows the Morgantown High Library in 1921. The young gentlemen are wearing suits and ties, while most of the young ladies are wearing navy-style tops with long skirts.

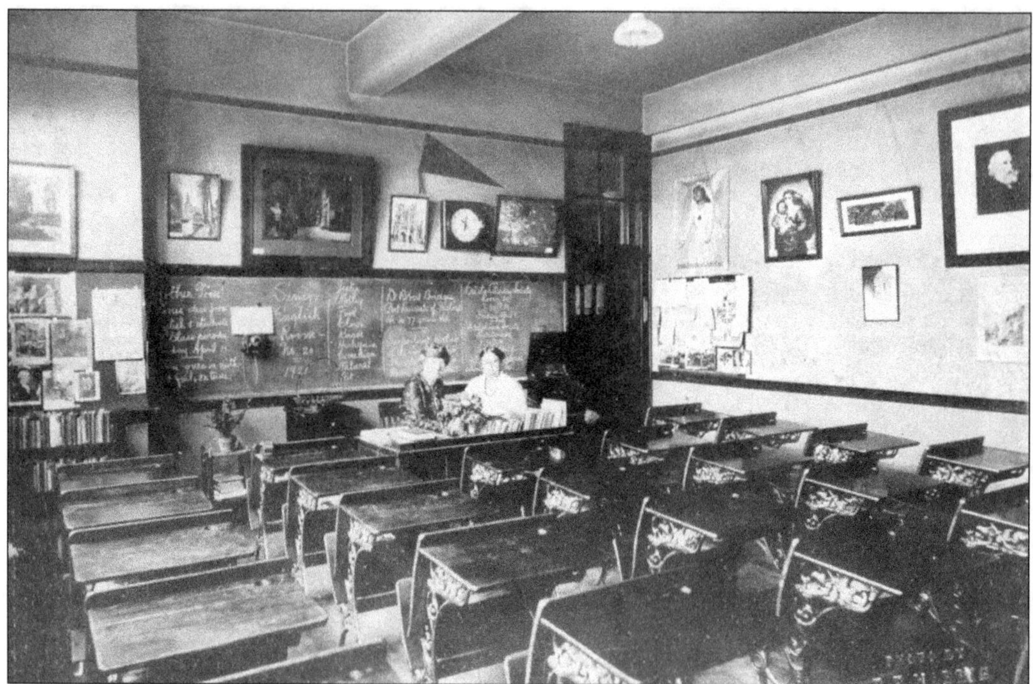

In 1921, Miss Donley, head of the English department, held classes for the seniors in this room in Morgantown High. The top of each student desk has a recess to hold a bottle of ink. The desks have floral cast-iron sides and lifting seats.

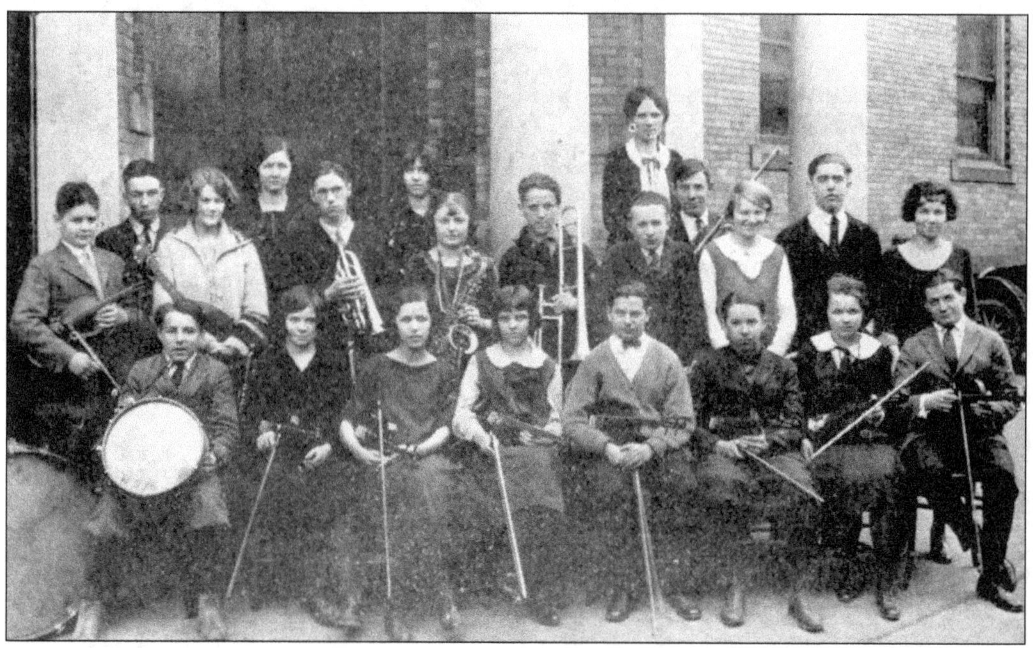

The Morgantown High yearbook *Whirlwind, Memories of 1924* included this picture of the school orchestra.

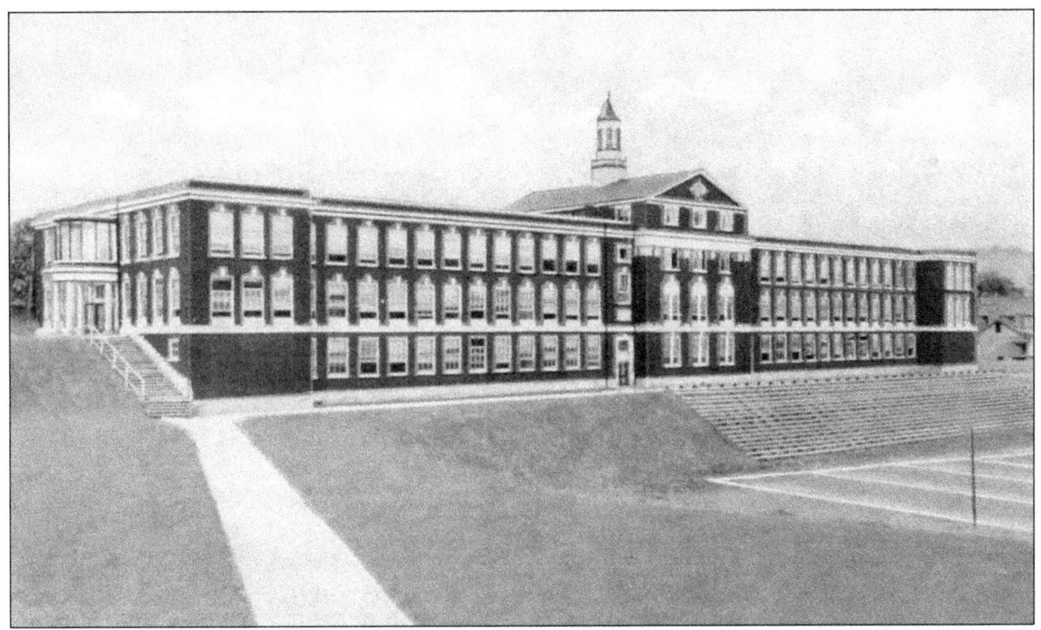

The current Morgantown High School opened in 1927 on a campus in South Park. The plan consisted of four buildings arranged in a capital "U." The inside of the U was to be used for the athletic field. The buildings around it were the academic and administrative building, the auditorium, the gymnasium, and the shop building. At the time, money was not available to construct the auditorium.

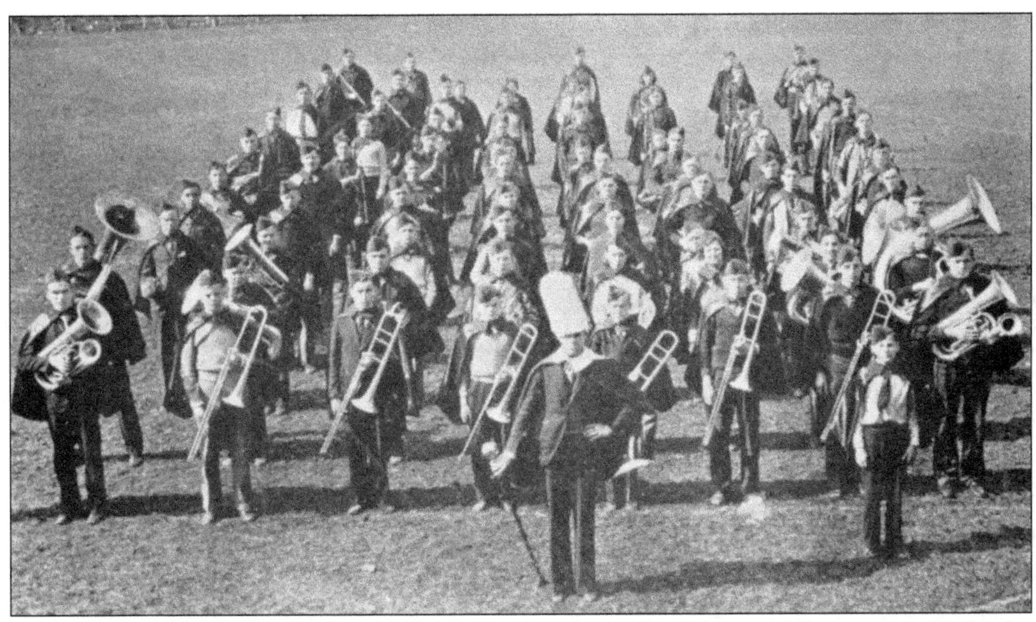

According to the caption in the 1931 *Mohigan*, the yearbook of the new Morgantown High, the school band had 81 musicians and practiced daily. Today the program includes about 250 students in the band and flag corps.

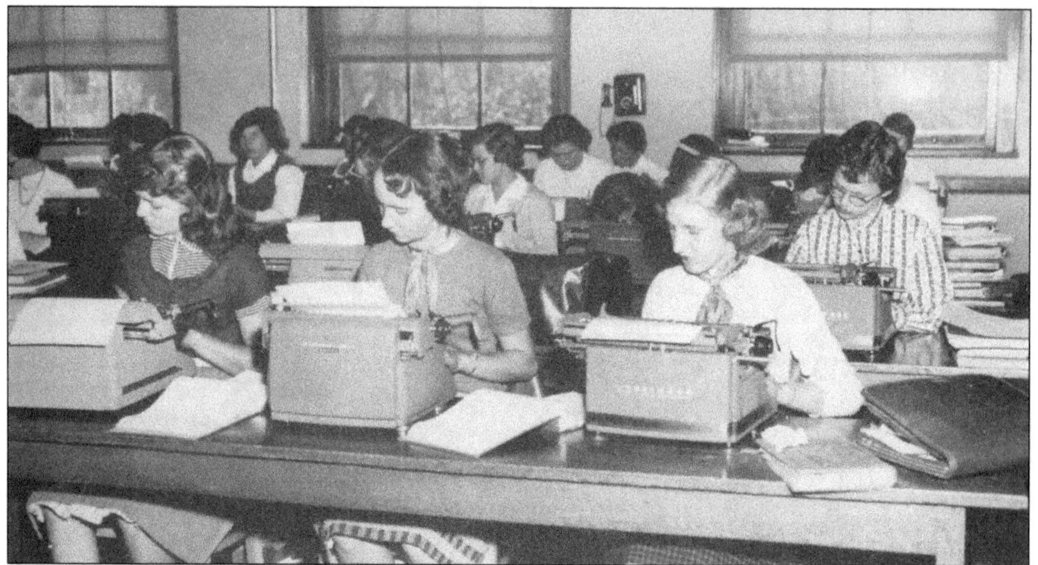

These students in a 1956 Morgantown High typing class were preparing for careers as secretaries. A good typist could type 90 or more words a minute. If an error was made in typing an important document, the typist would have to start again with a clean sheet of paper. She would also learn to take dictation in shorthand. It would be more than a quarter-century before computers became common.

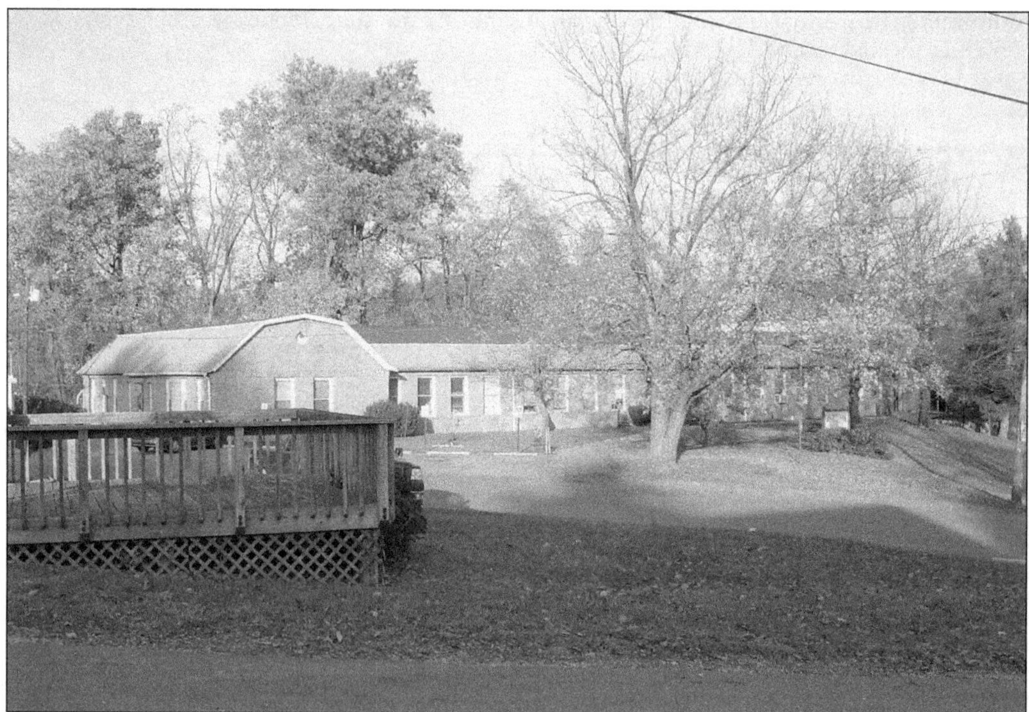

This school building was constructed by the Works Progress Administration (WPA) in 1935 as the county's Negro High School. Eleanor Roosevelt spoke at the dedication. Morgantown High School was integrated soon after the *Brown v. Board of Education* decision by the Supreme Court, and today the building houses Westover Elementary School.

Nine

After Hours

As a community with both a university and an industrial base, entertainment in Morgantown spans an extraordinarily wide range for a small town. University athletic events are regional in scope and draw crowds that exceed the city's population.

The university's music faculty has hosted classical orchestra performances by both local and visiting musicians for about a century, as well as producing opera, ballet, concert band, jazz band, and chamber music events. As individuals, university students and faculty support a dynamic alternative and folk music schedule.

Country and rock bands play on campus, as well as in local "watering holes." A community brass band plays in the parks on patriotic holidays.

The university, high schools, and independent organizations stage both light and serious dramatic performances in both large and small theater spaces, and circuses erect tents on the outskirts of town.

The community also hosts several large outdoor festivals each year.

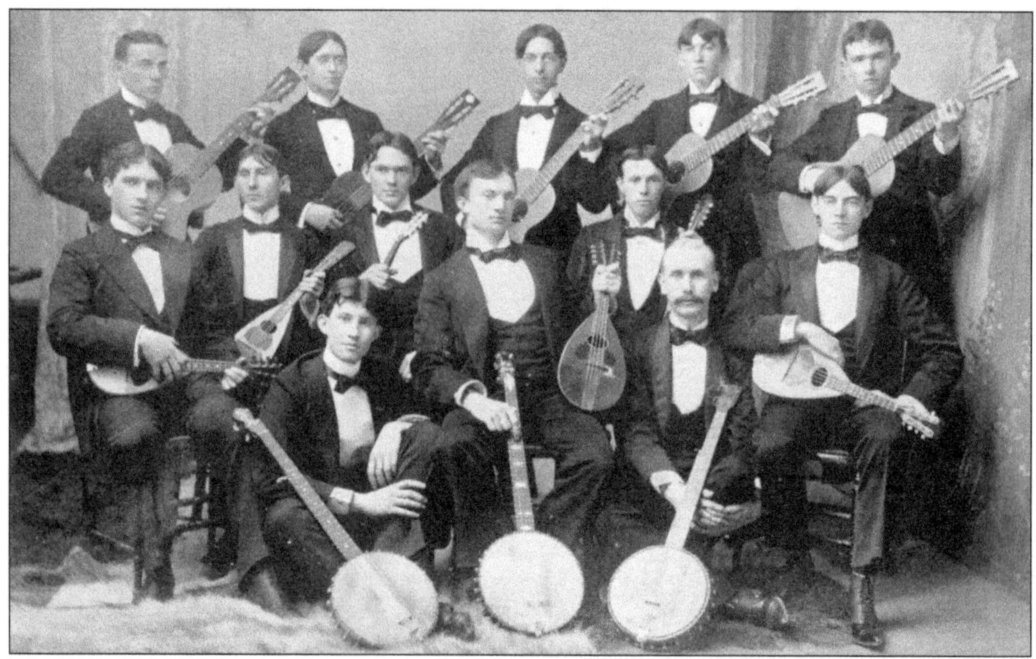

The 1896 edition of the WVU yearbook included this group photograph of the Banjo, Mandolin, and Guitar Club. At the end of the 19th century, similar string bands enjoyed international popularity.

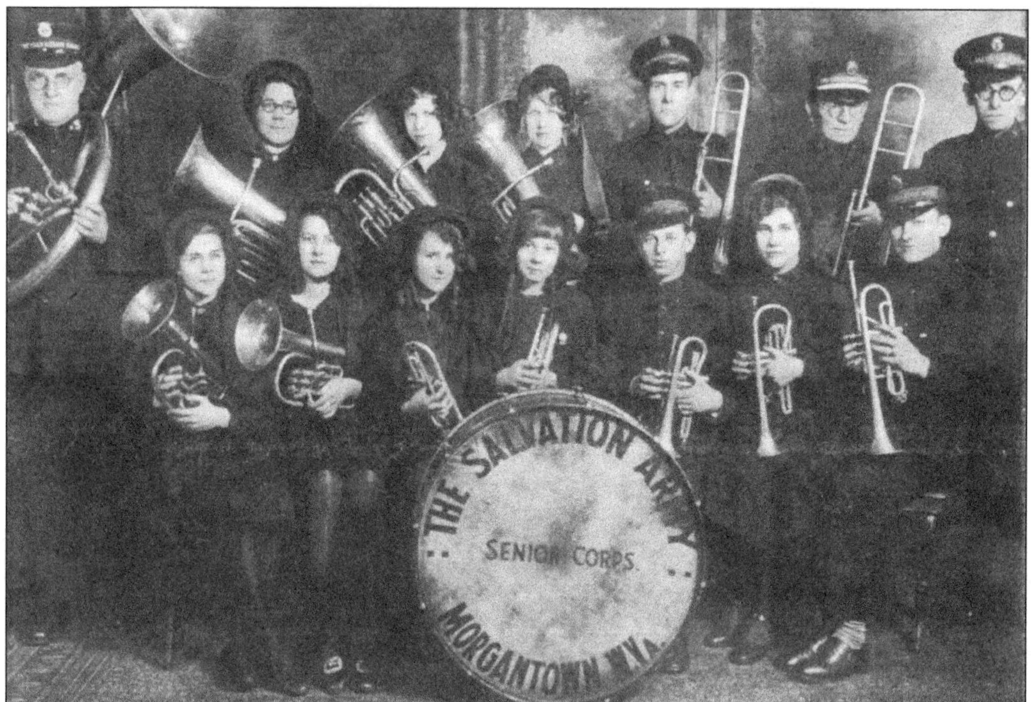

James and Elizabeth Stanton came here in 1897 and established the Salvation Army in Morgantown. This band was started soon after. The Salvation Army continues to be an important part of the local social services network, although the band has disappeared.

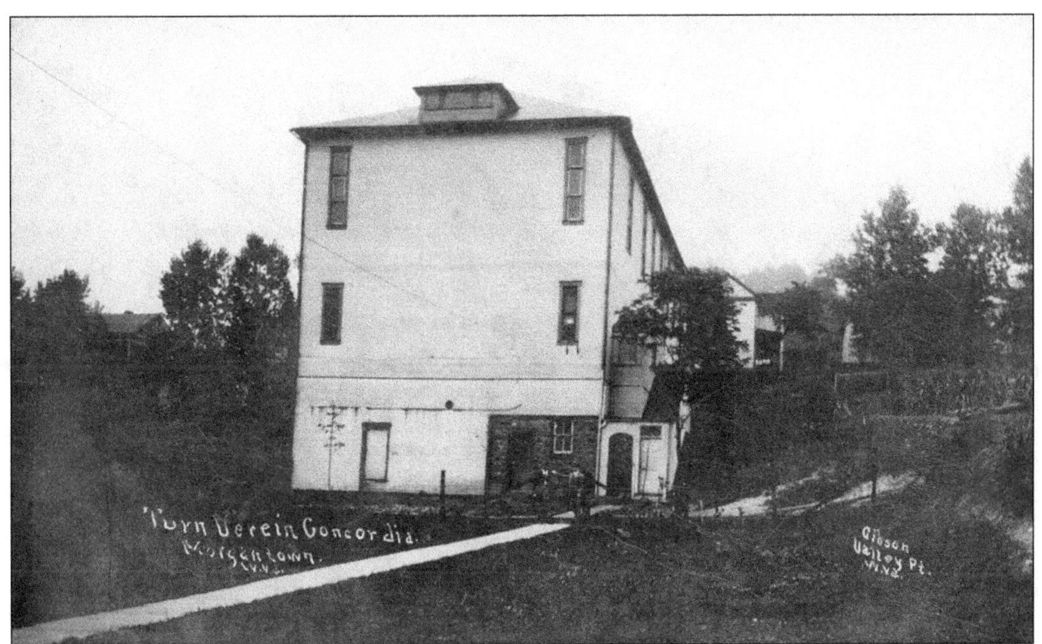

The Turn Verein (German for athletic club) built on Grant Avenue in the town of Seneca symbolized dramatic social changes in the Morgantown area. It was built by the German workers of the Seneca Glass Company as a place to hold dances and union meetings and to have a drink. In an area dominated by Baptists and Methodists, there must have been many who questioned the appropriateness of such a building. (Ron Rittenhouse.)

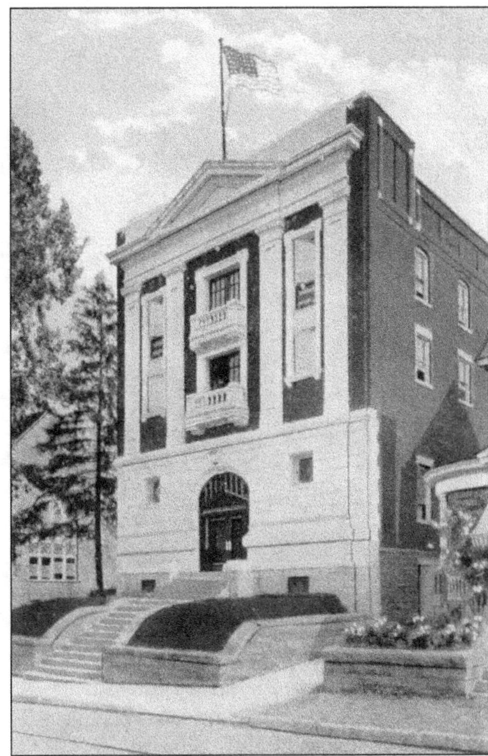

The Masonic Lodge has marble veneer and stylish detailing on its exterior. It was opened in 1916, and hundreds of visitors came to its dedication. The building still stands on the corner of High and Willey Streets, but it is no longer used for lodge activities and faces an uncertain future.

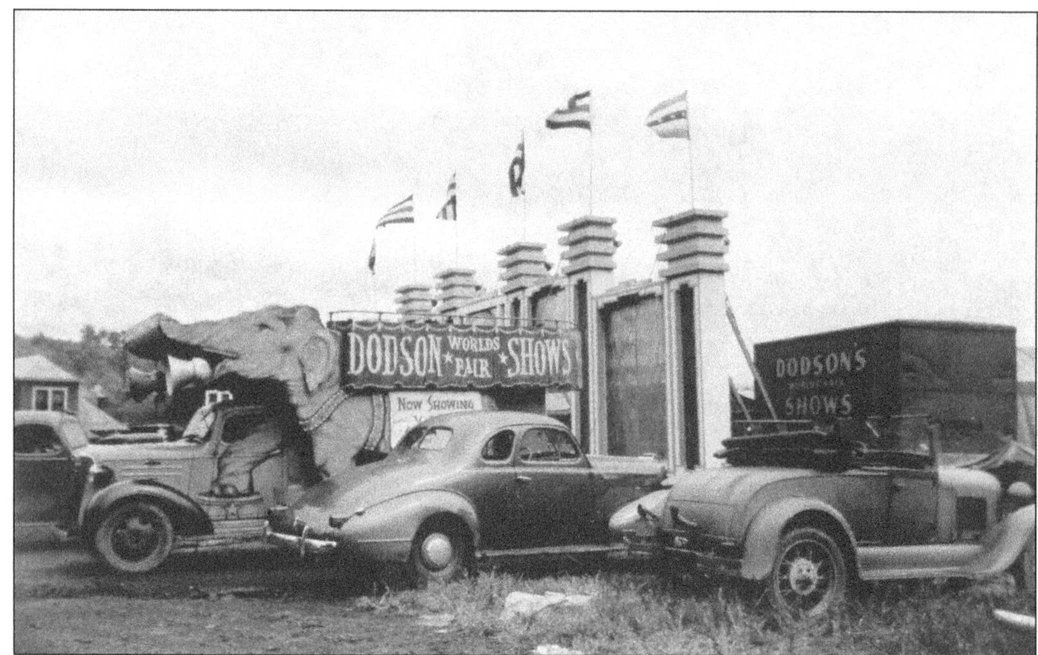

A Farm Security Administration photographer caught the vehicles of Dodson's carnival in Granville in 1938. The caption implied that the local miners only had access to outside entertainment once a year, but the whole gamut of Morgantown entertainment was only a short bus ride away from Scotts Run. (National Archives.)

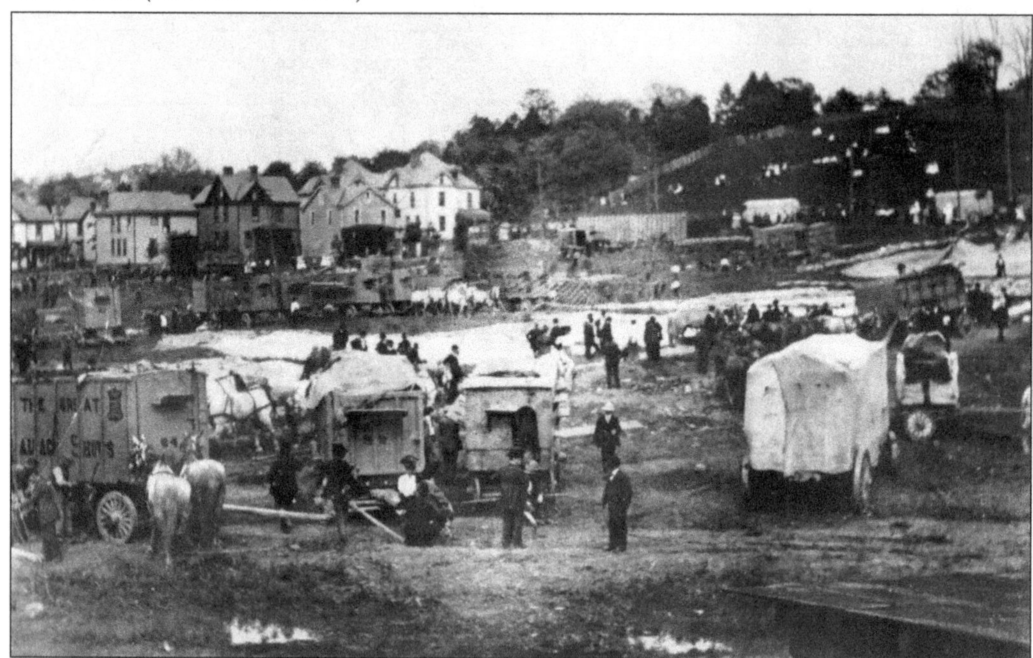

Many different circuses have visited Morgantown, particularly since the construction of the railroad. This undated picture shows the Great Palace Shows setting up the big top between the railroad yard and what is now Don Knotts Boulevard. Shows playing under canvas still visit the area. (Morgantown Public Library.)

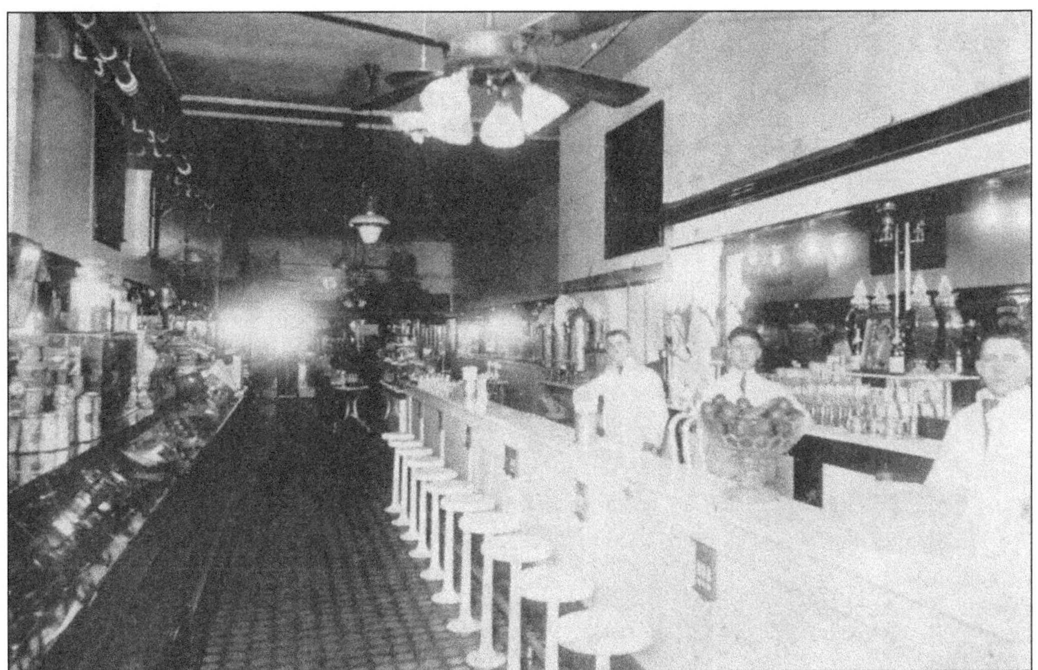

John and Theodore Batlas opened the Boston Confectionery, which offered soda, fizzies, and exterior glitz for atmosphere. It was located at 244 High Street. This view shows the soda jerks behind the counter in 1921. The Batlas name still appears on the building, which later housed the G. C. Murphy 5-and-10.

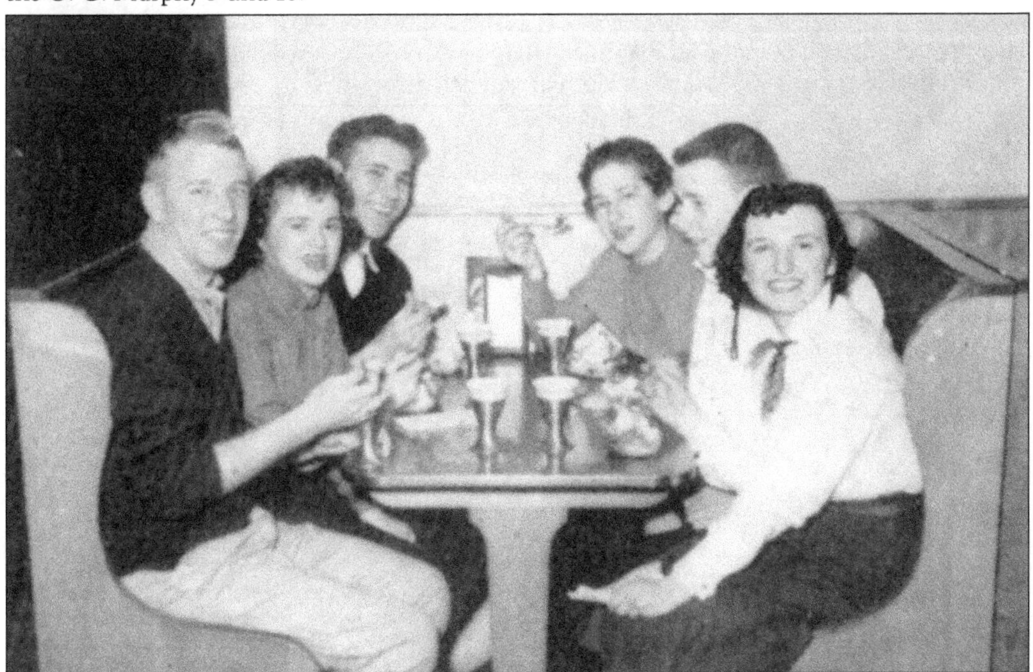

The Chico Dairy, on Beechurst Avenue, was a popular place with both locals and university students for many years. Chico's served huge sundaes and other treats. This photograph appeared in a 1954 advertisement. The ice cream parlor closed in the 1980s. (Morgantown Public Library.)

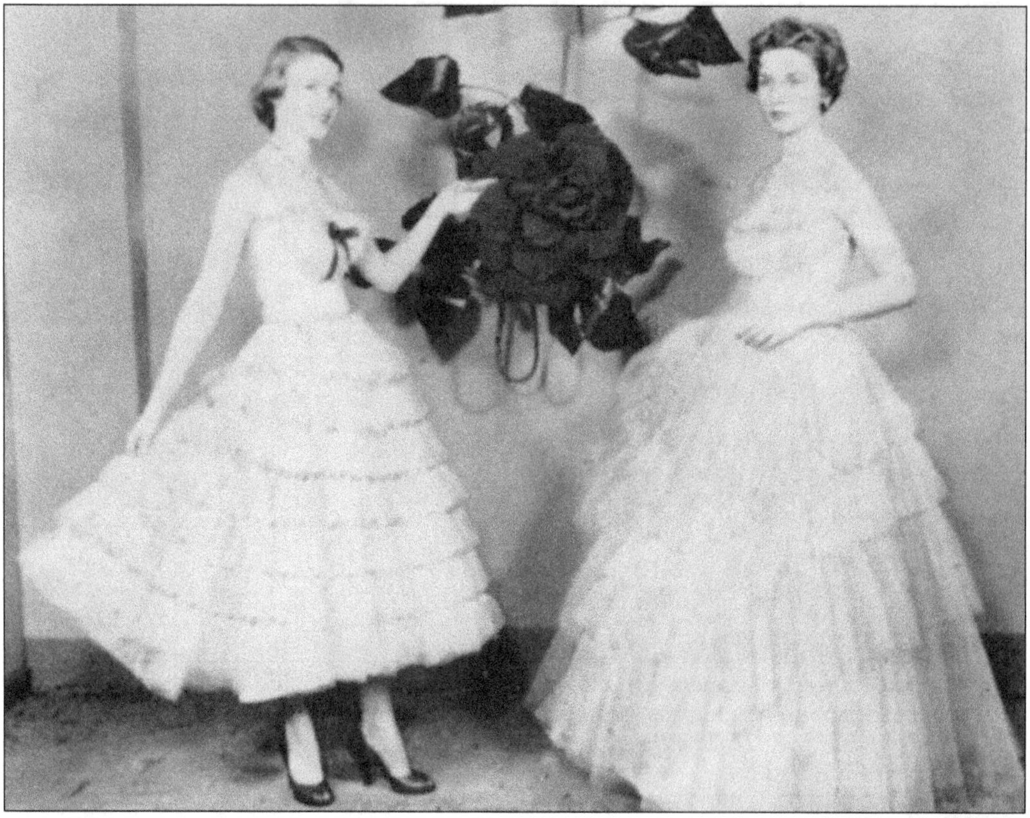

This 1955 photograph from the Morgantown High yearbook shows two students modeling gowns from Whitesides, once a well-knowing clothier on High Street.

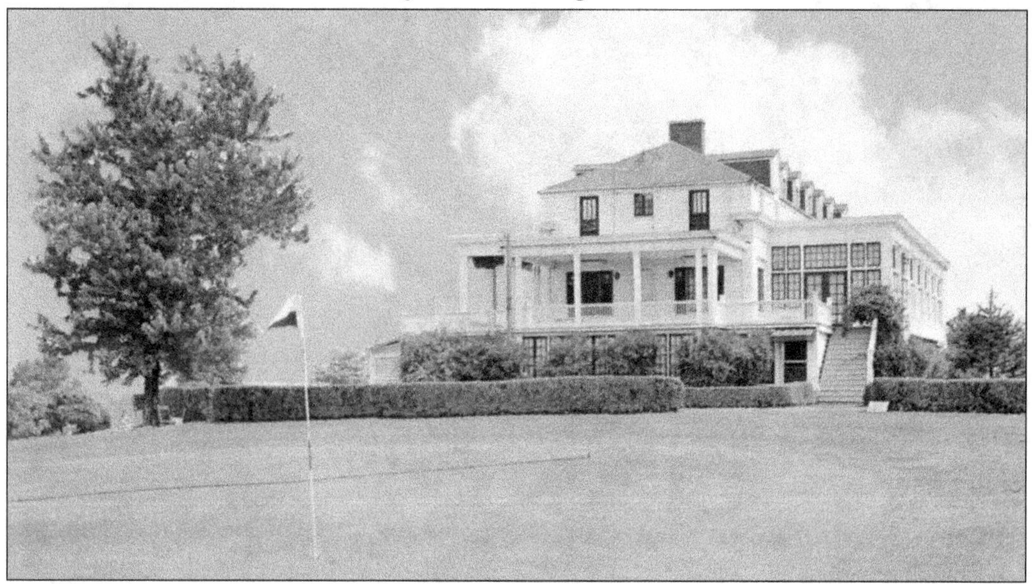

The Morgantown Golf and Country Club was established in 1924. Its location on a hilltop off University Avenue offered golfing with scenic views. The building was torn down about 1973 and is now the site of the West Virginia University Law School.

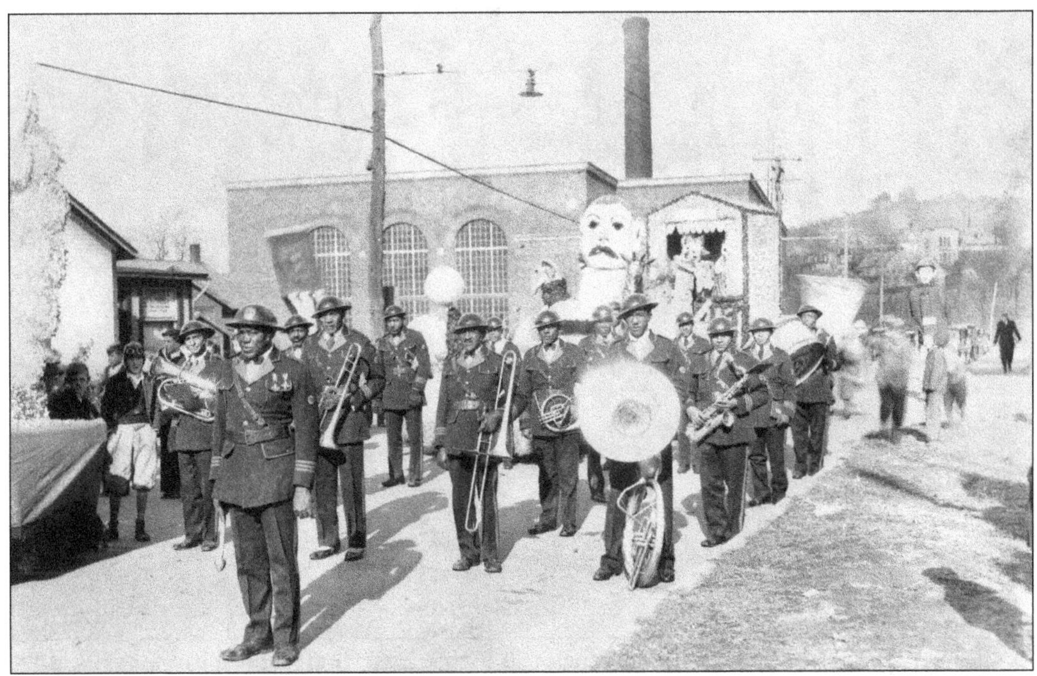

This photograph shows an African American band and parade floats lined up in front of the African Methodist Episcopal church on what is now Beechurst Avenue. The undated photograph must have been taken about 1929, when the Field House was built. State law resulted in segregation of many activities until the 1950s, but "colored" groups regularly took part in civic activities. (West Virginia and Regional History Collection, West Virginia University Libraries.)

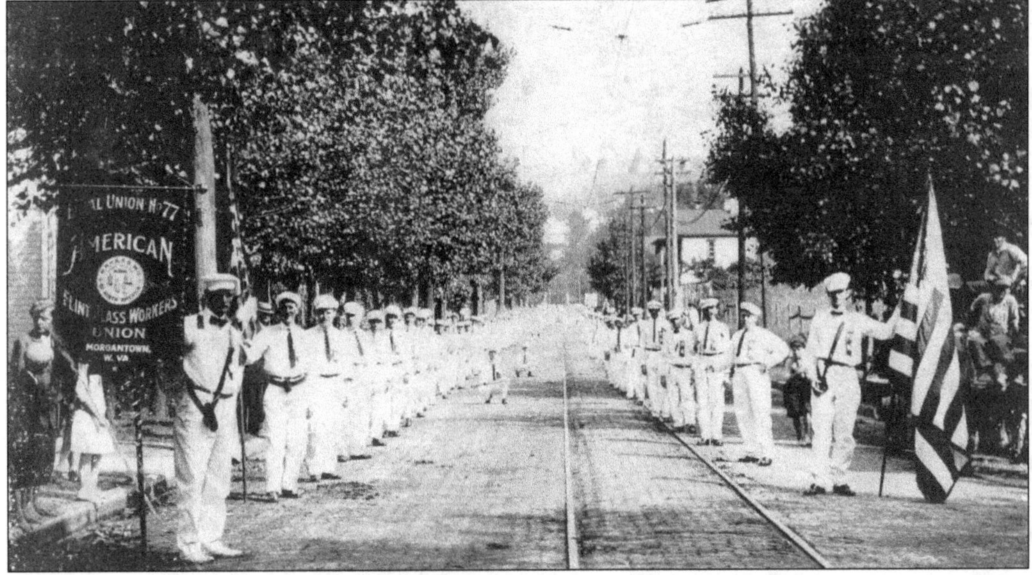

Members of the American Flint Glass Workers' Union lined up for a Labor Day parade. Many of the workers carry glass canes. It is said that some of the canes were hollow and contained refreshments for consumption along the parade route. Making special glass items for parades was common in glassmaking communities, but few of these pieces survived because they were often smashed at the end of the route.

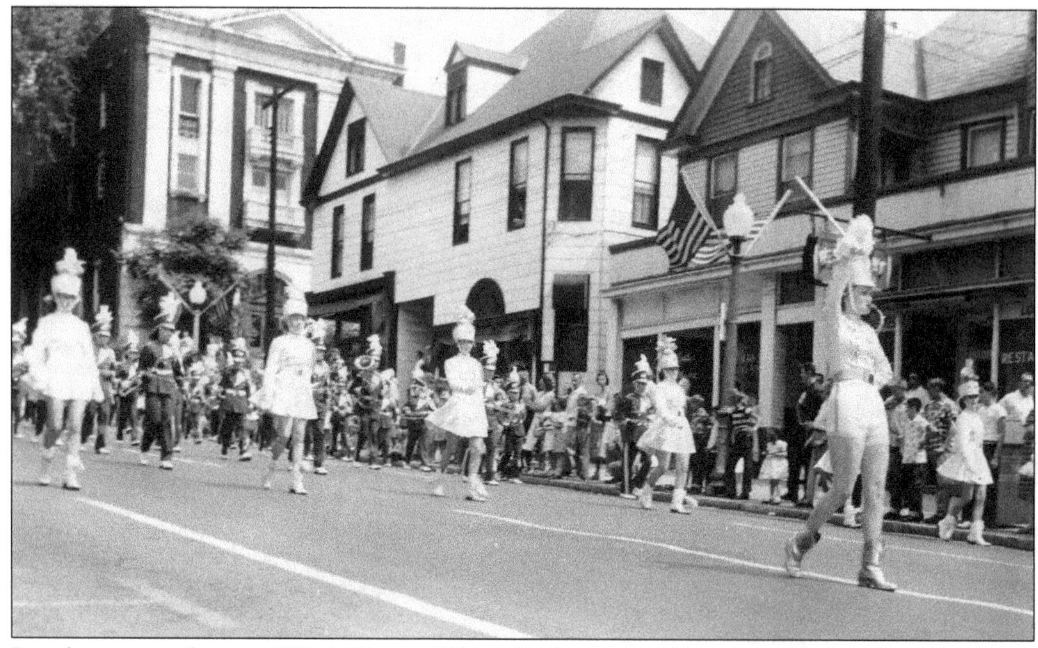

Parades start at the top of High Street. When this high school band paraded in the 1950s, even the spectators dressed up for the occasion. (Morgantown Public Library.)

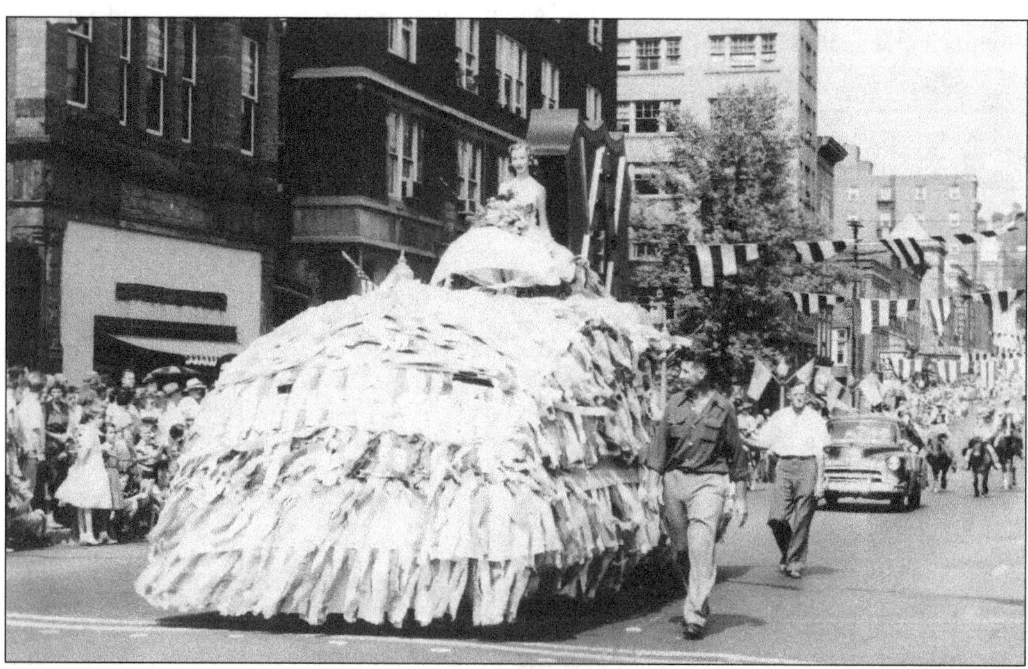

This float was part of a Labor Day parade on High Street in the early 1950s. There is an equestrian unit passing the courthouse. While parades down High are still held several times each year, floats tend to be limited to university and high-school homecoming parades, and horses, if included, are now in the rear. (Morgantown Public Library.)

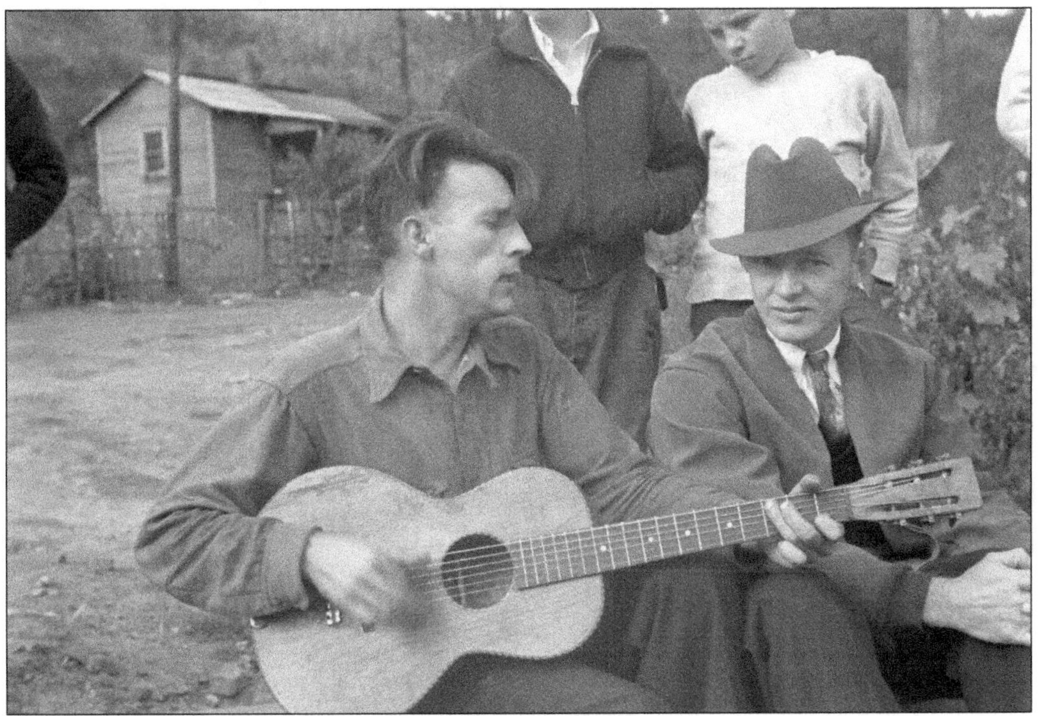
This guitar-playing singer was captured in one of the Scotts Run mining camps in 1935 by a photographer from one of the federal projects. (National Archives.)

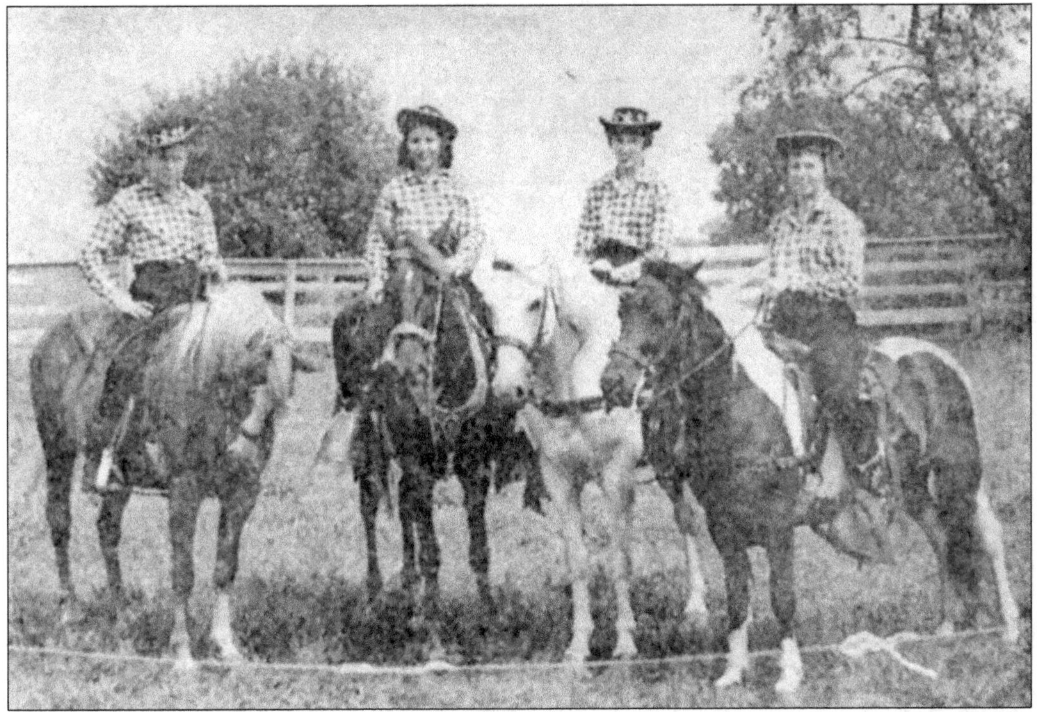
An annual horse show took place in Westover Park during the 1960s. Both English and Western classes were included.

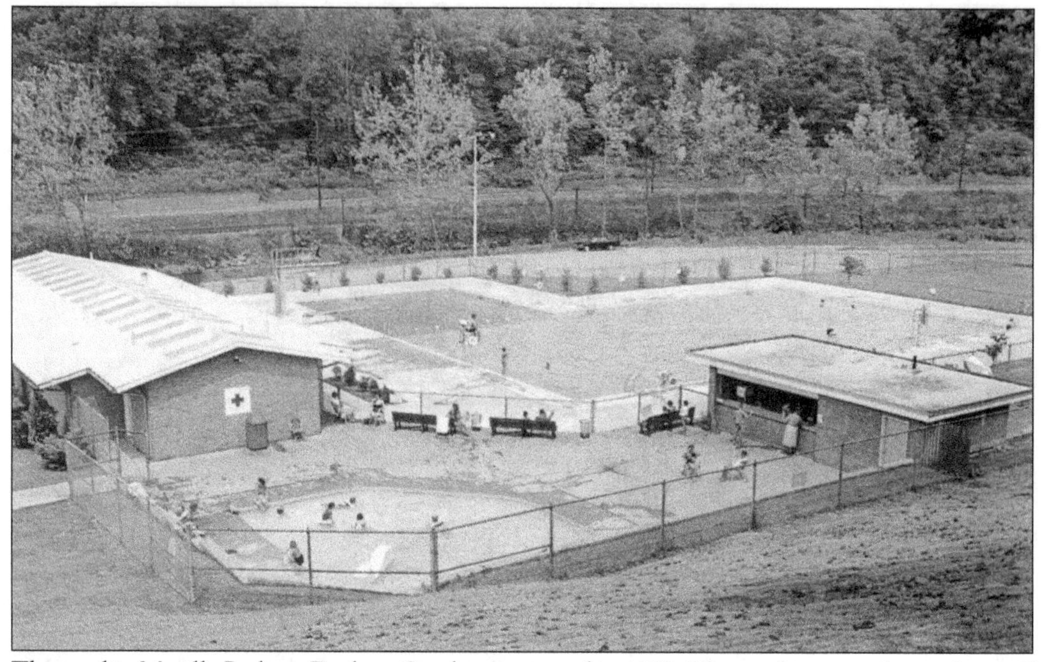

The pool in Marilla Park on Deckers Creek was opened in 1958. The pool is a popular cooling-off spot on hot summer days. Water slides have been added to the facility.

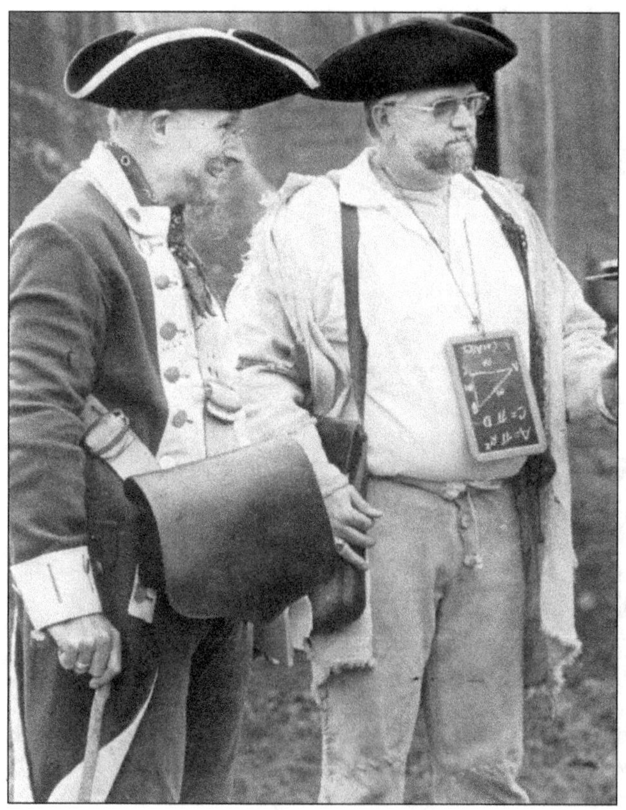

Prof. Willem Van Eck (left) and Judge Larry Starcher (right) portrayed Charles Mason and Jeremiah Dixon respectively at the first Mason-Dixon Festival in 1987. The festival, which includes a historical pageant, has continued to be a fall fixture in the Riverfront Park.

Ten

PLACES WE VISIT

The area around Morgantown includes hundreds of square miles of scenic beauty. The area to the east has been a recreational destination for both locals and visitors for over 100 years.

The original immigration route from the east followed essentially the same route as I-68, passing close to Coopers Rock and crossing the Cheat River as it approaches the city. Local residents took pleasure trips out along the highway in horse-and-buggy days.

The construction of paved highways and the Lake Lynn reservoir, popularly known as Cheat Lake, accelerated interest in the area for recreation, and the shores and nearby hills have become popular residential areas. The waters of the lake have become a good fishing area.

A second route to the east follows the Deckers Creek valley to the county line and then heads to Kingwood, the seat of Preston County. There are many scenic spots along the creek, but it had relatively few visitors until the Morgantown and Kingwood Railroad (M&KRR) was built in the early 1900s. With the opening of passenger service on the M&KRR, picnic trips up the valley became popular with rich and poor alike. A large amusement park was built near the county line. When automobiles replaced trains for recreational trips, interest in the valley declined, but the construction of a rail-trail has brought new visitors.

During much of the 20th century, the Monongahela River was highly polluted by mine wastes, but the water is now of fairly high quality. River fish are edible, and there is strong interest in fishing for bass and muskellunge. Some locals have always used the river for fishing, boating, and swimming, but since 1990, interest in riverfront construction and river recreation has increased rapidly. New boat docks and launch facilities are appearing, and an annual triathlon includes a river swim.

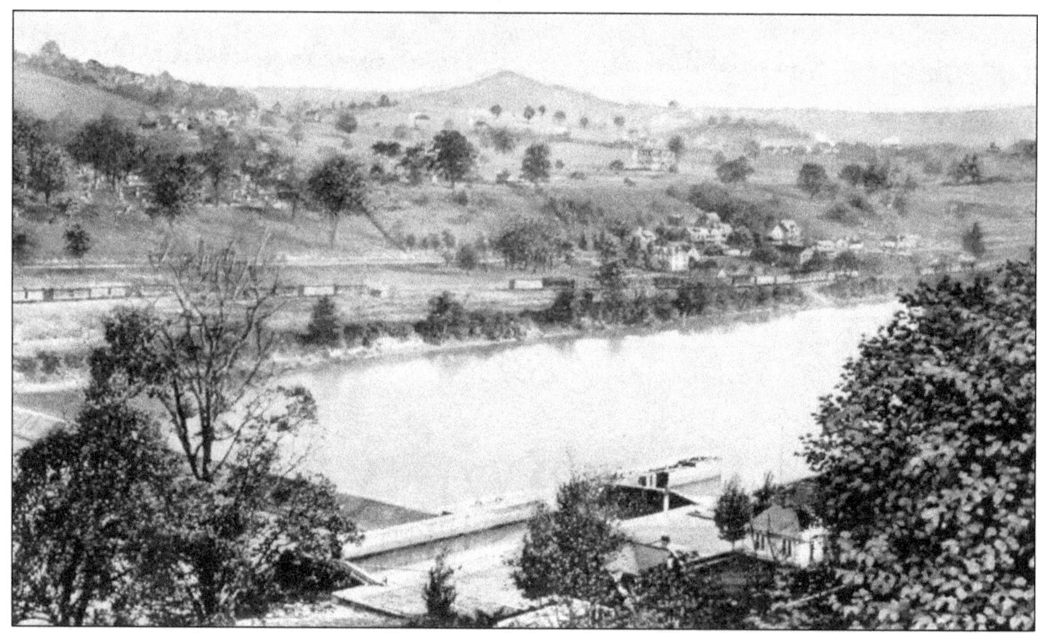

This view features Lock 10 on the Monongahela River. Dorsey's Knob is in the background, and its height and shape made it a well-known landmark.

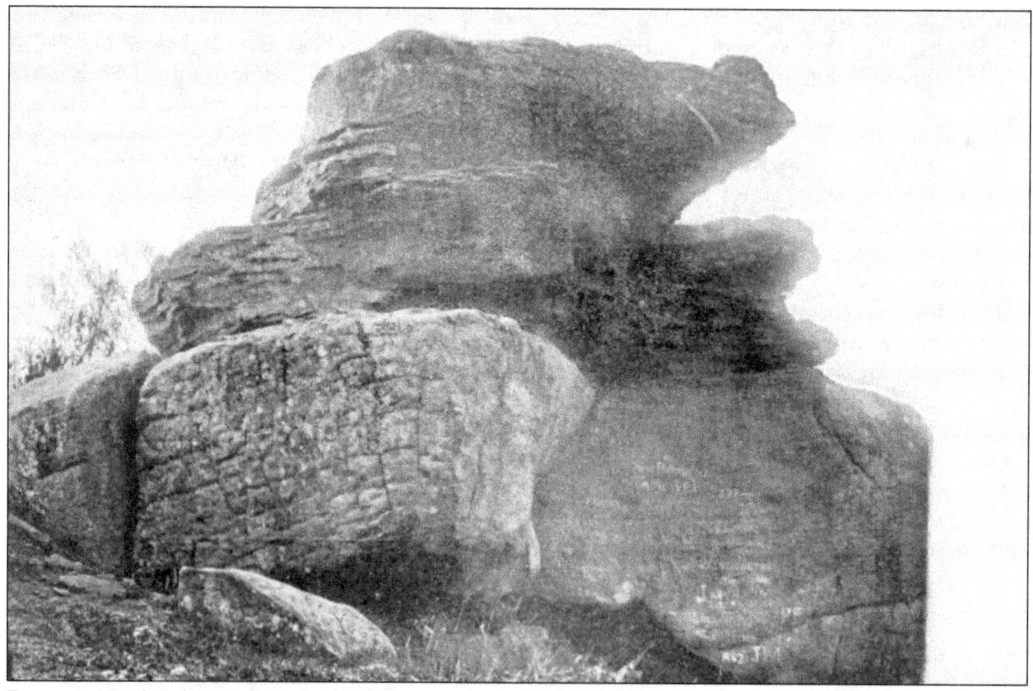

Dorsey's Knob is located south of Morgantown and overlooks the Monongahela River. Silhouetted 600 feet above the river, the rock structure made of hard sandstone is visible for miles around, making it a well-known landmark. It was named for the George Dorsey family, who owned the land in 1811. Today Sky Rock, as it is also called, is the site of a new park and lodge.

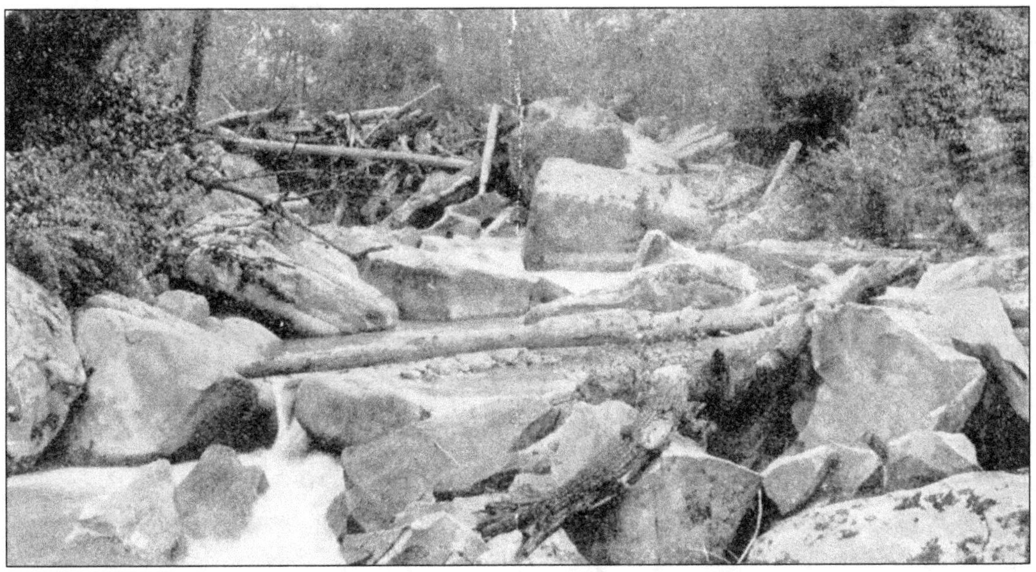

The rail-trail from Morgantown to Reedsville passes along this scenic view of the gorge on Deckers Creek.

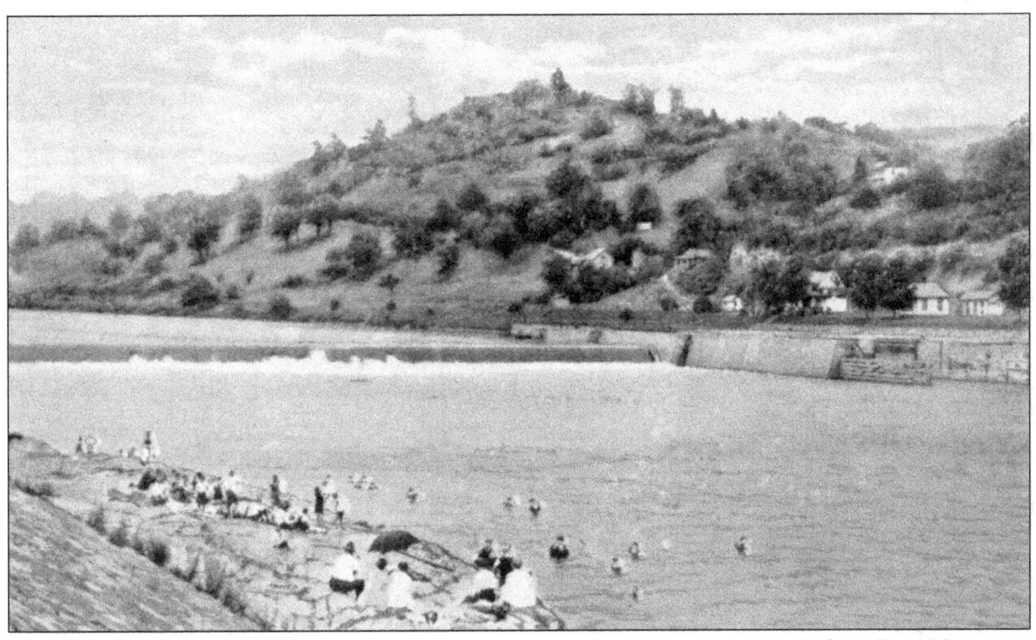

In 1920, the shelf of red rocks below Dam 10 was a public swimming area. When Dam Nine was replaced by the Point Marion Dam, most of the rocks were flooded by a higher water level.

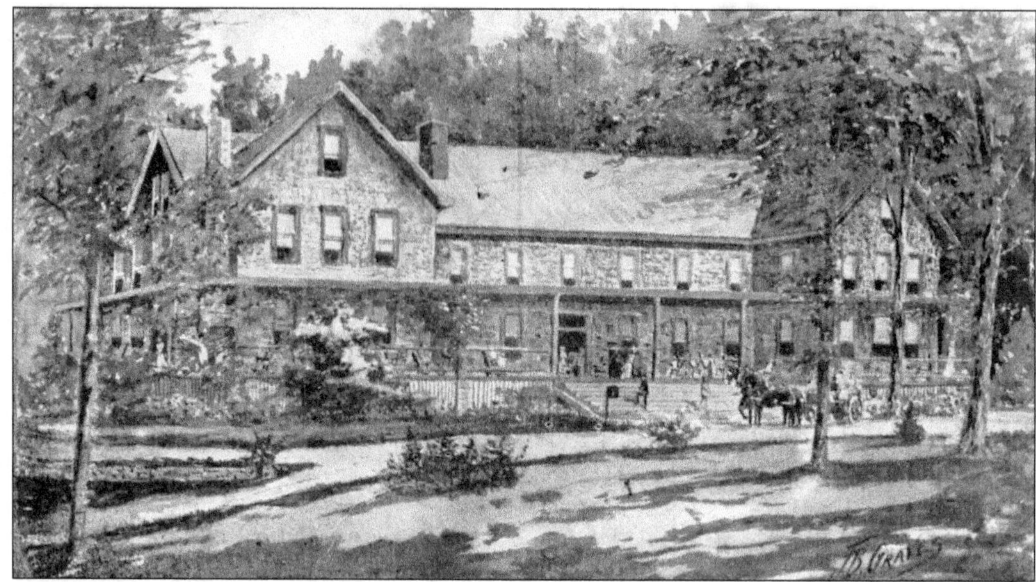

Mont Chateau Hotel was built in 1894 some 150 feet above the Cheat River. It was on the main road to the east, and carriages brought guests from Morgantown. In 1920, a private club from Pittsburgh purchased the hotel. In 1955, the State of West Virginia bought it for use as a state park. In 1956, the old building burned but was rebuilt. Today it houses the West Virginia Geological Survey.

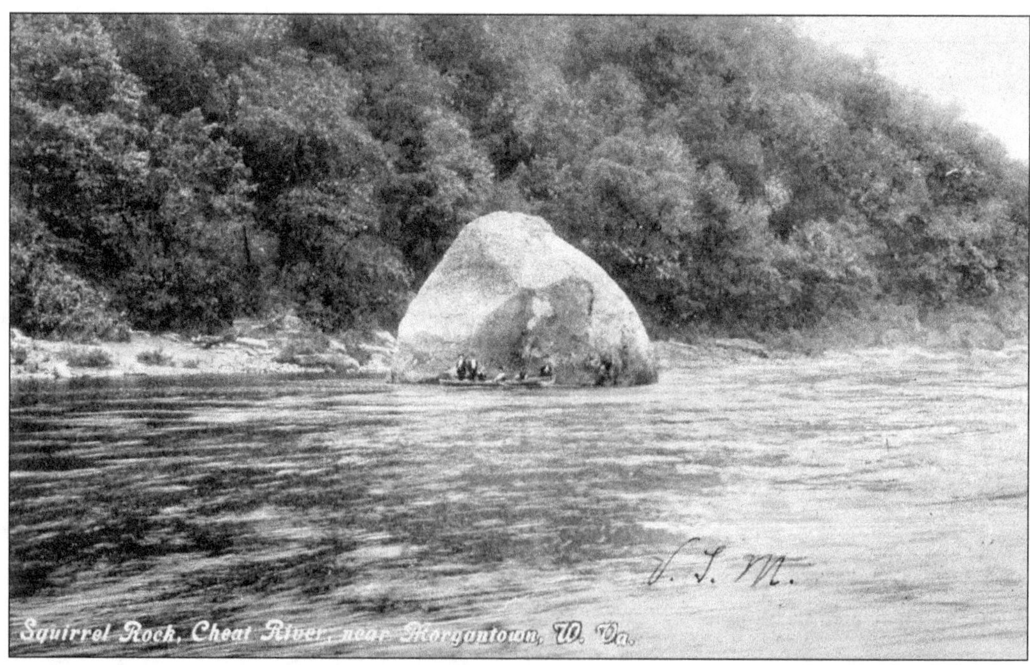

Squirrel Rock was once a well-known landmark located in the Cheat River near Mont Chateau Lodge. The imposing rock was submerged when the Cheat Lake Dam was completed in 1926.

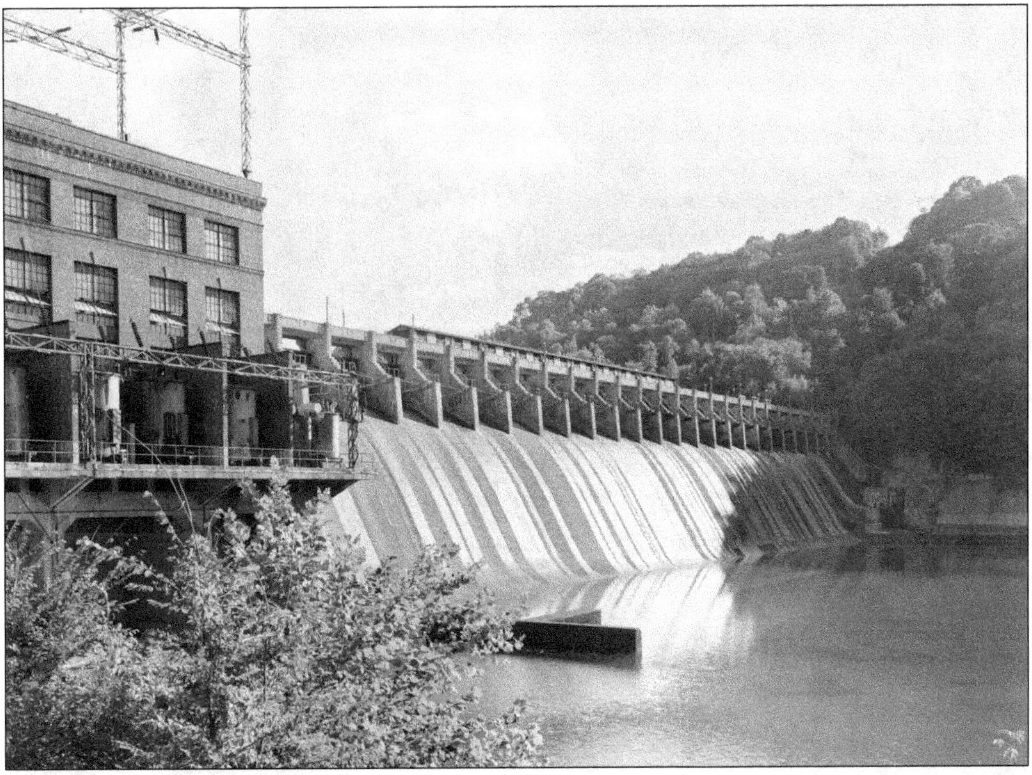

The Lake Lynn Power Station and Dam were completed in 1926 by the local power company. The lake is popularly known as Cheat Lake. Although there is limited shoreline access for the public, the lake is a popular place for boating and fishing. (HABS/HAER Library of Congress.)

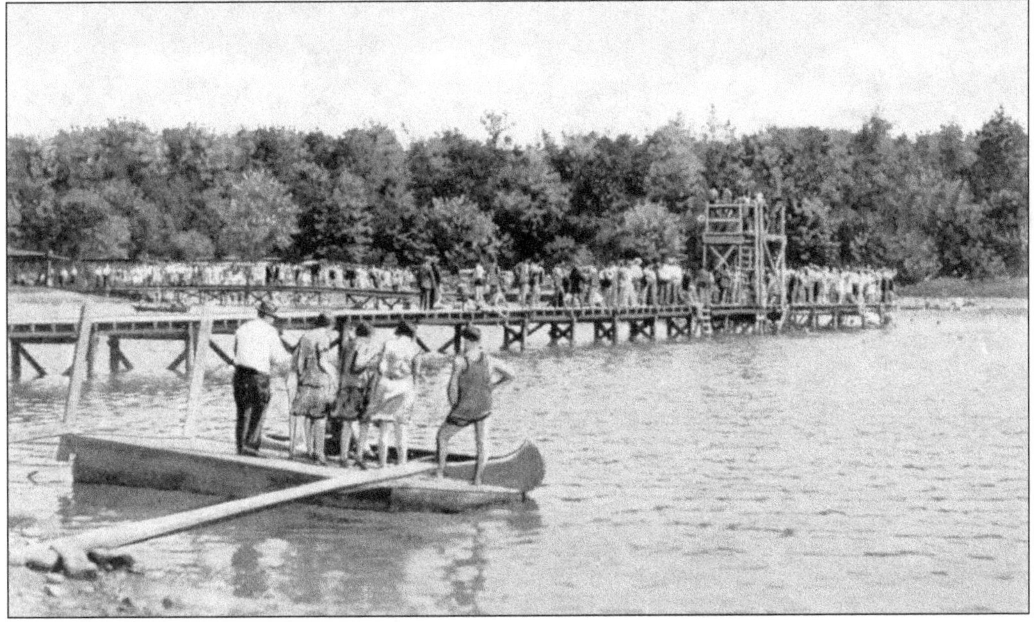

In the 1930s, Sunset Beach, on Lake Lynn (Cheat Lake), was a place for swimming and canoeing. For the past 40 years, it has been devoted to boat docks.

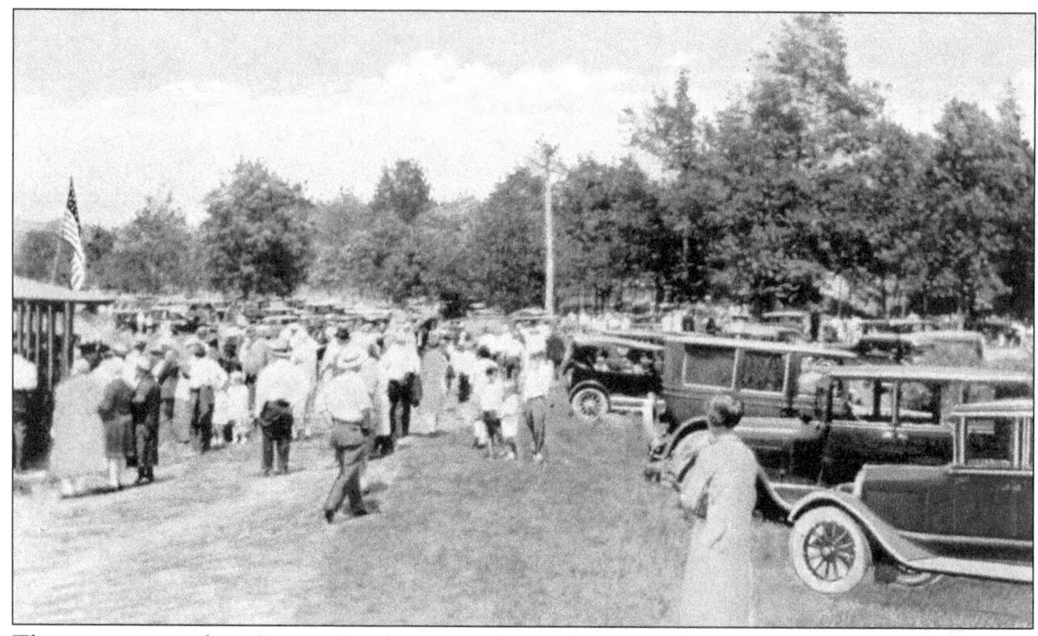

The picnic grounds at Sunset Beach attracted crowds, especially after paved roads reached it in the 1930s, when this picture was taken.

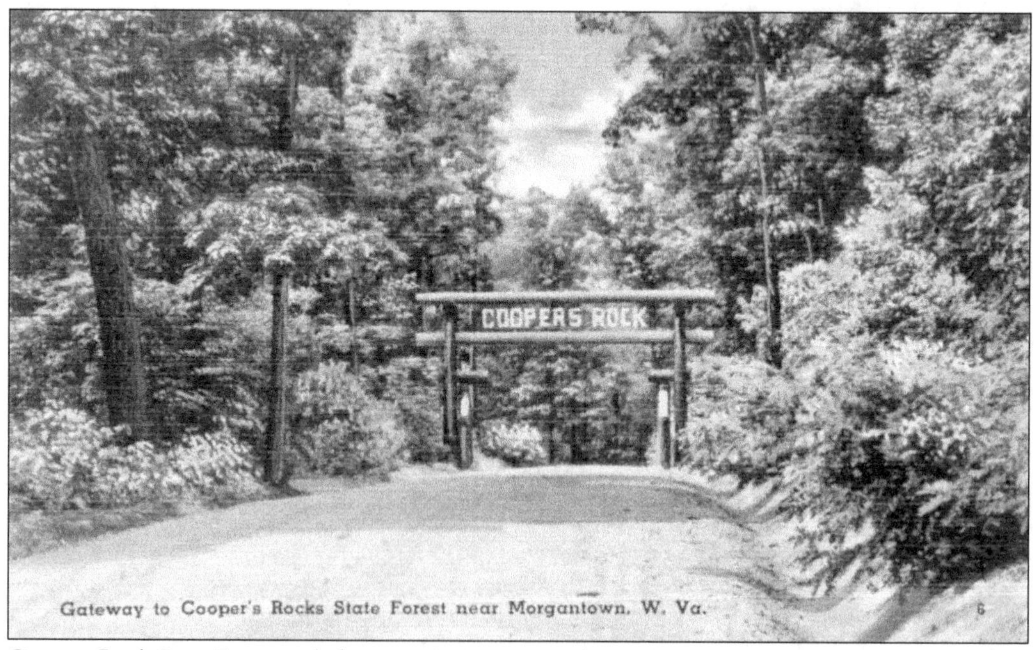

Coopers Rock State Forest includes over 12,000 acres and is used for recreation, timber management, and wildlife protection. Some land is leased by West Virginia University for forestry research and teaching. The forest was established in 1933, and the Civilian Conservation Corps built impressive stone steps and rustic picnic shelters. Coopers Rock is famous for its panoramic and scenic view.

Rock City, a natural walled city with vertical sandstone cliffs, is located at Coopers Rock State Forest. Rock City has long been a popular hiking location. This postcard of the location was mailed in 1909.

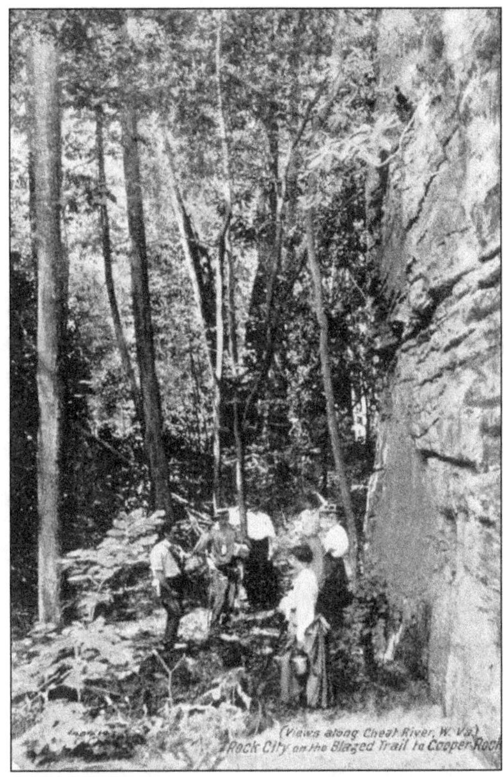

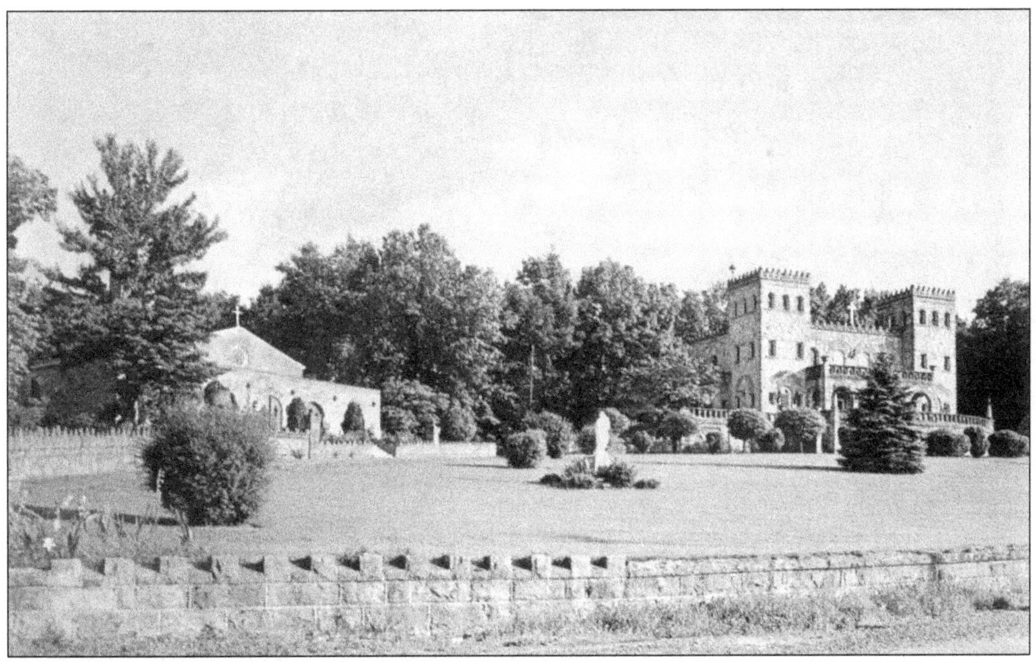

Thoney Pietro came to Morgantown as a bricklayer and became a contractor for brick street projects. He built this 23-room mansion on Tyrone Road in 1933. It was too far from town for his friends to come visit him as often as he wanted, so he donated it to the Catholic church and returned to town. Known as the Friary, it is used as a retreat center.

www.ingramcontent.com/pod-product-compliance
Lightning Source LLC
LaVergne TN
LVHW081528100826
845153LV00004B/230
* 9 7 8 1 5 3 1 6 2 6 8 0 8 *